THE PSYCHOLOGY OF LEARNING AND MOTIVATION

Advances in Research and Theory

VOLUME 19

CONTRIBUTORS TO THIS VOLUME

John Ceraso

Leslie B. Cohen

Keith J. Holyoak

John F. Kihlstrom

Janet Kolodner

Richard E. Mayer

Barbara A. Younger

THE PSYCHOLOGY
OF LEARNING AND MOTIVATION

Advances in Research and Theory

EDITED BY GORDON H. BOWER

STANFORD UNIVERSITY, STANFORD, CALIFORNIA

Volume 19

1985

ACADEMIC PRESS, INC.

(Harcourt Brace Jovanovich, Publishers)

Orlando • San Diego • New York • London
Toronto • Montreal • Sydney • Tokyo

ACADEMIC PRESS, INC.
Orlando, Florida 32887

United Kingdom Edition published by
ACADEMIC PRESS INC. (LONDON) LTD.
24–28 Oval Road, London NW1 7DX

LIBRARY OF CONGRESS CATALOG CARD NUMBER: 66-30104

ISBN 0–12–543319–0

PRINTED IN THE UNITED STATES OF AMERICA

85 86 87 88   9 8 7 6 5 4 3 2 1

CONTENTS

Contents

LEARNING IN COMPLEX DOMAINS: A COGNITIVE ANALYSIS OF COMPUTER PROGRAMMING

Richard E. Mayer

POSTHYPNOTIC AMNESIA AND THE DISSOCIATION OF MEMORY

John F. Kihlstrom

UNIT FORMATION IN PERCEPTION AND MEMORY

John Ceraso

HOW INFANTS FORM CATEGORIES

Barbara A. Younger and Leslie B. Cohen

CONTRIBUTORS

Numbers in parentheses indicate the pages on which the authors' contributions begin.

John Ceraso, Institute for Cognitive Studies, Rutgers University, Newark, New Jersey 07102 (179)

Leslie B. Cohen, Department of Psychology, University of Texas at Austin, Austin, Texas 78713 (211)

Keith J. Holyoak,[1] Department of Psychology, University of Michigan, Ann Arbor, Michigan 48103 (59)

John F. Kihlstrom, Department of Psychology, University of Wisconsin, Madison, Wisconsin 53706 (131)

Janet Kolodner, School of Information and Computer Science, Georgia Institute of Technology, Atlanta, Georgia 30332 (1)

Richard E. Mayer, Department of Psychology, University of California at Santa Barbara, Santa Barbara, California 93106 (89)

Barbara A. Younger, Department of Psychology, University of Alabama at Birmingham, Birmingham, Alabama 35294 (211)

[1]Present address: Department of Psychology, Carnegie-Mellon University, Pittsburgh, Pennsylvania 15213.

ix

MEMORY FOR EXPERIENCE

Janet Kolodner

GEORGIA INSTITUTE OF TECHNOLOGY
ATLANTA, GEORGIA

1

I. Introduction

Memory for experience is an integral part of our day-to-day lives. We often get "reminded" of previous experiences similar to a current situation. Those experiences may give us clues as to how to deal with the current situation. When we empathize with another person's problems, we may be remembering a previous similar experience of our own. When we understand more of a story than is told to us, or when we hypothesize missing details of some event we are trying to recall, our knowledge about generalized or generic events is being used. Yet it is not at all clear how experience (individual and generic) is stored in memory, by what processes it is possible to recall a previous episode, or what kinds of cues allow recall of a previous event.

This article presents an organization for experience in very long-term memory that supports both recall and recognition of events. The theory is implemented in a computer program called CYRUS and is based on our observations that much of the remembering people do is reconstructive. We therefore include a set of reconstructive retrieval strategies to allow recall of poorly specified events. Since we have new experiences from moment to moment and must be able to store almost all of them in memory, we also include a set of strategies for updating memory while maintaining its organization and therefore the accessibility of events over time. These strategies include both a means of indexing experiences in conceptual schemata and a way of reorganizing memory through learning new, more specialized schemata based on the similarities between experiences encoded in memory. These strategies provide several explanations of forgetting and retrieval confusion.

This research is certainly not the first to claim that long-term memory is reconstructive. Psychologists as far back as Bartlett (1932) have described memory as reconstructive. A number of recent experimental results illustrate the reconstructive nature of human memory. In asking people to name persons in their high-school classes, Williams (1978) found that his subjects recalled features of a person's name, such as its first letter, the number of syllables, and what it rhymed with, and used that information to come up with the name. When he asked people to recall whether a karate expert in a particular story had broken a block, Spiro (1979) found that they used their knowledge about karate experts in general to answer the question rather than retrieving actual story details. Brewer and Treyens (1981) found that people used generalized knowledge about places to recall the layout of a room rather than remembering in detail exactly how it was laid out. In each of these cases, only partial information was retrieved from memory and, using generalized knowledge, "reasonable" items were reconstructed.

The work presented here comes from the field of artificial intelligence (AI).

As such, we are interested in discovering how we can make the computer do many of the intelligent things people do. One way to do that is to model the way people do those things. Because most psychological theories are not constructed with computer implementations in mind, however, we often find that we must discover much of the psychology underlying the intelligent processing we are trying to implement. Such was the case in developing the model presented here. Our goal, in this case, was to develop a large computer memory that could be accessed in natural language.

We initially based our ideas on observations we made of people attempting to remember obscure things from their pasts, such as who their girl or boyfriend was in 1968, what museums they had been to, and who was the most famous person they had ever met. Each question required significant reasoning, and we asked people to think aloud as they were attempting to remember. These were our initial data. Using them, we constructed an initial theory of reconstruction and began building our computer program, CYRUS. The program acted as a theory tester. In the course of building it, we discovered things it could not do that people did and also discovered things that it did that we had not seen in people. We studied each of these through collection of additional protocols, augmenting as necessary the program and the hypotheses it was based on. Of course, we also kept in mind what the psychological literature had to tell us about the processes we were investigating. In this way, we were able to derive a model of reconstructive memory that is consistent with many of the observations psychologists have made and which additionally specifies in detail a structure for events and a set of strategies which act on it.

Our memory model is implemented in a program called CYRUS (Computerized Yale Retrieval and Updating System) (Kolodner, 1978, 1981, 1983a, 1983b, 1984; Schank & Kolodner, 1979). CYRUS stores and later remembers events in the lives of important dignitaries. Questions are posed to it in English. It translates those questions into a conceptual representation (Schank, 1972, 1975) and uses its reconstructive strategies to elaborate on that representation in its search of memory for an answer. The representations it stores in its memory are also conceptual representations and are organized around schemata called E-MOPs. CYRUS integrates new events into its memory and reorganizes it as necessary when new events are added.

The protocol in Table I is of CYRUS answering a number of questions about former Secretary of State Cyrus Vance. We include some of the intermediate reasoning CYRUS does to answer the questions. However, it is hard to include enough detail in the output to illustrate that CYRUS' reasoning is consistent with what we would expect of a person with the same knowledge. The ways in which CYRUS adds events to and searches its memory will be explained in detail throughout the article.

TABLE I

DIALOG WITH CYRUS

>When was the last time you were in Egypt?
    inferring a diplomatic trip
ON DEC 10 1978.

>Why did you go there?
    answering question using previous context
TO NEGOTIATE THE CAMP DAVID ACCORDS.

>Who did you talk to there?
    answering question using previous context
    inferring undifferentiated political meeting
WITH ANWAR SADAT.

>Has your wife ever met Mrs. Begin?
    inferring a social political occasion
YES, MOST RECENTLY AT A STATE DINNER IN ISRAEL IN JAN 1980.

>What heads of state have you met?
    inferring a diplomatic meeting
    searching directly for $MEET
    . . .
    applying strategies to search memory
    . . .
    searching for sM-CONFERENCE
    . . .
    searching for sM-VIPVISIT
      searching sM-VIPVISIT instance for $MEET
    . . .
    searching for I-NEGOTIATE
    . . .
KING HASSAN, MENACHIM BEGIN, MUSTAFA KHALIL, IAN SMITH,
PRESIDENT ASSAD, KING HUSSEIN, AND ANWAR SADAT.

>Last time you went to Saudi Arabia, where did you stay?
    inferring a diplomatic trip
IN A PALACE IN SAUDI ARABIA ON SEP 23 1978.

>Did you go sightseeing there?
    answering question using previous context
YES, AT AN OILFIELD IN DHARAN ON SEP 23 1978.

II. Background and Motivation

The model we present falls within the realm of "schema theory." Schemata
are the knowledge structures used to represent the *generic* concepts stored in
memory. They summarize the components, relationships, and attributes of specific exemplars they are abstracted from (Rumelhart & Ortony, 1977). A schema
is a *structured* memory object. It provides a generalized framework with *vari-*

ables as placeholders. During processing, schemata are *instantiated* and the variables get filled by the real values of the current instance. Filling of one slot may constrain the types of fillers other slots can have. Schemata and the generalized knowledge they contain permit *predictions* to be made during understanding (Schank, 1975), often on the basis of incomplete information. They are thought to be formed by a process of *induction* which creates and successively refines a schema based on the similarities and differences between the instances that comprise it. Two types of *organizational hierarchies* have been proposed for schemata (Thorndyke & Yekovich, 1980): a generalization/specialization hierarchy and a set of hierarchies representing the various relationships schemata can have to each other. When we refer to episodic schemata, for example, we can envision one episode being embedded in another one (e.g., museum visits happen during trips) or two episodes being related through causality (successful negotiations result in treaty signing).

Several theories have been put forth showing how schemata are used for encoding and retrieval. Encoding-oriented theories have concentrated on *understanding* or *comprehension* (e.g., Graesser & Nakamura, 1982; Minsky, 1975; Rumelhart & Ortony, 1977; Schank & Abelson, 1977; Thorndyke & Hayes-Roth, 1979), while retrieval-oriented studies have concentrated on the influences of schemata in recall (e.g., Bower, Black, & Turner, 1979; Rumelhart, 1975). Several recent articles review schema theory, schema properties, and the range of functions schemata are held responsible for (e.g., Alba & Hasher, 1983; Brewer & Nakamura, 1984; Rumelhart & Ortony, 1977; Thorndyke & Yekovich, 1980). We summarize below.

Schemata perform a wide range of functions during both encoding, or understanding, and retrieval. They *guide selection* of those aspects of a current item which will be noticed and recorded, the result being that only information relevant to active schemata is encoded. In the process, the content of the item is *abstracted,* while the surface form is lost. The content is also *interpreted* in such a way that it is consistent with the schema. This results in an *elaborated* representation, fleshed out and sometimes changed (e.g., Bartlett, 1932) by the generalized knowledge and defaults the schema holds. This is a process of *integrating* the new item with knowledge already in memory. During integration, new schemata may also be formed. In the end, a *representation* of the original item is created, with some of the original detail lost, some elaboration (inference) of details not explicitly stated, and sometimes with large changes in meaning. This, of course, later results in recall errors. During retrieval, schemata guide recall by combining the details selected for representation with memory's generalized knowledge. This process is called *reconstruction*. Schemata active during retrieval introduce detail where memory encodings are sketchy or confused. Faulty remembering also arises as a result of this process (e.g., Brewer & Treyens, 1981).

Several different general descriptions exist of these processes (e.g., Bartlett, 1932; Bobrow & Norman, 1975; Brewer & Nakamura, 1984; Rumelhart & Ortony, 1977) and a great deal of experimental work supports them (e.g., Brewer & Treyens, 1981; Owens, Bower, & Black, 1979; Spiro, 1979; Williams, 1978). In addition, several researchers have proposed more specific models of representation (e.g., Graesser & Nakamura, 1982; Lichtenstein & Brewer, 1980; Minsky, 1975; Schank & Abelson, 1977) and of schema creation (e.g., Anderson, Kline, & Beasley, 1979). Though much work and many years of experimentation have gone into these and other approaches to schemata, we are left with only a vague notion of any specifics with respect to the processes which work on schemata, exactly what they look like, and how they are activated and used. Indeed, psychologists are beginning to question this vagueness (e.g., Thorndyke & Yekovich, 1980; Brewer & Nakamura, 1984), some even wondering if schema theory as it stands is too vague to be a theory at all. Though it seems plausible and certainly is descriptive, Thorndyke and Yekovich (1980) question whether schema theory, as it stands today, is too vague to be predictive or testable.

In presenting our theory of remembering, we attempt to combat the vagueness problem in schema theory by specifying in detail the processes and knowledge structures involved. We have put forth specific strategies and memory structures that define a *process model*. In requiring that the model be programmable on the computer, we ensure that the processes and structures of the model are defined explicitly. Because remembering involves both encoding and retrieval processes, our model addresses schema processes and structures involved in both. Our model concentrates on the processes involved in integrating a new item into memory and on those involved in retrieval. Rather than looking at encoding, storage, and retrieval as separate entities, we define and examine them in relationship to each other. Integration of new items into memory (our analog to encoding), for example, both reflects retrieval capabilities we've observed in people and takes the underlying memory organization into account. Similarly, in considering memory organization (our analog to storage), we've examined the constraints implied by human retrieval—its successes, failures, and the strategies used.

Because we wanted to define what drives retrieval and organizational strategies, and because we were implementing our model on the computer, we have had to very explicitly define the structures in memory that organize individual memories with respect to each other. This is what we have called *memory organization*. While psychologists have been looking for some time at memory organization in the form of schemata (e.g., Graesser & Nakamura, 1982), the organization proposed here goes beyond current schema theory in a number of ways. First, it provides ways of organizing schemata with respect to each other. Second, it examines change in schemata over time. Third, it studies the use of schemata in organizing individual items represented by a particular schema (i.e., episodic traces). By organize, we mean very specifically *organize in a well-structured framework.* By putting an explicit organization on the knowledge in memory, we can define specific processes for finding things stored in memory's structures and for learning new, more specialized schemata from individual experiences. We will refer to two types of schemata: *organizing* and *nonorganizing.* The first organize individual memories, have a discernible structure, and can be searched strategically. The latter hold generic knowledge and some memories, but do not organize large numbers of individual items. Each has different functions in guiding retrieval.

Though we do not cover in detail the interpretation processes which are part of encoding, our research stems from work in understanding (Schank, 1975; Schank & Abelson, 1977). That research has shown that the episodic structures that store generalizations about day-to-day events (e.g., scripts, plans, and goals) form the core of our ability to understand language and get around in the world. Our model focuses on the schemata that organize and describe day-to-day events. In addition, we make some predictions about which details of an event will be encoded. In particular, our claim is that *schema-relevant differences are recorded.* These differences can take the form of specializations of the default schema values or of inconsistences; but to be schema relevant, they must make schema-related predictions. While our study focuses on memory for events, the principles and algorithms we have discovered are meant to be applicable to memory as a whole.

In the next sections, we present our memory model in as much detail as space allows. After detailing our model, we present its implications and compare it to closely related studies in psychology. We close by considering the completeness and viability of our model as a model of people. For more information about the model, we refer you to Kolodner (1984, 1983a, 1983b). The first presents the entire model as an AI model, the second presents the memory organization and retrieval processes, and the third presents processes for integrating new items into memory.

III. An Illustration of Reconstructive Memory

For the most part, people are expert at recalling information about their pasts. When people try to retrieve specific information about a particular episode in their lives, however, they often find they don't have the entire episode immediately available. In that case, they attempt to *reconstruct* the rest of the episode. When asked to recall a recent trip, one person started his reconstruction as follows:

> Let me see. When we got there, we must have had to find a hotel. Yes, I remember, we had a guide book with a lot of hotels in it, and we called a few of them until we found one with a vacancy. It was late afternoon, so we must have gone out to eat soon after that. . . .

Clearly, the trip was not stored in memory in one large chunk. Instead, it must have been stored in bits and pieces requiring reconstruction to put them back together. Such reconstruction can happen through application of generalized knowledge. In the protocol above, the knowledge that "one must have a hotel to stay in during a trip" and "usually after arrival, the next step of a trip is to check in at the hotel" allowed "finding a hotel" to be recalled.

The process seems to involve building a description of "what must have happened" and then filling it out with "actual" details. We can thus conclude the following about human memory for events:

Memory Principle #1

Human remembering is often a process of reconstructing what must have happened, rather than directly retrieving what did happen.

This process of *reconstruction* is almost always used by people trying to remember episodes, as evidenced by the fact that people tend to "remember" details incorrectly so often. In fact, retrieval confusions and false recall must be inherent to a process which produces probable rather than actual explanations.

IV. Memory Organization in Support of Reconstructive Retrieval

In discovering a memory organization for reconstructive memory, we must find one that not only supports such retrieval, but also *requires* it. We start by considering how people are able to find the right events in memory to answer specific questions. If memory were arranged in lists, then we could imagine a process which searched down an appropriate list until the correct episode were found. This seems unreasonable, however, for a memory with hundreds or thousands of events of the same type: Searching down a long list is a slow process which becomes slower as additional items are added to the list. People's memories do not slow down as they learn more (Smith, Adams & Schorr, 1978).[1]

Furthermore, if people searched down long lists in their memories to retrieve events, then it would be easy for them to enumerate experiences of particular types. For instance, a question such as the following would be easy to answer:

(Q1): Recall all the times you have been to museums.

[1]In fact, there is some debate about this among psychologists. Anderson (1974, 1976) cites the "fan effect" as evidence that retrieval slows down with the addition of new items about a particular concept. Smith *et al.* (1978), on the other hand, have shown that retrieval does not slow down with the addition of new items when context is guiding the retrieval. Reder and Anderson (1980) conclude that when people make consistency judgments rather than retrieving actual facts from memory, there is no interference to slow down the retrieval process.

This question, however, is not easy for people to answer, as suggested by the following protocol:

> I know I've been to a lot of museums in Europe. I've been to England, and I went to a number of museums there—some in London—the British Museum, the National Gallery, and a few smaller galleries, . . . I was at a museum in Brighton—the Royal Pavilion. I've been to museums in Paris—the Louvre and some smaller ones. In Rome, I've been to. . . . In Naples, to. . . . In Florence, to. . . .

The lists of experiences people enumerate are constructed on the fly as they are answering a question. In the protocol above, the person tried to recall "experiences in museums," "experiences in museums in Europe," "experiences in museums in England," "experiences in museums in London," and so forth, filling in (or reconstructing) additional details with each iteration. Generalizing from that, we can make the following hypothesis:

Memory Principle #2

Remembering requires progressive narrowing in on a description of the event to be remembered.

We can describe that process as a process of specifying details which can differentiate the targeted event from other events in memory.

The protocol above and others like it suggest that narrowing the description of a sought event or focusing in on an event by providing more detail is a *necessary* part of remembering (Williams, 1978). Thus, we can state the following principle of memory retrieval:

Memory Principle #3

In a reconstructive memory, memories are not directly enumerable. Instead, the features that describe individual memories must be reconstructed.[2]

Reconstructive retrieval seems to be a process of building up a plausible description of the target item. One step of the process involves narrowing a broad retrieval specification (that describes too many similar items) by specifying additional features. After that context is narrowed to describe only one item, that item can be found in memory. Based on this observation, we propose a memory structure based on the following organizing principle:

Memory Principle #4

Similar items in memory are organized around the same concept and are indexed under that concept by their differentiating features.

---

[2]Of course, there must be a capability for doing some types of enumeration. People remember short lists, for example, the 12 months of the year. Our thesis is that these lists are either committed to memory or are derived from a well-structured concept which serves as a map or chart. People report generating the list of 50 states, for example, by mentally scanning over a map of the United States.

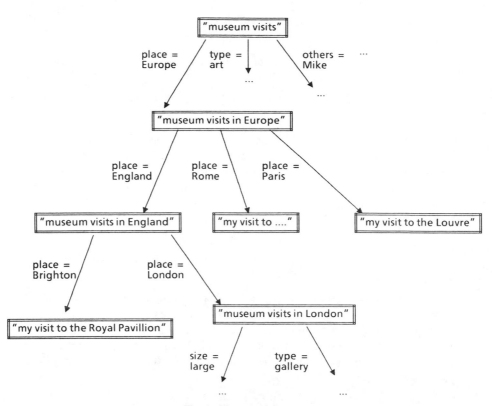

Fig. 1. Museum visits.

Concepts, then, serve as schemata, and play a multifaceted role. Items encoded by the same schema (i.e., represented by the same concept) are also organized in it by those specific features which differentiate them from the general schema.[3] Thus, the proximity of items in memory reflects the closeness of their content.

We thus see memory as networks of schemata with individual memory traces at the leaves. Arcs of the network are labeled by *features of items organized by the schema*. Specification of one of these features will allow traversal of the corresponding arc, arriving in memory at a more specific schema or an individual memory trace. Part of the memory structure implied by the protocols above is exhibited in Fig. 1.

The organization we propose is not yet complete. There are two additional restrictions we must put on the proposed organization to reflect the reconstructive processing above. First, *a schema's arcs must not be directly enumerable*. If they

---

[3]These features are similar to those that represent the "tag" in Graesser's and Nakamura's (1982) "schema copy plus tag" model. We shall see, however, that the implications of our theory are quite different.

were, then so would be all of the associated nodes and thus all associated items. This particular restriction also helps explain the "false start" phenomenon. Consider the following protocol:

Was I in a museum in Oxford? No, I was only there for a couple hours, and I only had time to see the outsides of the buildings.

In this fragment, the answerer has attempted a reconstruction of a possible museum visit by considering a "museum visit in Oxford." However, after further reasoning, he decides that this event never happened. In a fully enumerable memory, this phenomenon would not occur. All examples could be retrieved and checked without guessing at details. No counterfactual episodes would be considered and no false starts would be observed. If arcs are not enumerable, however, then their labels must be reconstructed during retrieval. This process can produce candidate memories which do not exist at all.

The second restriction follows from the first: *Arcs may be traversed only if their labels have been specified.* Such an organization will prohibit enumeration, but will allow directed traversal through memory. Intuitively, we can think of these structures as *locked conceptual networks*. The arcs can be thought of as locks which can only be opened (and thus traversed) if the correct key is available to open them (i.e., if the label on the arc can be specified). In this way, each concept organizes all of the concepts related to it, but retrieving any of these related concepts requires specifying the feature designated as its path "lock" or key. Reconstruction is thus seen as a method of directing search to only relevant items in memory.[4]

A. E-MOPs

We will be concerned henceforth with the organization of events in event schemas. The schemata which organize *events* in memory will be referred to as

---

[4]Note that if we had a strength associated with each arc in a traditional ISA/INSTANCE-OF network, and thresholds for cutoff or output interference, then we would obtain a memory that forgets and that cannot enumerate. While reconstructive retrieval strategies could be laid on top of such a structure, the structure itself would not provide enough information to guide and control reconstruction. We could also add associative strengths and cutoffs to the structure in Fig. 1, and our structure would forget and be unable to enumerate instances without the additional restrictions we propose here. However, such a memory structure would not, by itself, account for false starts and other strategic memory phenomena. It also would not provide an accounting of how the organization of memory can direct traversal of memory structures. As we shall see, the restrictions we put on the memory structure explain the need for and guide reconstructive retrieval processes. We have not considered the interaction of associative strength with these strategies, but its role should be explored.

Episodic Memory Organization Packets (E-MOPs).[5] Labels of arcs in an E-MOP are called its *indices* and are said to *index* the items organized by an E-MOP. When an event is entered into one of these structures, the features which differentiate it from other items in the E-MOP are extracted and used to index it. To retrieve events from an E-MOP, features of a targeted event are specified, the corresponding arcs are traversed, and the concepts indexed by the specified features are retrieved.

The E-MOPs implicitly and explicitly referred to in the examples are "diplomatic trips" and "diplomatic meetings." In general, we can expect an event memory to have E-MOPs for each major type of event it knows about. Thus, E-MOPs for day-to-day events might include "getting up in the morning," "eating in a restaurant," "going to the movies," "driving to the office," and so forth. Memory for a diplomat will also include E-MOPs for "diplomatic trips," "diplomatic meetings," "negotiations," "speeches," and other diplomatic activities. The E-MOPs for any particular person will depend on that person's activities and experiences.

A script is the simplest form of an E-MOP. Like scripts, E-MOPs provide conceptual categorization for events. The emphasis of E-MOPs is different, however. While script research emphasized the structure of generalized episodes and their uses in understanding and recall, the emphasis in studying E-MOPs is the organization of individual episodes with respect to each other and to appropriate generalized episodes. Scripts were thought of primarily as processing structures while E-MOPs are looked at as both storage and processing structures.

B.   The Internal Organization of an E-MOP

An E-MOP is a network in which each node is either an E-MOP or an event. Each E-MOP has two important aspects: (1) generalized information characterizing its episodes, and (2) tree-like structures that index those episodes by their differences. As for Schank's (1980) MOPs, the generalized information associated with an E-MOP is called its *content frame.* An E-MOP's content frame

---

[5]These structures are related to Schank's (1980) MOPs and to Lebowitz's (1980) S-MOPs, but the concerns in defining MOPs and S-MOPs were different from those in defining E-MOPs. In particular, Schank's (1980) concern was with showing the interrelatedness of structures in memory. Thus, in his example domain of professional office visits, he described how visits to doctors, dentists, lawyers, and other professionals are similar, and how the structures they are stored in are related. Our concern, on the other hand, is with the processes for retrieval of individual episodes and the organizational requirements those processes place on memory. If our domain were professional office visits, we would be describing how particular visits are stored in memory in relation to each other and the generalized information that would allow them to be retrieved.

Lebowitz (1980) used S-MOPs to store terrorism events derived from newspaper stories. E-MOPs are more experientially oriented and hold more detailed information than his S-MOPs.

larger episodes:
  "negotiations" (I-NEGOTIATE)
    participants = diplomats of same nationality as meeting participants, and of
         other countries involved in meeting topic
    topic = generalization of meeting topic
  "diplomatic trips" (sM-VIPVISIT)
    destination = country or area involved in meeting topic, or country of
         residence of meeting participant
  "conferences" (sM-CONFERENCE)
    participants = diplomats of same nationality as meeting participants, and of
         other countries involved in meeting topic
    location = location of meeting
    topic = generalization of meeting topic

enables:
  "treaty signing" ($TREATY)
    sides = sides of meeting topic

sequence of events:
  participants MTRANSing to each other about meeting topic

preceding and following events:
  "diplomatic meetings" ($MEET)
    participants = subset of meeting participants
    topic = aspect of meeting topic

more general E-MOPs and classifications:
  "political meetings (sM-MEETING)
    all components correspond
  "diplomatic activities"
    all components correspond

role fillers:
  participants: foreign dignitaries of countries involved in contract being
      discussed
  location : conference room in capital city of country of residence of some
      important participant
  topic: international contract
  duration: one to two hours

Fig. 2. "Diplomatic meetings" ($MEET)—generalized information.

holds information describing its events, including their usual cast of characters, settings, props, and topics, and their usual relationships to other events.

One of the E-MOPs CYRUS uses is "diplomatic meetings." Each of the diplomatic meetings entered into CYRUS's memory is indexed in that E-MOP. Figure 2 shows some of the normative information CYRUS knows about "diplomatic meetings."

Notice that the relationships between E-MOPs cannot be stored as simple links. Rather, E-MOPs must specify correspondences between their components. Thus, CYRUS's "diplomatic meetings" MOP specifies not only that it is related to "negotiations," but that the participants in those "negotiations" are the countries the participants of the meetings represent, and that the topic of the negotiation includes the topic of the meeting.

The second important feature of an E-MOP is its *indices*. An E-MOP's indices can index either individual episodes or specialized E-MOPs. When an E-MOP holds only one episode with a particular feature, the index corresponding to that feature will point to the individual episode. When two or more episodes in an E-MOP share the same feature, its corresponding index will point to a specialized sub-MOP (with the structure just described) which organizes the subset of events with that feature. In this way, MOP/sub-MOP hierarchies are formed.

Events are indexed in E-MOPs by all of their differences from the E-MOPs norms. In general, there can be hundreds of differences ranging from microscopic to abstract in level of detail. Differences indexed in E-MOPs are domain dependent and derived from specified content frame features. Thus, the features CYRUS uses are related to Vance's professional goals and include occupational, diplomatic, and social features. In addition, good indexing features make predictions about other features of the events they organize. Choosing indices will be discussed in Section VI.

Consider, for example, how the following two events are indexed in CYRUS' "diplomatic meetings" MOP:

>   EV1: "diplomatic meeting" with
>   actor (*VANCE*)
>   others (*BEGIN*)
>   topic (*CAMP-DAVID-ACCORDS*)
>   time (TIME546)
>   place (*BLAIR-HOUSE*)
>
>   EV2: "diplomatic meeting" with
>   actor (*VANCE*)
>   others (*GROMYKO*)
>   topic (*SALT*)
>   time (TIME342)
>   place (*UN*)

Both are diplomatic meetings with foreign diplomats about international contracts. EV1 is with Begin about the Camp David Accords, and EV2 is with Gromyko about SALT. These two meetings are discriminated in CYRUS's "diplomatic meetings" MOP ($MEET) as shown in Fig. 3.[6]

---

[6]The drawings of memory we present in this article are oversimplified in several ways. The content frame has been simplified in this and subsequent drawings. In addition, all of the indexing is not shown. Rather just enough is shown to illustrate the memory organization. Finally, our figures show full event representations stored at the leaf nodes of the memory networks. In our computer implementation, that is what is stored. We realize that this is unrealistic, and Section IX, Λ discusses our predictions about what should be stored in those places.

content frame:

differences:

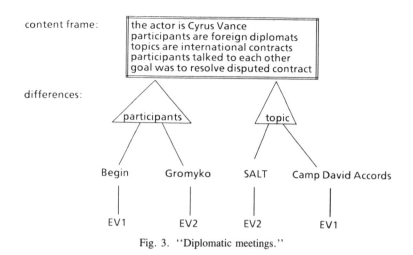

Fig. 3. "Diplomatic meetings."

As additional meetings are added to memory, generalized content frame information is refined, and additional indices for events are created. As that is happening, new E-MOPs are created where multiple episodes are indexed. Each of those new E-MOPs has a content frame based on the similarities between the episodes it indexes. Episodes are indexed in each new E-MOP according to their differentiating features. These newly created specialized E-MOPs inherit content frame properties from the more general E-MOPs they are specialized from and, in addition, have their own more specialized content frame information. Thus, E-MOPs and their specializations form a hierarchy discriminated by differences from content frame features.

After many meetings with Begin are added to the memory structure in Fig. 3 above, for example, its organization includes the arcs and nodes in Fig. 4. MOP1, "diplomatic meetings," is a refined version of the diplomatic meetings MOP in Fig. 3, while MOP2 and MOP3—"diplomatic meetings with Begin" and "diplomatic meetings about the Camp David Accords," respectively—are at the points in MOP1 where the meeting with Begin about the Camp David Accords is indexed. SALT and Gromyko remain indices to EV2, an individual event, since no additional similar meetings were added to the MOP. Thus, there would be no MOPs created at those index points until additional meetings about SALT or with Gromyko were added. Index points (2) and (3) index meetings with Dayan and about Jerusalem, respectively, in "diplomatic meetings." Index points (6), (7), (8), and (9) are new indices in MOP2 and MOP3 and index differences from the content frames of those newly created MOPs. The meeting with Dayan and the meeting about Jerusalem are indexed in MOP1 and also in appropriate specialized E-MOPs.

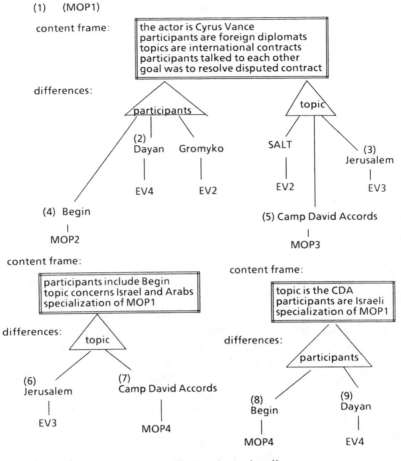

Fig. 4. "Diplomatic meetings."

V.   Searching a Reconstructive Memory

A.   TRAVERSING AN E-MOP—THE BASIC RETRIEVAL PROCESS

Because events are organized by their differentiating features, an event can be found in an E-MOP by following indices corresponding to its features. This process is a *traversal* process. Traversal involves following appropriate indices down the tree until the sought item is found. An event to be retrieved from an E-MOP is called a *target event,* and the features which describe it make up its *context specification.* A target event, or event which must be retrieved, can be said to be *targeted for retrieval.*

Traversal of an E-MOP is guided by the particular event targeted for retrieval. Consider, for example, the following questions:

(Q2): Have you ever discussed SALT with Gromyko at a diplomatic meeting?
(Q3): Have you ever attended a diplomatic meeting about the Camp David Accords with Dyan?

As a first step, answering a question requires extraction of its "target concept," that is, the concept that must be searched for in memory. The target concept for (Q2) is a "diplomatic meeting about SALT with Gromyko." Answering (Q2) requires retrieval of an event with that description.

The next step in the process involves choice of indices. Index selection is based on features specified in the target event. Indices chosen for use in retrieving any target event should be features that would have been chosen as indices for that event if it had previously been indexed in the E-MOP, i.e., features which would have differentiated it from other events already in the E-MOP.

A "diplomatic meeting about SALT with Gromyko" can be retrieved from the structure in Fig. 4 by traversing either of the indices "has topic SALT" or "has Gromyko as a participant," retrieving the event found at each of those points (EV2), and checking to make sure it has all the required features. Since EV2, found at both index points, is a meeting with Gromyko about SALT, it has all the features of the target event and can be used to form an appropriate response to the question.

When a target event specifies an event feature which is unique in an E-MOP, the event can be found by traversing the index associated with that feature. Question (Q2) had two unique features in the "diplomatic meetings" MOP—its participants and its topic. Either can be followed to retrieve the appropriate event.

Because there is no way of knowing before traversal whether or not a feature is unique to an E-MOP, the indices associated with each feature selected for retrieval are traversed in parallel. If one is unique, an event will be found and traversal can end. Otherwise, traversal continues at the next E-MOP level. Thus, in answering (Q3), both indices "has Dayan as a participant" and "has topic the Camp David Accords" are traversed. Since one is unique, an event is found, and traversal can stop. If, however, the index "has Dayan as a participant" had not been unique (i.e., if there had been more than one meeting with Dayan indexed in the E-MOP), then traversal would have had to continue within the E-MOP at that point and also within the "meetings about the Camp David Accords" MOP.

Traversal, then, is a *recursive process* involving choice of indices and traversal of those indices. It stops when an event is found or when there are no more specified indices to be traversed. If there are multiple paths to a target event, it will be retrieved from the shortest path that has all of its indices specified in the target event. We can think of traversal as a *breadth first search* which imple-

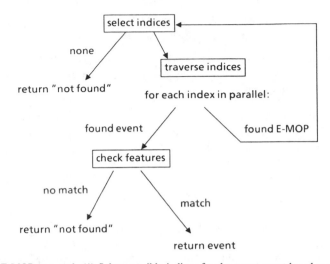

Fig. 5. E-MOP traversal. (1) Select possible indices for the target event based on its specified features and their differences from the norm of the E-MOP being traversed. (2) IF there are no indices, THEN return "not found." (3) ELSE follow all of those indices in the E-MOP. (4) IF events are found, THEN check that they have all features of the target event. If any do, return them and finish. (5) IF E-MOPs are found, traverse them in parallel using this algorithm.

ments *parallel traversal of all appropriate indices.* Figure 5 specifies the algorithm for traversal.

B.   WHERE TRAVERSAL BREAKS DOWN

If we assume that traversal is the basic or core retrieval process, then the entire retrieval process can be defined as follows: Choose a conceptual category (i.e., schema) for search, and traverse the indices of that category to find the target concept.

Three kinds of failures derive from this algorithm:

1. A question may not specify a category for search. In that case, one must be chosen.
2. Features specified in a question may not match those indexed in memory. In that case, hypothetical features must be derived.
3. A target event (extracted from the question) may describe many rather than only one event in memory. Because enumeration is not allowed, there must be some other way of getting at individual events. If the process in 2 is unsuccessful, then hypothetical related events must be derived and remembered.

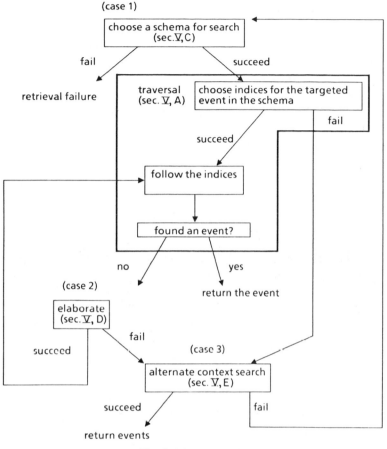

(case 1)

choose a schema for search
(sec. $\underline{V}$, C)

fail   succeed

retrieval failure

traversal
(sec. $\underline{V}$, A)   choose indices for the targeted
event in the schema

fail

succeed

follow the indices

found an event?

no   yes

(case 2)

return the event

elaborate
(sec. $\underline{V}$, D)

fail

succeed   (case 3)

alternate context search
(sec. $\underline{V}$, E)

succeed   fail

return events

Fig. 6. Memory search.

Strategic retrieval processes are necessary to compensate for each of these problems. Figure 6 shows how strategies to take care of each of these cases interact
with the traversal algorithm in the complete retrieval process. Boxes corresponding to the three cases above are marked. In sections below, we explain each in
detail.

C.   CHOOSING A CATEGORY FOR SEARCH

In order to use the traversal algorithm in Fig. 5, a category (i.e., schema) to be
searched must first be specified (case 1 in Fig. 6). Consider, for example, the
following question:

(Q4): Mr. Vance, when was the last time you saw an oil field in the Middle East?

If "seeing oil fields" were one of memory's E-MOPs, then this question would be fairly easy to answer. "Seeing oil fields" would be selected for search. If it indexed an episode in the Middle East, that episode could be retrieved from it. Similarly, if "seeing objects" were a memory category, it could be selected as a schema for retrieval, and events in the Middle East and at oil fields could be retrieved from it.

Suppose, however, that neither of these schemata existed in the memory being searched. In that case, an E-MOP for search would have to be chosen. We can imagine that the following reasoning process might take place during the process of answering (Q4):

A1: An oil field is a large sight, perhaps I saw an oil field during a *sightseeing* episode in the Middle East.

If one used information about episodic contexts associated with "large sites," a "sightseeing" category could be chosen for retrieval. Its contents could be searched for an episode at oil fields in the Middle East. If episodes in the sightseeing category were organized by the type of site and part of the world where they took place, and if there had been an episode in the Middle East at an oil field, then "a sightseeing episode at an oil field in the Middle East" could be retrieved.

To see that this process also occurs in human memory access, consider this question and a typical response:

(Q5): Who is the most famous person you have ever met?

The following protocol is typical of the answers to this question:

First I thought how somebody could be famous, and politics was the first thing I thought of. Then I thought about circumstances where I could have met a famous politician. I searched for political experiences I have had—mostly political rallies I participated in and experiences campaigning for candidates. I remembered that I had met McGovern. But since you said "most famous," I went on to think of other famous people I might have met. Next I thought of entertainers, and how I could have met them. I remembered going backstage a few times after seeing shows, but I couldn't remember who I had met. I started going through TV programs and the entertainers on those programs. I couldn't think of meeting any of those. Then I thought of famous scientists, and where I could have met them.

The diverse kinds of situations recalled in answering this question suggest that this person had no conceptual category (E-MOP) for "meeting famous people." Rather, he seemed to use knowledge about "famous people" to choose types of situations in which he could have met one. Using that information, he was able to direct search for episodes where he might have met politicians, entertainers, and scientists. His knowledge about politicians directed his search toward political rallies and campaigns where he could have met politicians. His knowledge about actors directed the search toward times he had been backstage after a show.

In general, in order to search memory, a *context for search* must first be set up. A context for search specifies a memory schema to be searched. Because CYRUS's memory is organized around event schemas, or E-MOPs, a context for search in CYRUS must include a specification of an E-MOP for traversal. Since people's memories may also be organized in other ways, a person can be expected to choose any appropriate organizing schemata in this step.

How can this be done? In CYRUS, the nonorganizing concepts in memory (e.g., individual and generic persons, contracts, places) point to E-MOPs they are commonly associated with. In general, context selection requires that nonorganizing concepts refer to those organizing schemata in whose context they normally occur. Appropriate categories for search can be chosen by selecting from the concepts associated with nonorganizational components of the retrieval cue. We thus propose the following principle:

Memory Principle #5

Retrieval from memory requires knowledge about the contexts associated with target items.

In this way, memory search is constrained and directed only to relevant schemata. A schema chosen for retrieval provides a context for search. "Political rallies" can be chosen as a context for search because they are associated with "politicians," one kind of famous person. "Sightseeing" can be chosen as a context for "seeing oil fields" if "oil fields" are defined as a "large site" and if "large sites" are associated with "sightseeing." To see in detail how this works, consider the following CYRUS example:

(Q6): Have you ever discussed the Camp David Accords with Dayan?

CYRUS knows about many different situations in which Vance might talk to other people (in fact, almost any situation could apply), but it does not have an E-MOP for "talking to people" or "discussing." Although Vance could talk to somebody during any of his activities, it would not be appropriate for CYRUS to search every one of its E-MOPs to find discussions about the Camp David Accords.

In answering (Q6), the topic and participants are used to infer a context for search. Figure 7 shows the knowledge CYRUS has about international contracts which allows an appropriate context to be chosen. The "Camp David Accords" is identified as an "international contract," and that, in turn, has the context "political meeting" associated with it. Similarly, but not shown, Dayan is identified as a "foreign diplomat," which has the event context "diplomatic meeting" associated with it. Furthermore, each associated context specifies the

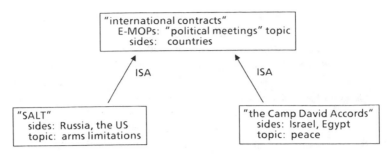

Fig. 7. International contracts.

role the component plays in it. Thus, "international contracts" not only lists "political meetings" as an E-MOP it is associated with, but it further states that it fits the topic slot of such a meeting. Using topic information, the context of a "political meeting" can be chosen to answer Q6. Using similar information associated with "foreign diplomat" (of which Dayan was one), "diplomatic meeting," a refinement of "political meeting," can be chosen. CYRUS thus searches its memory for a "diplomatic meeting about the Camp David Accords with Dayan."

D. ELABORATING FEATURES DURING RETRIEVAL

Traversing a category's indices to find a target event requires selecting potential indices from the event's features and traversing those indices. Features specified in a question, however, may not correspond to those indexed in memory. We must therefore look for some means of automatically deriving features which *are* indexed in memory from the available cues (case 2 in Fig. 6).

Consider again the question above:

(Q7): Mr. Vance, when was the last time you saw an oil field in the Middle East?

We mentioned earlier that if a "sightseeing" E-MOP organized its episodes according to their geographic location or the type of site, then finding a sightseeing event in the Middle East would be easy. Suppose, however, that our "sightseeing" category does not organize its episodes by either of those features. In that case, the following *elaboration* of the event sought in the question might be appropriate to answer the question:

A2: Which countries in the Middle East have oil fields? Iran and Iraq have oil fields, and so does Saudi Arabia. Have I seen an oil field in any of those places? . . .[7]

---

[7]Note that while we have prohibited enumeration of events from memory categories, this answer requires enumeration of countries in the Middle East. We do not address the process of such

If sightseeing episodes are organized by country, then *elaborating* "the Middle East" and specifying particular countries in that area of the world would enable retrieval of sightseeing episodes that took place in each of those places. Instead of searching for "sightseeing at an oil field in the Middle East," one could search for each of the more specific episodes, that is, "sightseeing at an oil field in Iran" or "sightseeing at an oil field in Iraq." The process that transforms given features of a target event into features which might be indexed in the current schema is called *index fitting*. Since the values of indices are not enumerable, this process is actually one of elaborating plausible features of sought items in the hope that one will be an index and "unlock" the network. Index fitting allows *downward traversal* in memory's networks to find nodes representing more specific concepts.

Elaboration is also necessary when a target concept is *too general* and no additional features are available to use for traversal. In that case, we call the elaboration process *plausible-index generation*. Consider, for example, the protocol above of a person recalling the museums he had visited. Previously, we observed that this person was trying to better specify or elaborate his descriptions of museum visits so that he could remember them one at a time. Because the person had been to many museums, however, "museum visit" is too general a specification of a target event—it describes too many events. The traversal process described above must fail because no features are available for it to use as traversal indices. In this case, elaboration provides additional hypothetical features of the target event. Thus, we can explain that this person was generating additional cues for downward traversal of memory structures.

Index fitting and plausible-index generation are used to elaborate features of a target event with respect to a particular schema. Those schemata are the ones at which traversal cannot continue. Thus, different plausible elaborations for a particular event might result when it is considered in two different E-MOP contexts.

To see how this fits into our model, consider the following question, asked of the MOP in Fig. 4:

(Q8): Describe all the instances in which you met with Begin about the Camp David Accords.

Because enumeration of events is impossible, answering this question requires individual retrieval of each appropriate meeting. In order to traverse E-MOPs to find those meetings, the indices to be traversed must be specified.

Using the features already specified in the question, traversal can proceed as

enumeration in this article. The way this could be done is by imagining a map of the Middle East and mentally walking around that map. Alternatively, it could be done by reconstructing the map. Thus, blind enumeration (i.e., enumeration of a list) is not necessary.

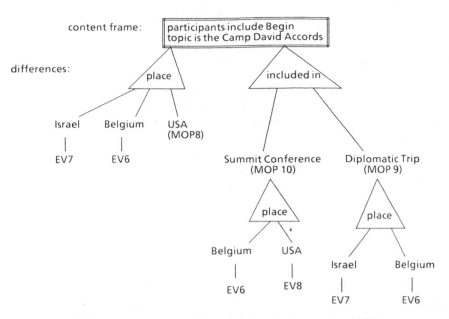

Fig. 8. Meetings with Begin about the Camp David Accords—MOP4.

far as MOP4, the subMOP which organizes "diplomatic meetings with Begin about the Camp David Accords." Because there are no additional features specified in the target concept which correspond to indices in that E-MOP, however, the traversal process must abort at this point. The retrieval specification "meetings with Begin about the Camp David Accords" is too general, and plausible index generation must be done.

Suppose now that MOP4—"diplomatic meetings about the Camp David Accords with Begin"—had the structure shown in Fig. 8. If possible places for these meetings or the types of events they were included in could be inferred, then actual meetings could be retrieved from the MOP.

Index fitting and plausible-index generation are done by *instantiation strategies*. Instantiation strategies are used to elaborate on two classes of event features: event components and event contexts. Event components include such descriptive features as participants, location, and topic. An event's context includes other episodes related to it through time, causality, or containment. Two classes of instantiation strategies are used to do elaboration: *Component-instantiation strategies* elaborate on event components, while *context-to-context instantiation strategies* are used to infer aspects of an event's surrounding context.

1. Component-Instantiation Strategies

Component-instantiation strategies are used to infer event components and role fillers of a target event. They get their guidance and information from three different sources: (1) the target event; (2) content frame information describing default values for components of items in some E-MOP the target fits into; and (3) the general relationships (less dependent on context) between components and other components.

Component-instantiation strategies take as input an event description and a MOP that event might fit into. They produce a set of possible values for the component in question. As a first step, each component-instantiation strategy gets as much detail as possible about the event component from the event itself and the E-MOP content frame. It then uses general information about the relationships between event components to fill in more detail. A set of tactics with these functions comprises the strategy, and strategies are associated with the particular types of nonorganizing concepts they are associated with (event components in CYRUS, e.g., topic, participants, place, and time).

Using the content frame of "diplomatic meeting" (Fig. 2), for example, the participants in a meeting about the Camp David Accords can be inferred to be Israeli or Egyptian diplomats. Had the content frame of "diplomatic meetings" not been sufficient to infer the location of a "meeting with Begin about the Camp David Accords," generalized information associated with location (i.e., that it is often the country of residence of one of the participants in diplomatic events) could have been used to make the same inference.

2. Context-to-Context Instantiation Strategies

The set of instantiation strategies which elaborate on the surrounding context (e.g., other events) of a target event are called *context-to-context instantiation strategies*. These strategies use content frame information from the schema a target event fits into to produce descriptions of other events plausibly related to the target. In general, these strategies allow inference and instantiation of organizing schemata plausibly related to the target item.

Context-to-context instantiation strategies produce a set of event descriptions as output. In CYRUS there is one such strategy corresponding to each possible relationship between events. Table II lists these relationships. In general, there must be one of these strategies for each relationship between organizing schemata. Input to these strategies consists of an event (real or plausible) and an E-MOP that event fits into. The event descriptions output by the strategy describe events plausibly related in the specified way to the input event. Table III lists the set of context-to-context instantiation strategies.

TABLE II

Relationships between E-MOPs

Causal relationships
   usual events and states that enable these events to happen
   their normal preconditions
   events and states that usually cause these events to happen
   events and states these events usually cause
   events and states these events usually enable
Containment relationships
   E-MOPs these events are usually part of
   the typical sequence of events for these episodes
Temporal relationships
   what kinds of events usually come before these episodes
   what kinds of events usually follow these episodes
   what kinds of events usually go on at the same time
Specialization/generalization relationships
   parent E-MOPs
   standard methods of achievement

Consider, for example, the strategy "Instantiate-Larger-Episodes" (in Fig. 9). It produces descriptions of episodes an event might have been part of. Each strategy has three steps. First, the appropriate content frame component of E-MOP is retrieved, for example, larger episodes for "Instantiate-Larger-Episodes," resulting episodes for "Instantiate-Results." Second, role fillers or components of EVENT are transferred appropriately to the event framework provided by execution of the first step. Third, component-instantiation strategies are applied to further refine the role fillers of any newly instantiated EPISODES.

Applying this strategy to a "diplomatic meeting with Begin about the Camp

TABLE III

Context-to-Context
Instantiation Strategies

Instantiate-Enablements
Instantiate-Preconditions
Instantiate-Results
Instantiate-Reasons
Instantiate-Enabled-Events
Instantiate-Larger-Episodes
Instantiate-Seq-of-Events
Instantiate-Preceding-Events
Instantiate-Following-Events
Instantiate-Standardizations

EVENT = the event whose larger episodes are to be instantiated, i.e., the
target event

MOP = the most specific E-MOP EVENT fits into

EPISODE = framework for episode to be instantiated

EPISODES = the newly instantiated events (i.e., the episodes which may
plausibly contain EVENT)

(1) If EPISODE is unspecified, then get the default larger episodes for MOP, else use
EPISODE.

(2) For each larger episode specification, transfer components as specified,
producing EPISODES, and make the following inferences when more specific
information is not available on the E-MOP:

    (a) Time specifications on each EPISODE include the time specified
       in EVENT.

    (b) Place specifications on each EPISODE include the place specified
       in EVENT.

    (c) Participants of EVENT are included in the participants of each
       EPISODE, groups and organizations they belong to might also
       be involved.

    (d) Topic of each EPISODE includes that of EVENT.

(3) Use relevant Component-Instantiation strategies to further specify components
of each EPISODE, using the already instantiated partial descriptions of each
component as constraints.

Fig. 9. Instantiate-Larger-Episodes.

David Accords'' (the target event of Q8), and using content frame knowledge
from the ''diplomatic meetings'' E-MOP (see Fig. 2), the following descriptions
are generated of episodes the meeting could have been part of:

A ''diplomatic trip'' to Israel.

A ''Summit Conference'' with Begin as a participant and whose topic was related to the Camp
David Accords.

''Negotiations'' with Israel about the Camp David Accords.

Production of these episode descriptions allows the following elaborations of that
target meeting:

''meetings with Begin about the Camp David Accords which took place during a diplomatic
trip to Israel''.

''meetings with Begin about the Camp David Accords during a summit conference which
included Begin as a participant and whose topic was related to the Camp David Accords''

"meetings with Begin about the Camp David Accords which were part of negotiations with
Israel about the Camp David Accords"

In answering Q8, this instantiation strategy is applied, and retrieval of each of
the elaborated meetings above is attempted. The first will find EV7 by following
the indices "included in a diplomatic trip" and then "place is Israel" in the E-
MOP in Fig. 8. Retrieval of the second will include traversal of the index
"included in a summit conference," and further elaboration will be needed to
retrieve an individual event. The third will not be successful in the E-MOP
illustrated.

E.   SEARCHING FOR SOMETHING OTHER THAN WHAT
WAS ASKED FOR

One of the observations we can make from many of the examples and protocols above is the following:

Memory Principle #6

Retrieval often requires search for something other than what was
requested.

Two reasons why it is often necessary to search for something other than what
was requested are that (1) a category for search might not be specified in a
question, and (2) a given specification might be insufficient for retrieval. In the
second case, the given context is elaborated as described above, and a better
specified context is searched for. Elaboration of plausible features is not always
successful, however. Unsuccessful elaboration is a third reason for searching for
something other than what was requested.

Consider again our sightseeing example from the previous section:

(Q9): Mr. Vance, when was the last time you saw an oil field in the Middle
East?

Suppose that there were not enough information available to choose indices for
traversal. In a memory where contextually related items refer to each other,
another way to find a sought item is to search for items it might have been related
to. Another related item might be more easily retrieved and, if found, might refer
to the targeted one. Since any sightseeing episode in the Middle East would have
happened during a trip to the Middle East, the following reasoning would be
appropriate to recall "sightseeing episodes in the Middle East":

A3: In order to go sightseeing in the Middle East, I would have had to have
been on a trip there. On a vacation trip, I wouldn't go to see oil fields, so
I must have been taken to oil fields during a diplomatic trip to the Middle
East. Which countries might have taken me to see their oil fields? Saudi

Arabia has the largest fields, perhaps they took me to see them. Yes, they did when I was there last year.

Search of this kind is quite often done by people, as shown in the following example of a person naming the museums he had been to:

Let me see. What other museums have I been to? The last time I was in England, I went to a bunch of museums in London—the British Museum, some gallery whose name I can't remember, and Mme. Taussaud's Wax Museum. And I also went to some palaces there that were museums—the Royal Pavilion in Brighton and some other palace in London, um, . . . it was called Hampton Court. When I went on my first trip to France, . . . I once went on a trip around New York State, and I went to the photography museum in Rochester and the Corning Glass Museum. During my trip to California, . . .

In each of these examples, we see search for a different kind of event than the one originally asked for. To find sightseeing experiences in A3, we see search for diplomatic trips during which the sightseeing might have taken place. In the human protocol, we see the person recalling trips to remember museum visits. Searching for a different type of event than the one targeted for retrieval is called *alternate context search* (case 3 in Fig. 6). Once a related event is retrieved, it can provide cues to use in reconstructing the originally targeted event. Features of a trip to England, for example, can be useful in filling in details of museum visits experienced during the trip.

While index fitting and elaboration direct depthwise search within memory, alternate context search is *lateral traversal* of memory. Search is within different E-MOPs, or schemata, than the one originally selected for retrieval. One problem associated with searching for alternate contexts is constraining the search. Search should be constrained to contexts that have a possibility of being related to an item targeted for retrieval. In general, for search to be constrained to relevant contexts, the following must be true:

Memory Principle #7

Memory schemata must hold generalized information concerning the relationships of their items to items in other schemata.

If "museum visit" holds the information that its items are often parts of "trips," "visits from out-of-town friends," or "visits to New York," then search can be constrained to only those three alternate contexts. Similarly, for constraining search of contexts related to "diplomatic meetings," generalized information associated with diplomatic meetings must be used. Figure 2 shows that information.

1. Guiding Alternate-Context Search

Executive search strategies direct search for alternate contexts. They have four steps: (1) Context-to context instantiation strategies (explained above) are called to construct descriptions of episodes plausibly related to the target event. (2) Control is passed to the traversal/elaboration process, which is directed to attempt retrieval of each of those hypothetical events. (3) If any such event is found, its episodic context is searched for the original target event. (4) If step (3) fails, events retrieved in step (2) are used to elaborate the target event, and memory is traversed looking for it.

Steps 1 and 2 of executive strategies have been described previously. Search of surrounding context (step 3) and elaboration of the target (step 4) must be described in more detail. Recall from the discussion of instantiation strategies that an event's context includes events it was related to through containment, time, or causality. Search of the episodic or surrounding context of one event for a target event means reconstructing the appropriate part of the first event to see if it corresponds to the target event. In our model, there are two mechanisms for doing this. First, an event itself might point to or describe another event related to it. If a particular museum experience was the highlight of some trip, for example, then the trip's description in memory may point directly to the museum experience or describe it in enough detail to retrieve it from its own MOP. In this case, to find a target event in the surrounding context of an alternate episode, the possible relationships between the two events are determined, and appropriate parts of the context of the alternate episode are checked to see if events it points to or describes correspond to the target.

If an event does not explicitly point to appropriate episodes related to it, but they are consistent with its context, a second procedure is available. The retrieved event is used to elaborate the target event. This is done through application of an appropriate context-to-context instantiation strategy. As an example of step (4), consider the following: The target event is "museum experiences." In searching for museum experiences, some trips are recalled, say a trip to England. While the sequence of events of the trip itself may not refer to any museum visits (step 3), transference of its features to a "museum visit" context might aid in describing a museum visit that did in fact happen. Its time, place, the weather, for example, applied to a museum visit might provide enough details to retrieve a valid visit to a museum.

"Find-from-Larger-Episodes" (see Fig. 10) constructs, finds, and searches the episodic context of events a target event could have been part of. To aid in finding a particular "diplomatic meeting with Gromyko," it would (1) call the context instantiation strategy "Instantiate-Larger-Episodes" to construct contexts for "summit conferences about a Russian–American concern," "diplomatic trips to Russia," and "negotiations concerning a Russian–American contract," (2) traverse memory searching for each of those, and (3) search the sequence of events of each episode found for an appropriate diplomatic meeting or (4) apply "Instantiate-Sequence-of-Events" to the recalled alternate context to elaborate the target event. There is an executive search strategy corresponding

IF the Target Concept could have been embedded in a larger episode

THEN

    (1) Use "Instantiate-Larger-Episodes" to hypothesize episodes the target concept could have been part of. Use Component-Instantiation strategies to fill in each description.

    (2) Search memory for those instances

    (3) If one is found, search its sequence of events and instrumental events for events which could match the Target Concept.

    (4) If no match is found, use "Instantiate-Seq-of-Events", plus the additional information found in the larger episodes, to better specify the target concept. Traverse memory for the new target concept.

Fig. 10. Find-from-Larger-Episodes.

to each relationship an event can have to other events. Table IV lists the set of executive search strategies.

2. When Is Alternate-Context Search Useful?

In guiding search for event contexts related to a target event, search strategies direct search for ''what must have happened'' or ''what may have happened'' if the target event had taken place. If an event that must have happened along with a targeted event can be found, its specification in memory might refer to the target or aid in its reconstruction.

Alternate-context search is helpful under two circumstances: (1) when the event being searched for is obscure, and (2) when many events corresponding to a general specification must be found. An obscure event is one which might be present in memory, but for which there is not enough generalized information available to do the necessary elaboration to get it out.

TABLE IV

Executive Search Strategies

Find-from-Enablements
Find-from-Preconditions
Find-from-Results
Find-from-Reasons
Find-from-Enabled-Events
Find-from-Larger-Episodes
Find-from-Seq-of-Events
Find-from-Preceding-Events
Find-from-Following-Events
Find-from-Standardizations

When retrieval fails because of inability to produce a sufficient elaboration, executive strategies are applied to search for alternate contexts related to the event which might be more easily retrieved. In one case, we observed a person searching memory for many different kinds of episodes related to renting cars to recall if she had ever rented a Chevy (an obscure event):

> I rent cars during trips when I need to be able to travel easily. In California, it is impossible to get around without a car. On my trip there last summer, I rented a Fairmont, and on my last trip there, I had a Toyota. Neither of them was a Chevy. What kinds of bad experiences have I had with rental cars? Was one of those cars a Chevy? I once missed a plane because I couldn't find the rental car place to return my car—that was a foreign car of some kind. Another time, I rented a car that was too big for me—I couldn't see over the steering wheel. It was the only car they had available. That might have been a Chevy, I have no idea if it was or not.

Searching for alternate contexts can aid retrieval since an alternate context might be less common than a target event and thus need less specification in order to be retrieved. Alternate-context search can also aid retrieval of a target event if the alternate context can be better specified with respect to the E-MOPs it is indexed in than the target event can. In extensive memory search, executive strategies can be applied in succession until a satisfactory answer is retrieved from memory.

VI.   Integrating New Items into Memory

Up to now, we have been assuming that memory would be well organized for application of retrieval strategies. Yet, we also stated previously that the memory we are considering is dynamic, that is, new experiences occurring from moment to moment must be added to the memory structures. As new events are added to memory, *good memory organization must be maintained.* Integrating new unanticipated items into memory requires a memory capable of organizing itself. The reorganization process must maintain the memory's structure and also build up the knowledge that retrieval strategies need in order to operate. Previous knowledge aids in deciding where and how to place new inputs in memory.

Memory update is very closely related to understanding. One aspect of understanding, for example, involves figuring out how a new item is similar to items already in memory. This is necessary in order to choose a schema for further processing the item. Choosing a schema for an item is also the first step in integrating it into memory. As in understanding, once a schema is chosen during memory update, it provides an appropriate point in memory from which to draw inferences and make assumptions. In fact, the end result of understanding and memory update is the same: The concepts that comprise and are related to an item have been specified, and the place for the item in memory's structures has been found.

To understand problems associated with memory update, we must look to both retrieval and understanding processes for guidelines. In understanding, for example, previously made generalizations are used to infer aspects not explicit in the event and to make predictions about what will be true in the future. During retrieval, that same generalized knowledge is used by reconstructive strategies for elaboration and to guide search of memory. It is also used during question answering to generate default answers and as part of the memory update process itself to control the proliferation of indices, subindices, and subschemas. To make much generic knowledge available, it must be built up as new items are added to memory. Both the new items and the generalizations that can be made based on their similarities to other items must be integrated into the memory.

In order for similarities to be noticed, similar items must be directed to the same place in memory. When a second item is directed to a place in memory where another already resides, their similarities are noted and generalizations are made. Of course, any generalization based on only two items might be faulty, so we must also provide for recovery from bad generalizations and control of later generalizations.

Noticing similarities is a crucial part of memory update. It would not be feasible, however, to have memory notice all similarities and differences. A person going to a meeting, for example, is not likely to connect the weather with the meeting unless it has some bearing on the meeting (e.g., how hard it is to get there). Generalization and noticing similarities must be directed and controlled. We have already proposed an indexing scheme based on differences that allows retrieval to be controlled by the input cues. In order to explain how generalization and the noticing of similarities can be controlled, we will have to give more detail about the way in which indices are chosen, both in adding new items to memory and in attempting retrieval of an item already stored.

In this section, a process for automatically adding new items to memory while maintaining its organization will be described. Extending what we know about memory organization, we can lay out the following algorithm for adding new items to memory: When a new item is added to memory, conceptual categories (schemata) are chosen for it. Differences between it and the norms of those categories are derived and features for indexing are chosen. After that, the item is indexed. In this way, index selection is controlled to avoid combinatorial explosion of indices and new schemata. As new specialized schemata are created through indexing, the generalized information that memory needs for understanding and retrieval is added to each one.

A. AUTOMATIC INDEXING

The first step in adding a new event to an E-MOP is to choose appropriate features of the event for indexing. Recall that this means choosing features which differentiate it from other events indexed in the same E-MOP. Consider, for example, how the following event should be indexed in memory under each of the following circumstances:

EV3: Cyrus Vance has a meeting with Andrei Gromyko in Russia about the Afghanistan invasion.

Case 1: Vance has met many times before with Gromyko, but never in Russia, and never about the Afghanistan invasion.

Case 2: Vance has been in Russia for the past 2 weeks meeting with Gromyko every day about the Afghanistan situation.

In the first case, the topic and location of EV3 can distinguish it from other meetings in memory. Therefore, either of those features would be reasonable indices for EV3 in a "diplomatic meetings" MOP. In the second case, however, its location and topic cannot distinguish this meeting from other meetings already indexed in that E-MOP. Indexing on those features will not be helpful in discriminating this meeting from others. There are two major problems to address in discussing index selection: What characterizes a good E-MOP index, and how can E-MOP indices be chosen?

B.   What Is a Difference from a Norm?

In introducing E-MOPs, it was stated that *indexing should be by differences from the E-MOP's norms*. The reasons for this stem from the two major purposes of an indexing scheme. First, it must *subdivide the categories* into smaller, more workable parts. Indexing must also serve to *make members of a category more accessible*. Through multi-indexing, the same item can be referenced in many different ways. Through subindexing, an item can be given a unique description and be made *discriminable*.

To see why this implies that indexing should be by differences, suppose indexing also included an E-MOP's norms. Since most events organized by any E-MOP have its norms as features, they would all have virtually the same indices. This would neither add to the discriminability of any item nor divide the category into smaller pieces. Organizing events according to differences allows events to be recognized individually. If a unique difference from a norm is specified in a retrieval key, the event that corresponds to that specification can be retrieved.

We identify four types of differences from norms: (1) a violation of the norm, (2) a variation of a norm (e.g., the norm plus additional features), (3) a specialization of the norm, and (4) a generalization of the norm.

In CYRUS, for example, the E-MOP "summit conference" has the norms shown in Fig. 11. Taking these into consideration, consider how the "Camp David Summit" would be indexed in the "summit conference" E-MOP. Its purpose was to negotiate an accord between Israel and Egypt, an important international contract. Its participants were the heads of state of Israel, Egypt,

content frame:

```
topic is an international contract
participants are heads of state of countries
 involved in contract and a group of their
 advisors
location is a resort area in neutral country
purpose is negotiations
includes many diplomatic meetings
duration is a few days
```

Fig. 11. Summit conference.

and the United States, plus their advisors. Its location was the U.S. president's private resort complex in the United States (not quite a neutral country). It lasted almost 2 weeks. Because the topic of the conference is *better specified* than the normal topic specification, this conference is indexed according to its topic. The participants are *a more general case* than the E-MOP's norms for participants (there is an addition), and that difference is indexed. The conference's location is indexed because it *violates* the norm. Because the purpose of the summit matches the norm (i.e., negotiation of its major topic), it does not get indexed. Finally, because this summit was longer than the norm (another violation), an index for its length is appropriate. Indices for each of these features are created.

C. What Makes a Good Index?

Although differences are appropriate for indexing, not all differences make good indices. Consider, for example, the following two situations:

An employer is interviewing a prospective employee for a job as a computer programmer.

An employer is interviewing a prospective employee for a job as a fashion model.

Because these are both interviews, it would be reasonable to index each using relevant features of the prospective employees. The features of the prospective employees that would make reasonable indices, however, differ greatly. It would be reasonable for the employer interviewing a prospective computer programmer to index the interview according to the interviewee's educational background. It would be less reasonable, however, for him to index the experience according to the color of the interviewee's hair (unless her hair is a weird color). On the other hand, it would be more reasonable for the employer interviewing a prospective model to index the experience according to the person's hair color and what he is wearing, rather than by his education.

Indexing Principle #1

The amount of detail that should be indexed for each feature of a situation depends upon the context in which the event is taking place.

How can this actually be done? We give several criteria for index selection. Because indices should divide a category into smaller pieces and differentiate events, *unique* features of events make good indices. A unique feature is one for which there is not already an index in the E-MOP. All aspects of unique features of an event should not be indexed, however, but only the *most general description of a unique feature*. One description is more *general* than a second if it can be used to describe the second, that is, if all of its aspects are also aspects of the second.

Indexing Principle #2

The more general a unique feature used as an index, the more retrievable the event being indexed will be.

A more general description of a feature will make a better index because it will be accessible in more cases. An index based on nationality, for example, will be traversable in more cases than an index for a particular person.

Perhaps the most important property indices should have is *predictive power*. A feature which is predictive often co-occurs with some other event feature. A useful generalization can be based on that co-occurrence. The nationality of participants in a "diplomatic meeting," for example, is predictive of one side of the contract being discussed. Thus, in a "diplomatic meetings" MOP, nationalities of participants are good predictive features for indexing.

A predictive feature is one which, if it indexed an E-MOP instead of an event, would correlate with other E-MOP features. It is important to index individual events by features which are potentially predictive so that, if additional similar events are added to memory, a new E-MOP with useful generalizations can be formed based on the similarities between events with that feature.

The first time we see a particular feature, however, we cannot be sure whether or not it will be predictive later. Predictiveness of features can be judged by previous experience. If a *type of index* (e.g., appearance of participants, nationality of participants, sides of a contract) has been useful previously for similar events, then there is a good chance it will be useful for a new event. If nationalities of participants have been predictive in indexing other "diplomatic activities," then "nationality of participants is Canadian" is likely to be predictive in any diplomatic context. This implies that schemata must know which features are likely to be predictive.

Indexing Principle #3

Indices should have predictive power or potential predictive power.

This implies that as new events are added to memory, the relative predictive power of different types of features must be tracked. Any found not to be predictive must be marked.

To further constrain the notion of predictive power in a MOP, we place the following additional constraint on E-MOP predictions: E-MOP indices should not only have potential predictive power, but they should make *context-related*

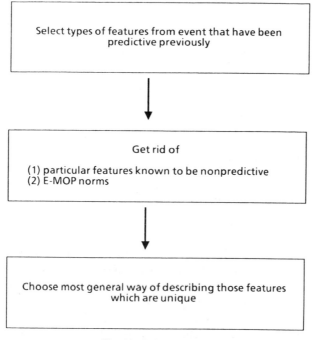

Select types of features from event that have been predictive previously

Get rid of

(1) particular features known to be nonpredictive
(2) E-MOP norms

Choose most general way of describing those features which are unique

Fig. 12. Index selection.

predictions. A context-related prediction is one which predicts schema-specific features.

Indexing Principle #4

The usefulness of an index depends on its context; a good index should make context-related predictions.

D. CHOOSING INDICES

These criteria for discriminability suggest the algorithm for index selection shown in Fig. 12. Since only features with predictive power should be indexed, the actual process of choosing indices must first use information about predictability to select possible indices for an event. Each of those possibilities can then be checked to make sure (1) that it has not been marked as nonpredictive, and (2) that it is not an E-MOP norm. In addition, each feature chosen as a potential index must be checked to see if there is a unique way of describing it. If so, the most general unique way of describing it should be used as an index.

In order for predictive power to be used in choosing indices, each schema must keep track of types of indices which have been useful and actual features which have not been useful and should no longer be used as indices. Similarly, in order to compute differences from a MOP's norms, its norms must be specified.

content frame:
    participants: diplomats of countries involved in contract being discussed
    location: conference room in capital city of country of an important participant
    topic: international contract
    duration: one to two hours

predictive:
    political roles of the participants
    classes those roles fit into
    nationalities of the participants
    occupations of the participants
    political leanings of participants
    topic, place, participant
    sides of the topic
    issue underlying the topic (e.g., peace)

nonpredictive features:
    participants' occupation is foreign minister
    participants' occupation is head of state

Fig. 13. "Diplomatic meetings."

Consider, for example, CYRUS's "diplomatic meetings" MOP after enough meetings have been added to it for it to know some of its nonpredictive features. The following are some of its predictive aspects, its norms, and the features it knows to be nonpredictive at that point in time.[8]

Using predictive information associated with this E-MOP, the first step of the index selection process would choose the following as potentially predictive features of the event below:

    EV4: Cyrus Vance has a meeting with Andrei Gromyko in Russia about SALT.

1. the meeting is with a foreign minister
2. the meeting is with a diplomat
3. the meeting is with a Russian
4. the meeting is with a Communist
5. the meeting is about SALT
6. the topic concerns the U.S. and Russia
7. the underlying topic is arms limitations
8. the meeting is with Gromyko
9. the meeting is in Russia

In the second step of the process, those features known to be nonpredictive or norms of the E-MOP are deleted from the set of potential indices. Taking into

[8]Note that CYRUS does not really have all of this information on the "diplomatic meetings" MOP itself. In order that features common to many of its MOPs do not have to be duplicated on each MOP, CYRUS has major MOP classifications which include most of the information about predictive features and some norms. Some of those classifications are "occupational activities," "social activites," and "meetings." Information lives on the most general E-MOP or MOP classification it belongs to.

account the norms and nonpredictive aspects of the ''diplomatic meetings'' MOP above, features 3–9 would remain as plausible indices for EV4.

VII. Creating New E-MOPs

After choosing features for indexing, events are indexed in E-MOPs by each of the chosen features. A feature chosen for indexing can have one of three relationships to the schema (Kolodner, 1980):

1. There is nothing yet indexed in the E-MOP with that feature.
2. There is one other item with that feature indexed in the E-MOP.
3. There is an E-MOP indexed by that feature.

A. INDEX CREATION

If there is not already an index for a feature (case 1), then one is created for it. Any time an event is indexed by a feature unique to an E-MOP, it can be retrieved from that E-MOP by specifying that feature. Thus, the more features an event has that are unique to an E-MOP, the more ways there will be of retrieving it uniquely. The rule that summarizes the process of creating a new index is in Fig. 14.

B. E-MOP CREATION

The second time an event with a particular feature is added to an E-MOP, a new sub-MOP is created. When a second event is indexed at a point where there is just one other event, the previous event is remembered. This is called *reminding* (Schank, 1980). Suppose, for example, that one of Vance's meetings had included a meal at a very fancy restaurant, and that it was his first working lunch at that restaurant. A second working lunch at the same or a similar restaurant would be indexed in memory in many of the same ways as the first, causing the first to be remembered.

Reminding triggers the creation of a new E-MOP. The current and previous events are compared for common aspects. Similarities between the two events are extracted, and a new E-MOP with generalized information based on those two occurrences is created, as specified in Fig. 15.

IF there is no prior index for a relevant feature of an event

THEN

(1) construct an index
(2) index the event's description there

Fig. 14. Index creation.

IF there is one event indexed at an index point for a new event

THEN

    (1) create a new E-MOP at that point
    (2) extract the similarities of the two events and add those as norms of the new E-MOP
    (3) index the two events in that E-MOP according to their differences from its norms

Fig. 15. E-MOP creation.

To see that this reminding and generalization process mimics the human process, imagine a person who has been to a French restaurant once in his life. According to the rules for indexing a first event, we imagine it is indexed under "serves French food" in his "restaurant" MOP. Suppose, now, that he goes to a French restaurant a second time. If both were expensive, and if in both there was good escargot as an appetizer, then he might make the generalizations that French restaurants are expensive and a good place for escargot. He would have to store that generalization somewhere, and the likely place to store it would be on a newly created E-MOP "restaurants that serve French food," an E-MOP created from the two experiences and indexed off of the "restaurant" E-MOP by the feature "serves French food."

C.   E-MOP REFINEMENT

When there is already a sub-MOP at the point where an event is being indexed (case 3), the new event is indexed in the sub-MOP by the same procedure used to index it in the more general E-MOP. In addition, the features of the new event are compared against the generalized information of both the parent E-MOP and the sub-MOP, and the validity of previous generalization is checked and refined. The rule in Fig. 16 summarizes that process.

To see that this is consistent with people's behavior, imagine a person going a third time to a French restaurant. The third and subsequent times a person goes to a French restaurant, the discrimination "serves French food" will direct the episode to the sub-MOP created above. Continuing with that example, if the third resturant were also expensive, it would confirm the generalization made previously. If not, it would weaken the generalization. The person would no

IF there is an E-MOP at an index point for a new event

THEN

    (1) index the event in that E-MOP
    (2) check the validity of its generalization
    (3) update its generalizations as necessary

Fig. 16. E-MOP refinement.

content frame:

differences:

Fig. 17. "Diplomatic trips to the Middle East."

longer automatically expect a French restaurant to cost a lot. If later visits proved that most French restaurants were indeed expensive, the generalization would be strengthened again, and the inexpensive one would be stored as an exception.

VIII. Generalization

Generalizations must be both made and refined. For now, we can assume that they are made by the initial generalization process explained above. Because initial generalizations made in creating an E-MOP might be incomplete, inaccurate, or wrong, the update process must also be able to monitor the correctness of generalized information in newly created E-MOPs. Consider, for example, the E-MOP in Fig. 17, created by adding two trips to the Middle East to memory. All episodes indexed in this E-MOP will have the feature "destination is the Middle East" since that is the index for this sub-MOP in "diplomatic trip." Probably most of these trips will continue to have the purpose of negotiating Arab–Israeli peace. We would not, however, expect that every trip to the Middle East will include a state dinner. There may also be attributes of trips to the Middle East not common to these first two trips.

As additional items are added to an E-MOP, the unreasonable generalizations must be discovered and deleted. In addition, new events must be monitored to see if additional generalized information can be extracted from them. Checking the correctness of generalizations requires monitoring both the norms and indices in an E-MOP. Undergeneralization or incomplete generalization is recognized when a particular feature indexes most of the events in an E-MOP. In that case, the corresponding sub-MOP is collapsed and its norms added to those of the parent MOP. A feature is overgeneralized if it is an E-MOP norm but does not correspond to later events added to the E-MOP. In this case, the feature is removed as a norm and an index to a sub-MOP is built for it. As new events are added to memory, their features are checked against the norms of the appropriate E-MOPs to see if either of these problems is true of any of them.

Index monitoring is also necessary as a way of keeping track of a feature's predictive power. If a particular feature does not correlate with other features, it is marked as nonpredictive so it will no longer be used as an index. We next explain recovery from overgeneralization or false generalization, generalization beyond the initial ones, and recovery from nonpredictive indices.

A.   ADDITIONAL GENERALIZATIONS

Any time a sub-MOP of an E-MOP indexes a large majority of the items in an E-MOP, the generalizations corresponding to that set of items will also be good generalizations for the entire set of events in the parent E-MOP. When this happens, additional generalizations about events in the parent E-MOP can be made by collapsing the sub-MOP and merging its generalizations with those of the parent. Figure 18 summarizes this process.

B.   RECOVERY FROM BAD GENERALIZATIONS

Recovery from bad generalizations is more complex. When new information and events contradict a previously made generalization, that generalization must be removed as one of the E-MOP's norms.

This raises a special problem. While a feature is one of the norms of an E-MOP, events are not indexed by that feature. On the other hand, if a feature is included in the norms of an E-MOP, then at least some of the events already in the E-MOP have it as a feature. Because events were not indexed by that feature, however, it would be expensive to go back and find all events supporting the generalization.

Generalization removal, then, can have grave implications in retrieval. If a retrieval key specified a feature that had been removed as a generalization, but which had not yet been indexed, then the retrieval processes would not be able to find any trace in memory of an event with that feature. It would have to conclude that there had never been such an event in memory.

To correct this problem, an index to an empty sub-MOP is created each time a feature is removed from a MOP's norms. In addition, the feature is marked as having once been "generalized." Upon encountering this marking, retrieval

IF a sub-MOP indexes a large majority of the events in its parent E-MOP

THEN

    (1) collapse the sub-MOP
    (2) get rid of its index
    (3) add the indexed feature plus other norms of the sub-MOP to the
        generalized information associated with the parent E-MOP

Fig. 18. Collapsing sub-MOPs.

IF a norm has been disconfirmed

THEN

    (1) remove it from the E-MOP
    (2) create an empty sub-MOP for it indexed by that feature
    (3) add other features removed from the E-MOP's norms at the same time
    (4) mark the new E-MOP as "once generalized"

Fig. 19. Recovery from false generalization.

functions are able to return the message "there may be events with this description, but I can't find particular ones" instead of failing completely if no distinct event can be found. This message triggers executive search strategies which attempt to find the sought event by some route other than the direct one. During later indexing, the new sub-MOP is treated like any other. The process of recovery from bad generalizations is summarized in Fig. 19.

C. MAINTENANCE OF PREDICTIVE POWER JUDGMENTS

The last kind of monitoring that must be done during memory update is monitoring for predictive power of features. The predictiveness of a particular type of feature is inherited from the more general E-MOPs a MOP is an instance of. Particular values of some type of feature, however, might turn out not to be predictive. An E-MOP indexed by a feature which is nonpredictive will have no generalized information to keep track of, and it will not be able to constrain indexing and new E-MOP creation, nor will it be able to help in understanding. Its indices will duplicate the indices in its parent MOP without it keeping track of useful generalized information. If this is the case, after a reasonable number of events have been added to an E-MOP (6 in CYRUS), the offending feature is marked as nonpredictive and is no longer used for indexing.

IX. Summary and Implications

Two types of retrieval strategies have been presented: instantiation strategies, which construct and elaborate contexts for search, and executive strategies, which guide search for and within alternate contexts. Strategy application depends on three types of knowledge being present in memory: (1) context-to-context relationships, (2) component-to-component relationships, and (3) relationships between type of components and contexts for search.

The retrieval process presented depends on memory's organization providing *discriminability* between items. With such an organization, specification of a unique set of features allows an item to be retrieved. Thus, although retrieval does not involve category enumeration, a series of similar events can be found in

TABLE V

Memory Principles

1. Human remembering is often a process of reconstructing what must have happened, rather than directly retrieving what did happen.
2. Remembering requires progressive narrowing in on a description of the event to be remembered.
3. In a reconstructive memory, memories are not directly enumerable. Instead, the features that describe individual memories must be reconstructed.
4. Similar items in memory are organized around the same concept and are indexed under that concept by their differentiating features.
5. Retrieval from memory requires knowledge about the contexts associated with target items.
6. Retrieval often requires search for something other than what was requested.
7. Memory schemata must hold generalized information concerning the relationships of their items to items in other schemata.
8. The closer a retrieval cue is to the encoding of an item at the time of retrieval, the easier retrieval of that item should be.

a directed way by reconstructing possible details and searching for events with those details, or by searching for an alternate context that might refer to a target event. Table V summarizes memory's organizational and retrieval principles.

Search, then, is directed only to relevant places in memory. If an E-MOP had hundreds or thousands of indices organizing tens of thousands of events, only those directly related to the targeted event would be traversed. Extra effort is put forth in directing search so that the search itself is highly constrained.

The potential problem in a richly indexed system is that indexing can get out of hand. We handle that problem through the notions of *salience, predictability,* and *generalization.* Indices are created only for salient features of a context; features are used for indexing only if they prove to have predictive power, and generalizations built in the course of memory update constrain selection of features for indexing. Table VI summarizes the indexing principles presented previously. Table V.II summarizes memory integration processes.

We continue by considering the implications of our model.

TABLE VI

Indexing Principles

1. The amount of detail that should be indexed for each feature of a situation depends upon the context in which the event is taking place.
2. The more general a unique feature used as an index, the more retrievable the event being indexed will be.
3. Indices should have predictive power or potential predictive power.
4. The usefulness of an index depends on its context; a good index should make context-related predictions.

TABLE VII

Memory Integration Processes

Index creation

IF there is no prior index for a relevant feature of an event, THEN (1) construct an index, and (2) index the event's description there.

E-MOP creation

IF there is one event indexed at an index point for a new event, THEN (1) create a new E-MOP at that point, (2) extract the similarities of the two events and add those as content frame features of the new E-MOP, and (3) index the two events in that E-MOP according to their differences from its norms.

E-MOP refinement

IF there is an E-MOP at an index point for a new event, THEN (1) index the event in that E-MOP, (2) check the validity of its generalizations, and (3) update its generalizations as necessary.

Additional generalizations

IF a sub-MOP indexes a large majority of the events in its parent E-MOP, and if the parent E-MOP is a stable size, THEN (1) collapse the sub-MOP, (2) get rid of its index, and (3) add the indexed feature plus other content frame features of the sub-MOP to the content frame of the parent E-MOP.

Recovery from bad generalizations

IF a content frame feature has been disconfirmed, THEN (1) remove it from the E-MOP, (2) create an empty sub-MOP for it indexed by that feature, (3) add other features removed from the E-MOP's content frame at the same time to the content frame of the new sub-MOP, and (4) mark the new E-MOP as "once generalized."

A. Reconstruction and Representation of Full Events

So far, we have shown how reconstructive strategies are used to direct search of memory, but have not considered reconstruction of full events. The model presented makes a set of predictions with respect to this task:

1. Pieces of episodes are spread throughout schemata (E-MOPs) in memory.
2. Schemata know their relationships to other schemata.
3. Anything abnormal in the relationship between events in a set of schemata will be recorded specially and used in reconstruction before default knowledge.
4. Strategies presented can elaborate any particular piece of an episode given a partial description, and can therefore predict what the pieces of the episode are and the details of each piece.

We have thus presented the core of the processes involved in full-event reconstruction. There are two additional considerations, however. First, we need a set of strategies to control the order in which reconstruction happens and the detail to which each piece of an episode is elaborated. There may also be additional strategies which are similar to, but missing from, those we have considered.

Second, we must better define our representations for events in E-MOPs. Up to now, we have been assuming that E-MOPs organize pointers to actual events and that events in memory point directly to other related events, an organization of tape recordings of events. If this were really the case, however, then we would never see intrusions, confusion, or omissions of details of events during reconstruction.

How, then, are events recorded? An important implication of the ability to make inferences during retrieval is that *all details of events need not be stored.* Because generalized knowledge is available to reconstructive strategies to use in inferring normative details of events, memory needs to store only those features of events which cannot be inferred through application of instantiation strategies, i.e., *those aspects of the event which are different than, or add to, the relevant E-MOP's specifications.* Merging those features and the E-MOP's norms during retrieval produces a specification of an entire event. References to events need only enough information to enable that reconstructive process to happen. The full representation of an event is thus distributed throughout the schemata and subschemata used to describe it.

B. FORGETTING

Of course, such incomplete specification is prone to retrieval failures. This is true because memory's structure is constantly changing. The set of features that describe an event are derived at the time an event is entered into memory. A reference that was unique at input time may not be unique at retrieval time. During retrieval, if the available specification of a contextually related event is no longer unique, then elaboration must be applied to reconstruct additional details that will enable its retrieval.

Elaboration, as a process of inferring plausible features, can be faulty. In that case, the wrong event or incorrect details may be recalled. If a recalled event or incorrect details are consistent with what is known, its differences will not be noticed, and false reconstruction will occur. Faulty retrieval of this kind corresponds to *recall intrusion* (Crowder, 1976; Owens *et al.,* 1979) and *recognition confusion* (Bower *et al.,* 1979; Gibbs & Tenney, 1980). In our retrieval process, these mistakes happen when some elaboration directs retrieval to the wrong episode, which is then substituted for what actually happened.

A prediction about retrieval can be made based on the fact that memory's structure is constantly changing:

Memory Principle #8

The closer a retrieval cue is to the encoding of an item at the time of retrieval, the easier retrieval of that item should be.

Psychologists have called a principle similar to this one *encoding specificity* (Tulving, 1972). According to that principle, the ease with which an item can be recalled from memory depends on the nearness of the retrieval specification to the description initially encoded in memory for the item. Because memory's schemata are constantly changing, we claim that *memory's changes must also be accounted for in predicting ease of retrieval.*

Other reasons for forgetting are based on features of the retrieval strategies and features of individual retrieval cues. Because the traversal algorithm requires that indices be specified before they are traversed, an item cannot be retrieved unless a set of suitable discriminating features can be generated for it. Strategies geared toward specifying plausible features cannot be used to generate deviant features. Thus, items whose features are different, but related to the norms will be easier to find than those whose features deviate excessively. The best example of this comes from examining one of CYRUS's mistakes. During memory update, CYRUS had incorrectly generalized that "diplomatic meetings are about Arab–Israeli peace." That generalization (in the content frame of "diplomatic meetings") had the following effect on retrieval. When asked to enumerate the diplomatic meetings Vance had attended, it used its knowledge about the topics of diplomatic meetings as a constraint on the elaboration it was doing. Thus, it searched for the meetings with features that would have been plausible if the topic were "Arab–Israeli peace," but didn't recall other meetings (e.g., meetings about SALT). Its retrieval strategies were working correctly at that point. The knowledge in memory which constrained their application to only relevant features also kept CYRUS from remembering items with deviant features (in this case, an alternate topic). *The constraints put on retrieval strategies by memory's generalized knowledge can cause forgetting.*

In addition, *the information available in a retrieval specification constrains retrieval.* Strategies are dependent on the information or cues available at the time of retrieval. This includes cues available from previous context and those present in a question. In choosing a context for search, for example, the proper context can only be chosen if some aspect of the retrieval specification refers to that context. If a person were answering "Who is the most famous person you've ever met?", we would not be surprised if he failed to remember meeting a famous person in a museum, since there is no obvious cue to initiate retrieval of museum experiences. On the other hand, if the person were prompted with "how about in a museum?", or if previous conversation had concerned museum experiences, there would be a better chance of his retrieving that experience. CYRUS also fails in this way. Vance's discussions about the Camp David Accords outside of political meetings, for example, are not recalled by CYRUS in answering "Who have you talked to about the Camp David Accords?", even though he may have given a speech about the situation or talked to somebody about the accords at some social function.

The same problems appear in alternate-context search. If, during processing, an executive strategy which would yield an answer is neglected, episodes which would have been found by that strategy might not be found. In addition, the generalized knowledge used for alternate-context search allows retrieval of only standard types of related episodes. CYRUS is fallible in this regard in trying to recall ceremonies. Because, for example, a ceremony commemorating the opening of air traffic routes by flying between the two airports is not a standard type of ceremony, alternate-context search is not sufficient for CYRUS to recall that ceremony. If flying had been a standard sort of ceremony, that episode could have been recalled by recalling flying ceremonies. In some cases, successive application of additional strategies during alternate-context search will yield an answer when one strategy fails. This, however, cannot be guaranteed. Another executive strategy, for example, uses the plausible reasons behind an event to aid in recall. Since opening air routes is not a standard reason for a diplomatic ceremony, however, that also would not work in this case.

C.   RECALL AND RECOGNITION

Psychologists have often noted that there are many items in memory that can be recognized but cannot be recalled. The CYRUS retrieval processes can be used to explain this. We assume that recognition probes have many more features of an event specified than do recall probes. Because a lot of information is given, there are multiple ways of searching memory without the need for extensive elaboration. Recall probes, on the other hand, provide fewer ways to search memory, and elaboration will be needed. Free recall will require more extensive elaboration than cued recall. Recognition is easier for two reasons: First, it offers more ways to search memory. Second, it allows more directed search of memory without the need to generate features to help direct the search.

D.   RETRIEVING GENERALIZED INFORMATION

In coming up with a memory organization that reflects human retrieval capabilities, we have defined one that integrates generic and episodic memory. Both are organized in the same structures and are thus accessed and updated via the same strategies. Thus, retrieval for a question such as "When you go to Europe, where do you usually stay?" will proceed exactly as for "Last time you were in Europe where did you stay?" To answer the second question, the particular trip to Europe would be retrieved by the traversal process (as described above), and its context would then be searched for where the actor stayed. In traversing memory to answer the first question, an E-MOP corresponding to "trips to Europe" would be returned by the traversal process in exactly the same way a particular event is retrieved. Generalized information associated with that MOP would then be used to answer the question. This is in line with recent studies that showed a blurred distinction between the two stores (e.g., Anderson & Ross, 1980; McKoon & Ratcliff, 1979).

E. MEMORY ORGANIZATION

In defining our model, we have made reference to two types of memory structures: organizing and nonorganizing. Organizing schemata are those that organize individual memories and other organizing schemata in a well-structured framework that can be searched strategically. We have presented specific strategies for searching E-MOPs, the organizing schemata which organize memories of events. Nonorganizing schemata hold generalized knowledge and some memories, but the individual memories they reference are not well structured in such a way that they can be searched strategically. Memories associated with nonorganizing schemata must be retrieved by considering hypothetical situations represented by organizing schemata. The process of context construction performs this task, but can only work if nonorganizing schemata refer to the organizing schemata they are associated with. Knowledge associated with organizing schemata also helps direct search by providing guidelines for elaboration and references to other organizing schemata.

Why is this important? For the most part, psychologists interested in reconstruction have explained to us why strategies are effective (e.g., Williams & Hollan, 1981) and have demonstrated that they are used by people (e.g., Spiro, 1979; Walker & Kintsch, 1985). The novel emphasis here, however, is in showing how a particular organization requires particular sets of strategies. The strategies themselves arise from the requirements of the memory organization. We have only been able to be as explicit as we have about the strategies because we have been specific about the memory organization.

Only by taking into account the memory structures that a retrieval process must search can particular strategies for retrieval be specified. If we were to add additional types of memory structures to our memory model (e.g., goals, themes), we would have to analyze the structure of each and propose strategies specific to each one. What our model does, however, is to predict the types of strategies we would expect to find for new schema types. If the new schema were of a nonorganizing type, we would have to be able to specify its relationships to organizing structures to allow context construction and its relationships to other nonorganizing schemata to allow elaboration. If a new type of organizing schema were added, we would have to specify the particular relationships it had to other organizing structures, and for each of those, the strategies for alternate-context search that would allow related items to be found. In addition, for each particular schema, knowledge which would allow the strategies to work would have to be available.

Some additional work has been done in this direction. Reiser, Black, and Abelson (1985) and Reiser (1983) have specified the differing properties of another set of knowledge structures for events and sets of strategies specific to each type of structure. Their experimental work has supported the claim that strategies are dependent on the function of the knowledge structure. Much of the work done by Schank's group (e.g., Schank & Riesbeck, 1981; Schank, 1980, 1982; Dyer, 1983) has also made the point that different processing is appropriate for different kinds of memory structures.

F. AUTOMATIC AND STRATEGIC PROCESSING

Because we have defined an explicit memory structure, we have been able to explicitly define *automatic and strategic retrieval processes* which work on those structures. Our automatic process is the traversal process, while the retrieval strategies we have defined are the strategic ones. As other researchers have found, our model supports the claim that strategic processes are not necessarily conscious ones (Shiffrin & Dumais, 1981; Reiser, 1985). Many of the strategies we propose come from observations of conscious retrieval (e.g., executive search strategies). Others arose from observations of the requirements on a memory which supported those processes (e.g., component-to-component instantiation strategies). While strategic, these processes are often unconscious. Still others fit both categories (context construction, context-to-context instantiation strategies). Each of these strategic processes makes use of knowledge associated with currently active schemata to direct memory search. The one automatic process, which does not depend on knowledge, but only on the data and memory structures available, is traversal. It, too, however, is constrained by strategic processing in two ways: first, by strategies which choose appropriate features for traversal from the huge set available; second, by the memory structures which have been created by strategic, but unconscious, organizational strategies and generalization procedures. These processes are strategic in that they choose from the available information and place constraints on memory. They are not, however, processes that a person would report awareness of.

All of this supports some recent claims about measurements of accessibility, namely, that accessibility of a particular item is a function of both automatic and strategic processing (Reiser, 1983, 1985; Shiffrin & Dumais, 1981; Neves & Anderson, 1981). In fact, we can take that further. Because strategic processes are so dependent on the knowledge they have available, we can claim that accessibility of an item can only be predicted by taking into account the automatic retrieval processes, the available strategic processes, the knowledge available to those strategies, and the memory's organizing structure.

X.   Related Work

There is much recent work in psychology that addresses some of the retrieval and organizational issues we address here. We present overviews and comparisons to those most closely related to our work.

Norman and Bobrow (1979) and Bobrow and Norman (1975) have proposed a theory of memory "descriptions" and constructive processes that operate on those descriptions. Their theory of reconstructive memory states that in order to find something in memory, its description must first be constructed. They have described reconstruction as a process comprised of (1) specification of a retrieval description, (2) search for that description, (3) evaluation of the memory record retrieved, and (4) failure diagnosis of that evaluation resulting in a new retrieval specification.

Although the reconstructive process they have described is similar in nature to that described in this report and used by CYRUS, Norman and Bobrow have chosen to ignore the problem of memory organization, and thus have not addressed the problem of what kinds of information are included in "descriptions" and how they might be organized with respect to each other in memory. They also do not address the problem of how any particular specified description is found. Rather, their concern is with very general processes that describe a retrieval mechanism independent of any particular organization.

Williams's (1978) work has drawn on the Norman and Bobrow theory of descriptions and is closest to that presented here. Williams (1978) has described the reconstructive process as a three-step retrieval process: Find a context, search, verify. Each of those steps, he explains, is a reconstructive process with the same three steps. Williams has gone on to describe some of the strategies people use in constructing the "descriptions" (Bobrow & Norman, 1975; Norman & Bobrow, 1979) that are necessary for remembering people they have known.

Although Williams identified some of the strategies people used for that task, his emphasis, like Norman and Bobrow, was in identifying and explaining very general memory phenomena independent of a specified underlying memory organization. As a result, he has uncovered many of the general reasoning processes people use in remembering and has explained some of the retrieval failures people have, but his explanations are on a very general level and do not explain how particular pieces of knowledge can guide reconstructive processing. He observes that contexts for search are chosen, for example, but does not describe how memory can guide that search.

In many ways, the work presented here is complementary to the work of Norman and Bobrow and of Williams. While they have proposed general mechanisms for retrieval without worrying about underlying memory organization, we propose a memory organization that supports reconstructive processing and well-specified processes for retrieval that depend on that underlying organization of information and knowledge in memory.

Some more recent work by Walker and Kintsch (1985) also supports our claims that retrieval is largely reconstructive. In their study, they found that few items of any category are directly retrievable, but rather that memory nodes associated with the retrieval topic are retrieved as intermediate cues, and from those, category items are generated. They found that the particular intermediate cues were personal and idiosyncratic, and highly dependent on episodic memory.

A theory that explains memory's low-level mechanisms is "spreading activation" (Anderson, 1976; Anderson & Bower, 1973), or "associative memory." This model has been used to describe many memory phenomena (e.g., Anderson, 1976; Anderson & Bower, 1973; Quillian, 1968). Although this model seems to explain memory's organization as a network of nodes and weighted links, it does not attempt to explain what the nodes, links, or associations in the network look like. It is not a model of memory organization, then, but rather a model of very low-level automatic memory processing. It is an attempt to explain low-level traversal from node to node in memory. We have presented a theory of the content of the nodes, their connections, and higher level strategic processes guiding communication between the nodes. In addition, we have specified constraints for the process of building the associative structures.

Some of CYRUS's features are reminiscent of EPAM (Feigenbaum, 1963), an early AI endeavor which modeled human memory. EPAM's discrimination nets provided an organization, encoding strategy, and retrieval process which modeled some of the results of human verbal learning experiments. Like CYRUS, EPAM placed new items in its network based on discriminating features and remembered items by traversing its networks. Like CYRUS, EPAM's processes explained forgetting and false retrieval found in people. There are a number of important differences between EPAM and CYRUS in their organization, encoding, and retrieval processes (Barsalou & Bower, 1984).

In terms of memory organization and encoding, EPAM's arcs hold negative rather than positive features, providing no place to store generalized information. In addition, only one discrimination is made at each level of the network in EPAM, while in CYRUS, multiple discriminations are made at each level.

There are a number of consequences for retrieval arising from this organization. In discrimination nets, search is guided by the structure of the network rather than the structure of the target item. Questions with no bearing on a target item will be asked of it in the course of memory traversal. An E-MOP's structure, on the other hand, allows retrieval to be directed by the retrieval key or target event itself. Second, EPAM provides only one path to each item. Because multiple discriminations are made at each level in CYRUS, there are multiple paths to each item in memory, allowing it to be retrieved through many different descriptions. CYRUS also provides context-driven strategies for elaborating descriptions and constructing alternate descriptions of items to be remembered.

While later versions of EPAM (Simon & Gilmartin, 1973) did allow redundant paths and positive features, EPAM did not take advantage of those features as CYRUS does. Also, there was no attempt to define retrieval strategies. EPAM was primarily meant as a model of perception rather than a general long-term memory.

Finally, it should also be pointed out that the items CYRUS stores (events) are significantly more complex and detailed than those EPAM worked with (nonsense syllables or chess positions). Thus, CYRUS has a great deal more contextual information available both to use in storing items in memory and in retrieving them. The use and organization of such knowledge were important parts of deriving CYRUS's structure and processes. While EPAM's organization and processes may be sufficient for explaining people's behavior in verbal learning experiments, they are not sufficient to describe the more complex phenomenon we observe in examining retrieval of episodic information from very long-term memory.

A final theory of long-term memory, developed concurrently with this one and also complementary to it, is Schank's (1980) theory of Memory Organization Packets (MOPs). Schank's MOPs are an attempt to explain how personal experiential memories can be organized in memory. He proposes that MOPs organize experiences according to their differences and also organize similarities between the events. This work has extended that theory by explaining in detail processes for index selection, memory organization maintenance, and retrieval. The major differences between Schank's MOPs and the E-MOPs presented here are differences in emphasis. He was interested in explaining the interconnectedness of memory structures, while this work has been more concerned with storage and retrieval of individual episodes.

In his most recent work, Schank (1982) goes beyond the organizational framework presented previously, looking at the organization of episodes with respect to the goals they are derived from and their relationships to steps in achieving those goals. As part of that larger framework, the model presented here explains in detail one way events are organized in episodic memory and gives a set of procedures for traversing that part of the memory organization. Though we do not specify in detail how to search more goal-related structures, the memory principles and processes presented here should carry over to those structures. Indexing by differences remains the preferred way to organize. New memory structures still need to be created based on similarities between events in memory. Retrieval strategies to choose contexts for search, to elaborate given event descriptions, and to direct search in alternate structures are still necessary to search memory. The knowledge those strategies and procedures use, however, becomes more diverse in considering goal-based structures, possibly creating the need for more control. Additional strategies particular to goal-based knowledge will also need to be derived.

XI. Is CYRUS a Good Model of People?

In previous sections, we have discussed our model's successes as a human model. In evaluating its generalizability to human memory, we must also consider features of human memory which CYRUS does not directly address.

First, our model depends on rich indexing of events in memory. Currently, in the implementation, each event is indexed by approximately ten features. Most real-life events that we experience have many hundreds or thousands of features. Thus, we must consider what would happen in a CYRUS-like memory which had to consider that many event features. Would the indexing get out of hand? Probably it would. There is a two-part solution to the problem that we outline, however. First, we need a better theory of "important feature selection" to select those features to be used as indices. In part, we have presented such a theory in Section VI, and it is presented in more detail in Kolodner (1983b, 1984). More attention, however, must be given to this aspect of the model. The second part to the solution is to use the memory principles and updating rules presented to derive a more compact graph structure. Though the current structure supports all of the principles we have presented, it has many redundancies in it. We are currently working on developing a more concise graphical organization based on the memory principles presented, but without the redundancies.

Another consideration in deciding if ours is a good model of people is the way it forgets. While its errors of omission are obvious, its errors of commission are not. It never really comes up with a wrong answer. In principle, it should be able to. In implementation, there is no mechanism for it. This is because the retrieval algorithm combines what is usually thought of as reconstruction (i.e., coming up with an event description) with verification of that description. If it cannot verify a memory, it will not produce it as an answer. Our program, CYRUS, considers many plausible but wrong memories as it searches memory, but suppresses all of them. It needs a way of judging the veracity of a plausible memory without explicitly "finding" it.

There are a number of features of human memory which we did not consider in developing this model. First, people seem to know what they know and do not know. Our model does not allow for that. Thus, a person can answer a silly question quickly, make judgments about whether he has remembered all instances of a type of event, make judgments as to whether further memory search will help, and so forth. Our implementation cannot do any of these things, not out of principle, but because they were not considered in developing the model. Second, we do not consider recency and frequency judgments. Again, this is a problem we did not consider in developing our framework, but it is an important consideration for furthering the theory. Similarly, we did not consider the role of practice in memory. Also, we did not consider how incorrect information in a cue affects the retrieval process, how memory changes in the course of retrieval, or how strategic processing and associative strength might interact.

Development of this model was an iterative process of observing people, coming up with a model to explain some behavior, evaluating it through implementation on the computer, adding features to it or changing it, then going back and looking at people, and so forth. Our initial aim was to address the broad problem of reconstructive retrieval from very long-term memory and to design a mechanism to explain it. The CYRUS program and the model presented are the results. We have been able to provide an algorithm for reconstructive retrieval and principles for memory organization. Some aspects of memory which we did not initially consider we got for free from our algorithms and memory structures—forgetting, generalization, and the combination of episodic and generic memory, to name a few. Other aspects of memory, such as those addressed above, did not come out of the model for free. Now is the time in the iterative process to consider those problems. It is time in the process to run experiments on people, testing the predictions made by our model, and also to see if the additional features of memory which we did not take into account can be made to fit *naturally* into the already existing framework.

Acknowledgments

This work was supported in part by the Advanced Research Projects Agency of the Department of Defense and monitored under the Office of Naval Research under contract N00014-75-C-1111 while the author was in residence at Yale University. It is currently supported in part by the National Science Foundation under Grant No. IST-8317711. The views expressed are solely those of the author.

I am indebted to Roger Schank, who helped guide this research when I was a graduate student, to all the members of the Yale AI project, who provided an environment conducive to good research, and to Gordon Bower, Mike Williams, Larry Barsalou, and Brian Reiser, who helped me to understand the psychological implications of this work. I am especially grateful to Larry Barsalou for the careful readings and comments he made on earlier drafts of this article.

The figures, tables, and portions of the text of this article are extracted from Kolodner, J. L., *Retrieval and Organizational Strategies in Conceptual Memory: A Computer Model*, Lawrence Erlbaum Assoc., Inc., Publishers, 1984.

References

Alba, J. W., & Hasher, L. (1983). Is memory schematic? *Psychological Bulletin*, **93**, 203–231.

Anderson, J. R. (1974). Retrieval of propositional information from a long term memory. *Cognitive Psychology*, **5**, 451–474.

Anderson, J. R. (1976). *Language, memory, and thought*. Hillsdale, NJ: Erlbaum.

Anderson, J. R., & Bower, G. H. (1973). *Human associative memory*. New York: Holt.

Anderson, J. R., Kline, P. J., & Beasley, C. M. (1979). A general learning theory and its application to schema abstraction. In G. Bower (Ed.), *The psychology of learning and motivation* (Vol. 13, pp. 227–318). New York: Academic Press.

Anderson, J. R., & Ross, B. H. (1980). Evidence against the semantic-episodic distinction. *Journal of Experimental Psychology: Human Learning and Memory*, **6**, 441–466.

Barsalou, L. W., & Bower, G. H. (1984). Discrimination nets as psychological models. *Cognitive Science*, **8**, 1–26.

Bartlett, R. (1932). *Remembering: A study in experimental and social psychology*. London: Cambridge Univ. Press.

Bobrow, D. G., & Norman, D. A. (1975). Some principles of memory schemata. In D. G. Bobrow & A. Collins (Eds.), *Representation and understanding*. New York: Academic Press.

Bower, G. H., Black, J. B., & Turner, T. J. (1979). Scripts in text comprehension and memory. *Cognitive Psychology*, **1**, 177–220.

Brewer, W. F., & Nakamura, G. V. (1984). The nature and functions of schemas. In R. S. Wyer & T. K. Srull (Eds.), *Handbook of social cognition*. Hillsdale, NJ: Erlbaum.

Brewer, W. F., & Treyens, J. C. (1981). Role of schemata in memory for places. *Cognitive Psychology*, **13**, 207–230.

Crowder, R. G. (1976). *Principles of learning and memory*. Hillsdale, NJ: Erlbaum.

Dyer, M. G. (1983). *In depth understanding: A computer model of integrated processing for narrative comprehension*. Cambridge, MA: MIT Press.

Feigenbaum, E. A. (1963). The simulation of verbal learning behavior. In E. A. Feigenbaum & J. Feldman (Eds.), *Computers and thought*. New York: McGraw-Hill.

Gibbs, R. W., & Tenney, Y. J. (1980). The concept of scripts in understanding stories. *Journal of Psycholinguistic Research*. **9**, 275–284.

Graesser, A. C., & Nakamura, G. V. (1982). The impact of a schema on comprehension and memory. In G. Bower (Ed.), *The psychology of learning and motivation* (Vol. 16, pp. 59–109). New York: Academic Press.

Kolodner, J. L. (1978). *Memory organization for natural language database inquiry* (Research Rep. No. 142). New Haven, CT: Dept. of Computer Science, Yale University.

Kolodner, J. L. (1980). Organizing memory and keeping it organized. In *Proceedings of the First Annual National Conference on Artificial Intelligence, Stanford, CA* (pp. 331–333).

Kolodner, J. L. (1981). Organization and retrieval in a conceptual memory for events. In *Proceedings of the International Joint Conference on Artificial Intelligence, Vancouver, B.C., Canada* (pp. 227–233).

Kolodner, J. L. (1983a). Reconstructive memory: A computer model. *Cognitive Science*, **7**, 281–328.

Kolodner, J. L. (1983b). Maintaining organization in a dynamic long term memory. *Cognitive Science*, **7**, 243–280.

Kolodner, J. L. (1984). *Retrieval and organizational strategies in conceptual memory: A computer model*. Hillsdale, NJ: Erlbaum.

Lebowitz, M. (1980). *Generalization and memory in an integrated understanding system* (Tech. Rep. No. 186). New Haven, CT: Dept. of Computer Science, Yale University.

Lichtenstein, E. H., & Brewer, W. F. (1980). Memory for goal-directed events. *Cognitive Psychology*, **3**, 412–445.

McKoon, G., & Ratcliff, R. (1979). Priming in episodic and semantic memory. *Journal of Verbal Learning and Verbal Behavior*, **18**, 463–480.

Minsky, M. A. (1975). A framework for representing knowledge. In P. H. Winston (Ed.), *The psychology of computer vision*. New York: McGraw-Hill.

Neves, D. M., & Anderson, J. R. (1981). Knowledge compilation: Mechanisms for the automatization of cognitive skills. In J. R. Anderson (Ed.), *Cognitive skills and their acquisition*. Hillsdale, NJ: Erlbaum.

Norman, D. A., & Bobrow, D. G. (1979). Descriptions: An intermediate stage in memory retrieval. *Cognitive Psychology*, **11**, 107–123.

Owens, J., Bower, G. H., & Black, J. B. (1979). The "soap opera" effect in story recall. *Memory and Cognition*, **7**, 185–191.

Quillian, M. R. (1968). Semantic memory. In M. Minsky (Ed.), *Semantic information processing*. Cambridge, MA: MIT Press.

Reder, L. M., & Anderson, J. R. (1980). A partial resolution of the paradox of interference: The role of integrating knowledge. *Cognitive Psychology*, **12**, 447–472.

Reiser, B. J. (1983). *Contexts and indices in autobiographical memory* (Cognitive Science Tech. Rep. No. 24). New Haven, CT: Cognitive Science Program, Yale University.

Reiser, B. J. (1985). Knowledge-directed retrieval of autobiographical memories. In J. L. Kolodner & C. K. Riesbeck (Eds), *Memory, experience and reasoning*. Hillsdale, NJ: Erlbaum.

Reiser, B. J., Black, J. B., & Abelson, R. P. (1985). Knowledge structures in the organization and retrieval of autobiographical memories. *Cognitive Psychology,* in press.

Rumelhart, D. E. (1975). Notes on a schema for stories. In D. G. Bobrow & A. Collins (Eds.), *Representation and understanding*. New York: Academic Press.

Rumelhart, D. E., & Ortony, A. (1977). The representation of knowledge in memory. In R. J. Anderson, R. J. Spiro, & W. E. Montague (Eds.), *Schooling and the acquisition of knowledge.* Hillsdale, NJ: Erlbaum.

Schank, R. C. (1972). Conceptual dependency: A theory of natural language understanding. *Cognitive Psychology,* **3,** 552–631.

Schank, R. C. (1975). *Conceptual information processing*. Amsterdam: North-Holland Publ.

Schank, R. C. (1980). Language and memory. *Cognitive Science,* **4,** 243–284.

Schank, R. C. (1982). *Dynamic memory: A theory of learning in people and computers.* London: Cambridge Univ. Press.

Schank, R. C., & Abelson, R. P. (1977). *Scripts, plans, goals, and understanding.* Hillsdale, NJ: Erlbaum.

Schank, R. C., & Kolodner, J. L. (1979). *Retrieving information from an episodic memory* (Res. Rep. No. 159). New Haven, CT: Dept. of Computer Science, Yale University. (Short version in *Proceedings of the Sixth International Joint Conference on Artificial Intelligence, Tokyo.*)

Schank, R. C., & Riesbeck, C. K. (1981). *Inside computer understanding: Five programs plus miniatures.* Hillsdale, NJ: Erlbaum.

Shiffrin, R. M., & Dumais, S. T. (1981). The development of automatism. In J. R. Anderson (Ed.), *Cognitive skills and their acquisition*. Hillsdale, NJ: Erlbaum.

Simon, H. A., & Gilmartin, K. J. (1973). A simulation of memory for chess positions. *Cognitive Psychology,* **5,** 29–46.

Smith, E. E., Adams, N., & Schorr, D. (1978). Fact retrieval and the paradox of interference, *Cognitive Psychology,* **10,** 438–464.

Spiro, R. J. (1979). *Prior knowledge and story processing: Integration, selection, and variation* (Tech. Rep. No. 138). Champaign: Center for the Study of Reading, University of Illinois.

Thorndyke, P. W., & Hayes-Roth, B. (1979). The use of schemata in the acquisition and transfer of knowledge. *Cognitive Psychology,* **11,** 82–106.

Thorndyke, P. W., & Yekovich, F. R. (1980). A critique of schema-based theories of human story memory. *Poetics,* **9,** 23–49.

Tulving, E. (1972). Episodic and semantic memory. In E. Tulving & W. Donaldson (Eds.), *Organization of memory,* New York: Academic Press.

Walker, W. H., & Kintsch, W. (1985). Automatic and strategic aspects of knowledge retrieval. *Cognitive Science,* in press.

Williams, M. D. (1978). *The process of retrieval from very long term memory* (Processing Memo CHIP-75). La Jolla, CA: Center for Human Information.

Williams, M. W., & Hollan, J. D. (1981). The process of retrieval from very long-term memory. *Cognitive Science,* **5,** 87–119.

THE PRAGMATICS OF ANALOGICAL TRANSFER

*Keith J. Holyoak**

UNIVERSITY OF MICHIGAN
ANN ARBOR, MICHIGAN

I. Introduction

One of the peaks of current achievement in artificial intelligence is the design of expert systems for problem solving. A typical system is provided with detailed knowledge about a specific domain, such as potential defects of an electronic device, and then uses this knowledge in conjunction with inference procedures to mimic the skill of an expert troubleshooter. There are reasons to suspect, however, that the current generation of expert systems is approaching an upper limit in efficacy. The extreme domain specificity of the knowledge incorporated in expert systems leads to what Holland (1984) terms "brittleness"—small changes in the domain to which the system is to be applied typically require extensive human intervention to redesign the knowledge incorporated into the system.

In psychological terms, brittleness reflects a lack of capacity to transfer knowledge based on past experience to novel situations. In fact, current expert systems

*Present address: Department of Psychology, Carnegie-Mellon University, Pittsburgh, Pennsylvania 15213.

THE PSYCHOLOGY OF LEARNING
AND MOTIVATION, VOL. 19

59

typically learn nothing at all from experience in solving problems. New knowledge is only acquired as the result of its implantation by the human programmer. In contrast, one of the hallmarks of human intelligence (as well as that of other higher animals) is that the knowledge of the system is self-amplifying; that is, current knowledge, under the guidance of various forms of environmental feedback, is used to modify and augment the knowledge store in an adaptive fashion. Furthermore, learning is possible despite various sources of uncertainty about the state of the environment or the consequences of possible actions that the organism might take.

Following Holland, Holyoak, Nisbett, and Thagard (1985), I will use the term *induction* to refer to all inferential processes that expand knowledge in the face of uncertainty. Developing a descriptive account of human induction may well be the key to providing a prescriptive remedy for the brittleness of systems designed to display artificial intelligence. Many forms of induction involve recombinations and transformations of existing knowledge to generate plausible hypotheses relevant to the organism's interactions with its environment. The focus of the present article will be on one variety of inductive recombination—the use of analogies (particularly analogies between situations drawn from relatively remote knowledge domains) to solve novel problems and to form generalized rules.

My intent is to integrate two lines of empirical and theoretical work in which I have been involved for the past few years. The first is a series of studies of analogical problem solving begun in collaboration with Mary Gick (Gick & Holyoak, 1980, 1983) and continued with others. The second is an overarching pragmatic framework for induction proposed by Holland *et al.* I will attempt to sketch the global view of analogy that emerges from the pragmatic framework as well as specific research issues and hypotheses. The central issues with which I will be concerned involve the need to specify the circumstances under which people are able to notice analogies and put them to appropriate uses. Accordingly, the first part of the article will present a synopsis of relevant aspects of the framework developed by Holland *et al.* This framework will then be used to outline a pragmatic view of analogy. In subsequent sections I will review empirical research, particularly relatively recent work, that explores the impact of various types of similarity on analogical transfer between problems.

II. A Pragmatic Framework for Induction

A. THE PRAGMATIC CONTEXT OF INDUCTION

In a cognitive system with a large knowledge base the set of potential inferences that might be drawn, and the potential recombinations that might be explored, will be indefinitely large. The immediate problem is that without some basic constraints virtually all the possible extensions of the knowledge base will be utterly useless. For example, if the system knows that snow is white, it might proceed to apply a standard rule of inference in propositional logic to deduce that "either snow is white or rhubarb grows in the Sahara." Such deductions, although assuredly valid, are almost as assuredly pointless. And if unconstrained deduction is a fruitless exercise, unconstrained induction can easily be fatal. If an organism drinks water repeatedly and thereby is led to the confident generalization that all liquids are refreshing, its first encounter with turpentine may have disastrous consequences.

Holland *et al.* argue that progress in understanding induction in philosophy, psychology, and artificial intelligence has been stunted by misguided attempts to specify purely syntactic constraints on induction without attention to the relationship between induction and either the goals of the system or the context in which induction occurs. Indeed, as noted above, the critique extends to traditional accounts of deductive inference as well. (See Cheng & Holyoak, 1985; and Cheng, Holyoak, Nisbett, & Oliver, 1985, for evidence favoring a pragmatic approach to human deductive inference.) In a later section I will illustrate the general critique with respect to a particular syntactic account of analogical transfer.

From the pragmatic perspective, the central problem of induction is to specify processing constraints ensuring that the inferences drawn by a cognitive system will tend to be (a) relevant to the system's goals and (b) plausible. What inductions should be characterized as plausible can only be determined with reference to the current knowledge of the system. Induction is thus highly context dependent, being guided by prior knowledge activated in particular situations that confront the system as it seeks to achieve its goals. The study of induction becomes the study of how knowledge is modified through its use.

Figure 1 sketches the organization of the kind of processing system that places induction in a pragmatic context. The key ideas are that induction is (a) directed by problem-solving activity and (b) based on feedback regarding the success or failure of predictions generated by the system. The current active goals of the system, coupled with an activated subset of the system's current store of knowledge, will provide input to inferential mechanisms that will generate plans and other types of predictions about the behavior of the environment. These predictions, coupled with receptor input (both perceptual representations of the environment and information about internal states of the system), will be fed back to other inferential mechanisms. A comparison of predictions and receptor input will yield information about predictive successes and failures, which will in turn trigger specific types of inductive changes in the knowledge store.[1]

---

[1]In addition to its role in induction, receptor input can directly alter both the knowledge store (by creating memory traces of perceptual inputs) and the active goals. Constructed plans can also alter goals (by generating new subgoals).

Keith J. Holyoak

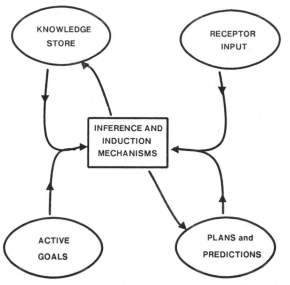

Fig. 1. A model of problem-directed, prediction-based induction.

As Fig. 1 indicates, no strong distinction is made between inferential and inductive mechanisms, since many specific mechanisms play a dual role. As we will see below, analogy provides a clear illustration of this duality of function in that a useful analogy will typically both guide generation of a specific solution plan and trigger induction of a generalized version of the plan.

Within the context of an information-processing system that succeeds in imposing pragmatic constraints on induction, the kind of "inference overload" described earlier is unlikely to arise. Indeed, a person confronted with a problem of an unfamiliar type may suffer not from a surfeit of ready inferences, but rather from lack of even a single plausible approach to the problem. In just this type of problem-solving context an analogy drawn from a different, better understood domain may plan an important role as an inferential and inductive mechanism.

B. MODELS AND MORPHISMS

According to the sketch in Fig. 1, the immediate input to inductive mechanisms is the product of a comparison between the system's internally generated predictions and receptor input. At the most general level, the inductive goal of the system is to refine its knowledge store to the point at which its predictions about the environment are sufficiently accurate as to achieve its goals in interacting with the environment. A representation of some portion of the environment that generates predictions about its expected behavior is termed a *mental model*. The function of induction is to refine mental models.

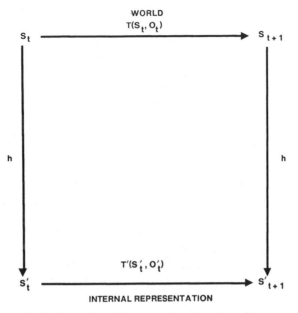

Fig. 2. A mental model structured as a homomorphism.

We can describe the notion of an internal model in terms of *morphisms*, as schematized in Fig. 2. The environment can be characterized in terms of *states* and a *transition function* that relates each state to its successor; that is, the state of the environment at time $t + 1$, S_{t+1}, is given by $T(S_t, O_t)$, where T is the transition function and O_t is the output from the cognitive system at time t (i.e., its overt actions). In a mental model, the components of environmental states as well as system outputs are aggregated into categories by a *mapping function* h_{t+1}, treating members of each category as indistinguishable for the purposes of the model. For example, many distinct objects in the environment may be categorized as chairs or as people. The model will specify a transition function T' that is intended to mimic sequences of transitions among environmental states up to a pragmatically appropriate level of precision. For example, a fragment of T' might correspond to a rule stating that if a person sits on a chair at time t, then the person will be supported at $t + 1$.

If a model constitutes a valid homomorphism, it will have the property of *commutativity;* that is, carrying out a transition in the environment and then determining the category of the resulting state will have the same outcome as determining the category of the initial state and then carrying out the transition in the model. Specifically,

$$h[T(S_t,\ O_t)] = T'[h(S_t),\ h(O_t)]$$

In a realistic mental model of a complex environment, commutativity will sometimes fail. This will happen in just those circumstances in which the model generates a prediction that does not correspond with subsequent receptor input. Such failures of a model are the triggers for inductive change. One of the most basic types of change is the generation of subcategories corresponding to aberrant cases (e.g., identifying a subtype of the category "bird," the members of which violate the expectation that birds will fly) along with a corresponding refinement in T'. For example, an initial expectation that might be stated as, "If a bird is pursued, then it will fly away," might be augmented with a new expectation, "If an ostrich is pursued, then it will run away." Note that the new, more specialized part of the transition function need not replace the more general one. If the system simply prefers more specific expectations in cases of conflict, then an overly general expectation may often serve as a useful default which will occasionally be overridden by a more specific exception. The categories and transitions at each successive level of specificity will further refine the predictive adequacy of the model. The overall structure of the model can be defined recursively as a nested set of morphisms, termed a *quasimorphism, or q-morphism.* (For a formal definition, see Holland *et al.,* 1985.) A q-morphism is equivalent to an extended notion of default hierarchy.

Several aspects of the above characterization of mental models as morphisms will prove important for an account of analogical problem solving. First, a solution plan can be viewed as a model in which the initial state is a problem representation, the final state is a representation of the class of goal-satisfying states, and the transition function specifies a plan for transforming the former into the latter. Second, we will see that a valid problem analogy can itself be viewed as a morphism. Furthermore, this characterization is useful in differentiating important from less important differences between analogs. Third, the initial solution plan constructed from an analogy is often imperfect in much the same way as a mental model may in general be imperfect, triggering similar sorts of inductive corrections.

C.   A RULE-BASED REPRESENTATION OF MENTAL MODELS

The characterization of mental models in terms of morphisms is one step removed from a description of a potential process model. This next step is taken by representing both the mapping function h and the internal transition function T' by *condition–action rules* (i.e., rules of the form "If ⟨condition⟩ then ⟨action⟩.""). Models based on condition–action rules are prevalent in both cognitive psychology and artificial intelligence; however, the framework proposed by Holland *et al.* (1985) is most directly derived from a type of parallel rule-based system termed a *classifier system* (Holland, 1975, in press). For the purposes of the present article it will not be necessary to describe the properties of such systems in detail. Only the relationship between types of rules and components of mental models is directly relevant.

The building blocks of mental models are *empirical* rules—rules that describe the environment and its behavior.[2] The rules that constitute the transition function, generating expectations about the behavior of the environment, are termed *diachronic* rules because they describe expected changes in the environment over time. The rules that constitute the mapping function *h* are termed *synchronic* rules because they have the function of performing atemporal categorizations of the components of environmental states. For example, a typical synchronic rule would be, "If an object is small, feathered, and builds nests in trees, then it is a bird." A diachronic rule might be, "If an object is a bird, and it is chased, then it will fly away."[3]

Synchronic rules capture the kind of categorical and associative information often represented in static semantic networks, while diachronic rules can represent information about the expected effects of system actions, such as problem-solving operators (Newell & Simon, 1972). An advantage of representing both categorical and action-related information in a common rule format is that both are then subject to the same inductive pressures. Similarly, activation of both types of information is determined by the same processing constraints. In the framework proposed by Holland *et al.* (1985), several important principles govern the organization and processing of rules. First, on a single cycle of activity a limited number of rules may operate in parallel. Executed rules post *messages*—pieces of declarative information—that determine the subsequent behavior of the system. Messages may also be generated by receptor inputs and by information retrieved from declarative memory stores. Some messages will specify current goals of the system; those goals will largely direct the activity of the system, and goal attainment will constitute a basic source of "reward" for rules.

On each cycle of processing activity, active messages are matched against the conditions of rules. Those rules that have their conditions fully matched become competing candidates for execution. These candidate rules then place "bids" to determine which of them will be executed. The size of the bid made by each rule is determined by three factors: (a) the *specificity* of the rule's condition (more specific rules make larger bids); (b) the *strength* of the rule (a numerical measure, subject to inductive revision, which indicates the past usefulness of the rule

---

[2]Holland *et al.* distinguish empirical rules, which directly model the environment, from more general *inferential* rules, which manipulate current information to modify the knowledge store (and hence constitute the "inferential mechanisms" indicated in Fig. 1).

[3]Although time is a critical dimension in problem solving, the synchronic/diachronic distinction can be viewed more generally as one between state re-descriptions versus state transitions, even when the transitions do not correspond to a temporal dimension.

in achieving the system's goals); and (c) the *support* accruing to the rule from the messages that matched it. The latter is a relatively volatile measure of the current activation level of the messages satisfying the rule's condition.

Rules thus compete for the "right" to post messages and hence direct subsequent processing. A number of rules may be jointly executed, allowing the system limited parallelism. The parallel nature of the system allows multiple rules to act together to describe complex (and possibly unique) situations. Inductive mechanisms will favor the development of *clusters* of rules that often work well together. A rule cluster will consist of multiple rules with identical or overlapping conditions. Because the only actions of rules are to post messages, problems of conflict resolution are minimized. Multiple rules can post contradictory messages, and these can coexist until either one message acquires sufficient support to effectively suppress its alternatives, or the need for effector action creates a demand for an unambiguous decision.

As the system operates, the rules will be subject to a variety of inductive pressures. The strengths of existing rules will be revised as a function of their efficacy in attaining goals. In addition, new rules will sometimes be generated in response to particular states of the system, such as failures of predictions, and the new rules will then compete with those already in the system. Analogy, the topic of the present article, is but one of many mechanisms for generation of plausibly useful new rules. (See Holland *et al.,* 1985, for discussion of other inductive mechanisms.)

III.   The Function and Structure of Analogy

Analogy is a broad topic, extending well beyond the domain of problem solving *per se* into the realms of argumentation and literary expression (Holyoak, 1982). In this article I will focus on the role of analogy in problem solving, in keeping with both the theoretical framework outlined above and the scope of our empirical work. In general, analogy is used to generate new rules applicable to a novel *target* domain by transferring knowledge from a *source* domain that is better understood. The overall similarity of the source and target domains can vary enormously along a continuum from the mundane to the metaphorical. At the mundane end of the continuum, it is commonplace for students learning such activities as geometry theorem proving and computer programming to use initial examples as analogical models for solving subsequent problems (Anderson, Greeno, Kline, & Neves, 1981; Pirolli & Anderson, 1985). Our own research has explored the use of problem analogies toward the metaphorical end of the continuum, involving structurally similar situations drawn from superficially dissimilar domains.

A. AN EXAMPLE: THE CONVERGENCE ANALOGY

In order to make our discussion more concrete, let us consider a particular type of analogy we have used in many experiments with college students. The target problem we have used most often is the "radiation problem" first studied by Duncker (1945). The problem runs as follows:

> Suppose you are a doctor faced with a patient who has a malignant tumor in his stomach. It is impossible to operate on the patient, but unless the tumor is destroyed the patient will die. There is a kind of ray that at a sufficiently high intensity can destroy the tumor. Unfortunately, at this intensity the healthy tissue that the rays pass through on the way to the tumor will also be destroyed. At lower intensities the rays are harmless to healthy tissue, but will not affect the tumor either. How can the rays be used to destroy the tumor without injuring the healthy tissue?

This problem is reasonably realistic, since it describes a situation similar to that which actually arises in radiation therapy. On the other hand, it is not a problem that typical college subjects can easily classify as an example of a familiar problem type. In terms of the kind of rule-based system described above, there are no diachronic rules immediately available to construct a transition from the initial problem state to a goal-satisfying state. The problem solver might imagine the possibilities of altering the effects of the rays or altering the sensitivities of the healthy tissue and/or tumor. However, such abstract operators do not specify realizable actions. As a result, the problem is seriously "ill-defined" (Reitman, 1964).

Analogy differs from other inferential mechanisms in that it is less directly focused on the immediate problem situation. To solve a problem by analogy one must attend to information other than the problem at hand. Precisely because few strong rules will be available for directly dealing with an ill-defined problem, weaker synchronic rules that activate associations to the target may have an opportunity to direct processing. Analogy provides a mechanism for augmenting the mental model of an unfamiliar situation with new rules derived from a source analog.

In the case of the radiation problem, an analogy might be used to generate rules that provide more specific operators. This possibility was tested in the initial experiment performed by Gick and Holyoak (1980). The experimenters attempted to demonstrate that variations in the solution to an available source analog can lead subjects to generate qualitatively different solutions to the target. In order to provide subjects with a potential source analog, the experimenters first had subjects read a story about the predicament of a general who wished to capture a fortress located in the center of a country. Many roads radiated outward from the fortress, but these were mined so that although small groups could pass over them safely, any large group would detonate the mines. Yet the general needed to get his entire large army to the fortress in order to launch a successful attack. The general's situation was thus substantially parallel to that of the doctor in the radiation problem.

Different versions of the story described different solutions to the military problem. For example, in one version the general discovered an unguarded road to the fortress and sent his entire army along it; whereas in another version the general divided his men into small groups and dispatched them simultaneously down multiple roads to converge on the fortress. All subjects were then asked to suggest solutions to the radiation problem, using the military story to help them. Those who read the former version were especially likely to suggest sending the rays down an "open passage," such as the esophagus, so as to reach the tumor while avoiding contact with healthy tissue. In contrast, subjects who received the latter story version were especially likely to suggest a "convergence" solution—directing multiple weak rays at the tumor from different directions. Across many comparable experiments, Gick and Holyoak found that about 75% of college students tested generated the convergence solution after receiving the corresponding military story and a hint to apply it. In contrast, only about 10% of students generated this solution in the absence of a source analog, even though most subjects would agree the solution is an effective one once it was described to them. The mapping between the source and target was occasionally revealed in the protocols of subjects who spoke as they worked on the problem:

> Like in the first problem, the inpenetrable fortress, the guy had put bombs all around, and the bombs could be compared to the healthy tissue. And so they had to, they couldn't go in *en masse* through one road, they had to split up so as not to damage the healthy tissue. Because if there's only a little bit of ray it doesn't damage the tissue, but it's all focused on the same spot. (Gick & Holyoak, 1980, p. 327)

B.   ANALOGICAL MAPPING AND SCHEMA INDUCTION

Analogical problem solving involves four basic steps. These are (1) constructing mental representations of the source and the target, (2) selecting the source as a potentially relevant analog to the target, (3) mapping the components of the source and target, and (4) extending the mapping to generate a solution to the target. These steps need not be carried out in a strictly serial order, and they will interact in many ways. For example, a partial mapping with the target is typically required to select an appropriate source. Also, because mapping can be conducted in a hierarchical manner, the process may be iterated at different levels of abstraction. Nonetheless, these four steps impose a useful conceptual organization on the overall process.

The correspondences between the convergence version of the military story and the radiation problem are shown in Table I. Even though the particular objects involved (e.g., army and rays, fortress and tumor) are very different, the

TABLE I

Correspondences Among Two Convergence Analogs and Their Schema

Military problem

Initial state
  Goal: Use army to capture fortress
  Resources: Sufficiently large army
  Operators: Divide army, move army, attack with army
  Constraint: Unable to send entire army along one road safely
Solution plan: Send small groups along multiple roads
Outcome: Fortress captured by army

Radiation problem

Initial state
  Goal: Use rays to destroy tumor
  Resources: Sufficiently powerful rays
  Operators: Reduce ray intensity, move ray source, administer rays
  Constraint: Unable to administer high-intensity rays from one direction safely
Solution plan: Administer low-intensity rays from multiple directions simultaneously
Outcome: Tumor destroyed by rays

Convergence schema

Initial state
  Goal: Use force to overcome a central target
  Resources: Sufficiently great force
  Operators: Reduce force intensity, move source of force, apply force
  Constraint: Unable to apply full force along one path safely
  Solution plan: Apply weak forces along multiple paths simultaneously
  Outcome: Central target overcome by force

basic structural relations that make the convergence solution possible are present in both. The goal, resources (and other objects), operators, and constraint are structurally similar, and hence can be mapped from one problem to the other. Because the military story provides clear problem-solving operators (e.g., "divide the army"), subjects are able to use the mapping to construct corresponding operators (e.g., "reduce ray intensity") that can be used to solve the ray problem.

The abstract structure common to the two problems can be viewed as a *schema* for convergence problems—a representation of the class of problem for which convergence solutions are possible. The convergence schema implicit in the two analogs is sketched at the bottom of Table I. The schema represents an abstract category of which the specific analogs are instances. As we will see below, analogy is closely related to the induction of category schemas by generalization. Indeed, schema induction can be viewed as the final step in analogical transfer.

Because the information in a problem schema can be represented by a set of interrelated synchronic and diachronic rules, a schema will be represented as a rule cluster of the sort described earlier.

C. The Pragmatics of Analogy

Within our pragmatic framework for induction, the most basic questions regarding analogy concern the manner in which it can be used to help solve problems. In particular, an account of analogy must address two related puzzles. First, how can a relevant source analog be found efficiently? The target problem will typically be related in some way or another to an enormous range of knowledge, most of which will be entirely unhelpful in generating a solution. Second, once a relevant analog is identified, what determines which of the properties of the source will be used to develop a model of the target problem? Especially when the source and target are highly dissimilar on a surface level, only a small subset of knowledge about the source can be transferred to the target.

In general, a useful source analog will be one that shares multiple, goal-related properties with the target. Goal-related diachronic rules attached to the source analog will provide the basis for the generation of new diachronic rules appropriate to the target problem. An analogy is thus ultimately defined with respect to the system's goals in exploring it. For this reason, as will be argued later, syntactic approaches to analogy, which do not consider the impact of goals on analogical transfer, are doomed to fail.

What does it mean to model a problem by analogy? Analogy involves "second-order" modeling—a model of the target problem is constructed by "modeling the model" after that used in the source problem. As schematized in Fig. 3, the model of the source problem is used as a model of the target problem, generating a new model that can be applied to the novel situation (cf. Fig. 3 with Fig. 2). In Fig. 3, the source model provides a morphism for some aspects of the world (labeled "World A"). A model of the aspects of the world involved in the target problem ("World B") is constructed by means of the analogical mapping (indicated by dark arrows) from the target to the source. As indicated in Fig. 3, in an ideal case the resulting target model will be isomorphic to the source model; that is, goals, objects, and constraints will be mapped in a one-to-one fashion so that corresponding operators preserve the transition function of the source (i.e., the function T'_B in the target model mimics the function T'_A in the source).

Note that even in the ideal case not all elements of the source situation need be mapped, but only those included in the model of the source, that is, those causally relevant to the achieved solution. In any problem model the components are directly relevant to the solution plan: the goal is a *reason* for it; the resources *enable* it; the constraints *prevent* alternative plans; and the outcome is the *result* of executing the solution plan. In terms of rules, the necessary mapping involves

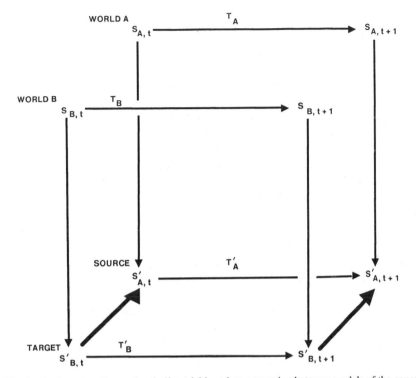

Fig. 3. Analogy as a "second-order" model based on a mapping between models of the source and target domains.

properties of the source included in the conditions of those diachronic rules that constitute the relevant transition function. By defining analogy in terms of relationships between problem models, it is possible to delimit the information transferred from source to target in a principled way. [Hesse (1966) was the first to stress the central importance of causal elements in analogical transfer.]

In practice, however, the initial target model derived by analogy will be less than isomorphic to the source, and even an adequate target model will typically fall short of this ideal. Since the target problem will not be adequately modeled *prior* to the mapping process (otherwise the analogy would be superfluous), the initial mapping with the source will inevitably be partial. Initiation of the mapping process will depend on the problem solver having first identified *some* element of the target problem that is similar to an element of the source model, that is, an element included in either the source model or some generalization thereof. In the case of interdomain analogies the similarities of the source and target are primarily relational. Hence the initial mapping will typically involve detection of an abstract similarity between corresponding goals, constraints, object descriptions, or operators, which constitute the implicit schema common to the two analogs.

Elements of the implicit schema that are identified in the target can serve as retrieval cues to access relevant source analogs as well as to initiate the mapping process once a source analog is available. More will be said later about the retrieval of source analogs. Once the relevance of the source is considered and an initial partial mapping has been established, the analogical model of the target can be developed by extending the mapping. Since models are hierarchically structured and the mapping will usually be initiated at an abstract level, the extension process will typically proceed in a top-down fashion. As the source model is "unpacked," the analogist will attempt to construct a parallel structure in the target model using elements appropriate to the new domain. New rules for the target domain can be generated by substitution of mapped elements in corresponding rules for the source domain.

For example, a subject in one of Gick and Holyoak's experiments might first establish a mapping between the doctor's goal of "using rays to destroy a tumor" and the general's goal of "using an army to capture a fortress," since both are instances of the implicit schema of "using a force to overcome a target." The rays are now (tentatively) mapped with the army; accordingly, the analogist will attempt to construct operators for acting on the rays which match those that act on the army in the source model. For example, since the army could be divided into small groups, it follows that the high-intensity rays could be "divided into small rays" (or, in terms more appropriate to the target domain, "divided into several low-intensity rays"). By substitution of mapped elements, a source rule such as, "If the goal is to get a large army to a central fortress, and a constraint prevents sending the entire army along one road, then divide the army into small groups and send them along multiple roads simultaneously," can be used to generate the critical target rule, "If the goal is to get high-intensity rays to a central tumor, and a constraint prevents administering high-intensity rays from one direction, then divide the high-intensity rays into several low-intensity rays, and administer the low-intensity rays from multiple directions simultaneously."

This process of model development will continue until an adequate target model is created or until a point is reached at which the analogy begins to "break down." What does it mean for an analogy to break down? Holyoak (1984b) distinguishes between four types of mapping relations. *Identities* are those elements that are the same in both analogs (e.g., the generalized goal of "using a force to overcome a target"). The identities are equivalent to the implicit schema. *Indeterminate correspondences* are elements that the analogist has yet to map.

The other two types of mappings involve known differences between the two analogs. For example, the mapped objects of "rays" and "army" obviously will generate a host of differences when the concepts are analyzed. However, differences do not necessarily impair the morphism (after all, the problems are only supposed to be analogous, not identical). *Structure-preserving differences* are those that allow construction of corresponding operators, and hence maintain the transition function of the source model. For example, an army is visible whereas radiation is not; however, since no operators necessary to achieving a solution are blocked simply because the rays are invisible, this difference is structure preserving.

Other differences, however, will be *structure violating* because they prevent the construction of corresponding operators. For example, an army, unlike rays, consists of sentient beings. Accordingly, the general can simply tell his men to "divide up," and the army can be expected to regroup appropriately without further intervention. Rays, of course, do not respond to such cavalier treatment. Although they can in a sense be "divided," the requisite operator will be of a very different type. Subjects often introduce multiple "ray machines" (with no counterparts in the source analog) which can be modulated appropriately.

An analogy breaks down, then, roughly at the level of specificity at which differences prove to be predominantly of the structure-violating sort. Analogies vary in their *completeness,* that is, their degree of approximation to an isomorphism in which all differences are structure preserving. The usefulness of an analogy, like the usefulness of any mental model, is determined by pragmatic factors. An imperfect analogy can be used to construct rules that provide a first approximation to a valid transition function for the target model. This approximate model will be useful if it can be refined by other inferential mechanisms. The process of refining an approximate solution derived by analogy is conceptually the same as refining a mental model by the addition of new categories and diachronic rules, and can be viewed as an extension of the overall problem-solving task (Carbonell, 1982). In general, the relationship between a source model and a successful target model constructed from it will correspond to a q-morphism, as described earlier.

D.   CRITIQUE OF THE SYNTACTIC APPROACH

The pragmatic framework predicts that the information transferred from a source to a target will be heavily influenced by the system's goal. The analogist will attempt to construct a set of diachronic rules for the target problem that embodies a transition function adequate to achieve the goal. This characterization of analogy differs sharply from syntactic approaches that attempt to predict the outcome of analogical transfer in terms of purely formal analyses of the structure of the source and target analogs, without making reference to goals. Gentner (1983) is the most emphatic proponent of the syntactic approach. In her theory, "the interpretation rules are characterized purely syntactically. That is, the processing mechanism that selects the initial candidate set of predicates to map attends only to the *structure* of the knowledge representations for the two analogs, and not to the content'' (Gentner, 1983, p. 165). A critical examination of Gentner's analysis will illustrate some of the difficulties that generally beset syntactic accounts of inductive mechanisms (Holland *et al.*, 1985).

Gentner distinguishes between ''attributes,'' which are one-place predicates, ''first-order relations,'' which are multiplace predicates with objects as arguments, and ''higher-order relations,'' which are multiplace predicates with propositions as arguments. The syntactic claim is that in using an analogy, people are most likely to map higher-order relations, next most likely to map first-order relations, and least likely to map attributes. For example, in the analogy between atomic structure and a solar system, the target and source share the higher-order relation that ''attraction depends on distance,'' and the first-order relation that ''objects revolve around each other.'' However, attributes of mapped objects, such as their absolute size, do not transfer. Gentner relates the preference for relations, especially higher-order relations, to what she terms a ''systematicity'' principle. This principle states that a highly interconnected predicate structure—one in which higher-order relations enforce connections among lower-order predicates—is most likely to be mapped.

At first glance Gentner's account looks quite reasonable. Indeed, in the case of interdomain analogies such as that between atoms and solar systems, the primacy of relations in the mapping is virtually definitional. However, a closer examination reveals problems for the syntactic approach. First, as Gentner acknowledges, the higher-order relations of interest typically are such predicates as ''causes,'' ''implies,'' and ''depends on,'' that is, causal elements that are pragmatically important to goal attainment. Thus, the pragmatic approach readily accounts for the phenomena cited as support for Gentner's theory.

Second, it is by no means clear that the systematicity principle distinguishes relations that transfer from those that do not. In the solar system analogy, Gentner mentions the relation ''the sun is hotter than the planets'' as an example of a relation that fails to transfer because it does not participate in an interconnected set of propositions. This claim is highly suspect. The relative heat of the sun and its planets is causally related to an indefinitely large number of other propositions, such as those describing why only the sun is a star, how the planets originated, the potential for life on the sun versus its planets, and so on. These interconnected propositions obviously have little or nothing to do with our understanding of the analogy with atomic structure, but the systematicity principle is quite unhelpful in showing why they are irrelevant.

Indeed, a basic problem with Gentner's analysis is that it seems to imply that the mappable propositions can be determined by a syntactic analysis of the source analog alone (since the relational status of propositions is defined independently of their participation in an analogy). It follows that the same information should be transferred in all analogies involving a given source. This is clearly false. As an example, let us take as our source analog the concept "elephant." Suppose we know a person of large girth with a penchant for stumbling over furniture. If I were to remark that "Sam is an elephant," the analogical basis of the metaphor would be quite clear. Now suppose that I tell you, "Induction is an elephant." You may be forgiven a moment of incomprehension, especially if you were misled into considering how induction might resemble our clumsy acquaintance Sam. You may grasp my meaning, however, if I remind you of the well-known story of the blind men who grasped different parts of an elephant and then gave totally different descriptions of what the beast is like. Induction may be as much an elephant as Sam, but only the latter has been insulted. Clearly, the basis of an analogy is intimately related not only to the source, but also to the target and the context in which the analogy is used.

Finally, not all analogies are so abstract as that between the solar system and the atom. Consider, for example, an analogy that 4-year-old children can often use to help solve a problem (Holyoak, Junn, & Billman, 1984). The target problem presented to the children required them to find a way to transfer a number of small balls from one bowl to another bowl that was out of reach. A variety of objects were available for possible use, including a rectangular sheet of paper. A source analog, presented prior to the target problem in the guise of an illustrated story, described how the television character Miss Piggy rolled up a carpet and used it as a tube to move her jewels from her jewel box to a safe. Many children were able to generate an analogous solution to the ball problem—rolling the paper to form a tube and then rolling the balls through the tube to the distant bowl.

In this simple analogy, the successful mapping between the carpet and the piece of paper on the attribute of shape is important because in each analog the shape enabled the critical "rolling" operator to be applied. In contrast, the relation of location failed to map (the paper was initially located on the table, whereas Miss Piggy's carpet was initially on the floor). However, this mapping failure was irrelevant because the initial location of the to-be-rolled object was not causally related to the solution achieved in the source analog.

The syntactic approach might attempt to discount this example of attribute precedence in mapping by claiming the story and target problem used by Holyoak *et al.* were too similar to constitute a "real" analogy. However, the resulting restrictive definition of analogy would be quite arbitrary. The pragmatic approach admits of analogies that range over the entire continuum from the mundane to the metaphorical. Even objects that Gentner would term "literally similar" can be analogically related if a goal is apparent. Because Gentner's theory is stated in terms of mappings between static propositions rather than rules, it misses the fundamental distinction between synchronic and diachronic relations, that is, between the mapping and the transition function. An analogy, like any model, must bring with it rules for predicting state changes. Thus, it is anomalous to say that "cats are analogous to dogs" (rather than "cats are *similar* to dogs") because no clear predictive goal is apparent. In contrast, it is perfectly natural to consider whether cats and dogs are analogous *with respect to some specified predictive goal,* such as determining if cats can swim given knowledge that dogs can do so (i.e., predicting the state change that would result from placing a cat in a large body of water).

The syntactic approach is unable to accurately predict the basis for analogical transfer because it fails to take account of goals. Differing goals can lead to different mappings for what is putatively the "same" analogy (Holyoak, 1984b). The perceived structure of an analogy is heavily influenced by the pragmatic context of its use. The aspects of the source analog transferred to the target will be determined by a variety of factors, including knowledge of what aspects of the source are conventionally taken to be important or salient (Ortony, 1979), the apparent goal in using the analogy (e.g., what aspects of the target need to be explained), the causal relations known to be central in the source (Winston, 1980), and what aspects can in fact be mapped without generating structure-violating differences. These complex and interactive factors, which are obscured by purely syntactic analyses of analogy, can be investigated within a pragmatic framework.

IV. Selection and Use of a Source Analog

Within the pragmatic framework, the structure of analogy is closely tied to the mechanisms by which analogies are actually used by the cognitive system to achieve its goals. As noted earlier, the analogy mechanism is most likely to come into play when initial solution efforts based on available diachronic rules that describe the behavior of the target domain fail to generate an acceptable solution plan. In such circumstances it may be necessary to attempt a less direct approach.

In the remainder of this article, I will focus discussion on the processes by which a plausible source analog can be initially selected (the second step of the four specified earlier). The selection step is crucial to the initiation of an explicit mapping procedure. In some cases source analogs are generated by systematic transformations of the target (Clement, 1982). In other cases the source analog will be directly provided by a teacher, as is the case, for example, when the solar system is used as an analogy to elucidate atomic structure. For present purposes, however, the cases of central interest are those in which the analogist notices the relevance of some prior situation to a target problem without external guidance.

The conditions under which people are likely to notice potential analogies are far from clear. Indeed, a consistent research finding has been that college subjects often fail to spontaneously make use of analogies (Gick & Holyoak, 1980, 1983; Hayes & Simon, 1977; Reed, Ernst, & Banerji, 1974). For example, whereas about 75% of the subjects in a typical experiment by Gick and Holyoak were able to generate the convergence solution to the ray problem given a hint to use the prior military story, only about 30% generated this solution prior to receiving an explicit hint. Given that about 10% of sujects produce the convergence solution without any analog, this means that only about 20% of the subjects may have spontaneously noticed and applied the analogy.

In fact, one could reasonably question whether there is any convincing evidence that people notice analogies between problems presented in substantially remote contexts. Even in the case of analogies between problems in the same domain, such as geometry, anecdotal reports suggest that students seldom notice analogies between problems presented in different chapters of their textbook. In all the experiments reported to date, the source and target analogs were presented consecutively within a single experimental session. It could be, for example, that the 20% of subjects in the Gick and Holyoak experiments who spontaneously used the analogy did so simply because they were sensitive to demand characteristics of the situation, which would surely suggest that the story and the problem immediately following might be somehow related.

A.   SCHEMA INDUCTION AND SPONTANEOUS TRANSFER

The strongest evidence that analogs drawn from remote domains are ever spontaneously noticed comes from studies in which multiple source analogs are provided. Gick and Holyoak (1983) had some groups of subjects first read two convergence stories (e.g., the military story described earlier and a fire-fighting story in which converging sources of fire retardant were used to extinguish a large blaze). Other groups read a single convergence story plus a disanalogous story. All subjects summarized each story and also wrote descriptions of how the two stories were similar. The latter task was intended to trigger a mapping between the two stories, which would have the incidental effect of leading to the induction of an explicit representation of the shared schematic structure. All subjects then attempted to solve the ray problem, both before and after a hint to consider the stories.

Gick and Holyoak found that subjects in the two-analog groups were significantly more likely to produce the convergence solution, both before and after the hint, than were subjects in the one-analog groups. Since demand characteristics were presumably comparable for both sets of subjects, the advantage of the two-analog subjects prior to the hint is evidence of spontaneous transfer.

Gick and Holyoak interpreted these and other more detailed results as indicating that induction of an explicit schema facilitates transfer. One might argue, however, that the results simply demonstrate that two analogs are more likely to produce transfer than one because subjects given two analogs have an additional analog that might be retrieved (i.e., if they fail to notice the relevance of one they might nonetheless notice the relevance of the other). However, in a recent experiment, Richard Catrambone and I (1985) have obtained further evidence that schema induction is the basis of the advantage afforded by multiple analogs. We replicated the comparison between groups receiving two analogs versus one analog plus a disanalogous control story. As in the procedure used by Gick and Holyoak (1983), all subjects wrote summaries of each individual story they read. However, we varied whether or not the subjects wrote descriptions of the similarities between the two stories. If this comparison procedure is in fact critical in triggering schema induction (because subjects do not spontaneously perform a detailed mapping between the two stories), then provision of two analogs should only be beneficial when subjects compare the two. On the other hand, if each story is retrieved independently, then two analogs should produce greater transfer than one, even if the stories are not compared to each other.

Table II presents the percentage of subjects in each of the four experimental groups who produced the convergence solution to the ray problem before receiving a hint to use the stories, after the hint, and in total. Twenty subjects served in each group. The results for the comparison conditions closely replicated the comparable conditions run by Gick and Holyoak (1983) in that subjects receiving two rather than one analog were significantly more likely to produce the convergence solution, both before the hint and in total once the hint was given. In particular, 60% of the subjects given two analogs produced the solution spontaneously, versus only 20% of those receiving one analog plus a control story.

The pattern differed for the groups who were not given comparison instructions. In this case only 35% of the subjects given two analogs produced the convergence solution prior to the hint. This figure was significantly lower than

TABLE II

Percentage of Subjects Producing Convergence Solution

Experimental groups	Before hint	After hint	Total
Two analogs			
Comparison	60	30	90
No comparison	35	45	80
One analog plus control			
Comparison	20	25	45
No comparison	20	15	35

that obtained for subjects in the two-analog comparison condition and did not differ significantly from that obtained for the one-analog conditions. However, once a hint to use the stories was given, the total percentage of subjects producing the solution did not differ as a function of comparison instructions, as both two-analog conditions significantly surpassed the one-analog conditions (overall means of 85 versus 40%).

These results support the schema induction hypothesis regarding the mechanism by which multiple analogs facilitate transfer. At least when the two potential source analogs are superficially dissimilar from each other, as was the case in the above experiment, college students are apparently unlikely to map the analogs and form an explicit schema unless directed to compare them. Consequently, simply providing two analogs, without comparison instructions, does little to foster spontaneous transfer. However, once a hint to use the stories is provided, subjects presumably could retrieve the analogs from memory and map them with each other and the target problem to form a generalized convergence schema. As a result, provision of two analogs aided total transfer once the hint was given, even in the absence of explicit comparison instructions.

It should be noted that in the experiment described above, as in the earlier Gick and Holyoak (1983) study, the groups given one analog in conjunction with a disanalogous control story exhibited lower levels of transfer (especially in terms of total solution frequency) than is typically observed when one analog is given alone. The presence of a "distractor" story makes it more difficult for subjects to identify and apply a source analog. However, the advantage of the two-analog comparison condition in frequency of spontaneous transfer is not attributable solely to the negative impact of the disanalogous story in the one-analog condition. The figure of 60% transfer prior to the hint for the former condition is about twice as great as that consistently obtained in conditions in which one analog is given without a distractor story (Gick & Holyoak, 1980, 1983).

The importance of schemas in mediating transfer across disparate domains can be readily understood in terms of the kind of processing system described earlier. A problem schema is an abstract category that will be linked to a cluster of synchronic rules for categorizing situations of that type and diachronic rules for constructing an appropriate type of solution. Indeed, once a person has induced a schema from initial examples, novel problems that can be categorized as instances of the schema can be solved without directly accessing representations of the initial analogs. It follows that while experiments illustrating the role of schemas demonstrate spontaneous interdomain transfer, they do not provide evidence of *analogical* transfer in the strict sense of direct transfer from a representation of a particular prior situation to a novel problem. Evidence of spontaneous analogical transfer thus remains elusive.

B.   Support Summation and Retrieval of Plausible Analogs

In order to pursue the question of whether and when people spontaneously notice interdomain analogies, let us again consider the operation of the processing system described earlier. When a target problem is established as the focus of processing, the messages describing the problematic situation will direct the ensuing rule-based search for a solution. These messages will describe the initial state, the goal state, relevant operators, and constraints on a solution. Among the rules executed early in the problem-solving attempt will be synchronic rules that support messages describing salient properties of the problem components. Given the ray problem, for example, the message representing "ray" will trigger rules that support messages such as "is a force," "passes through dense matter," "is invisible," and so on. Such property messages will in turn trigger rules supporting messages describing other entities that also share these properties.

The resulting "aura" of associations to the components of the target problem will initially be quite diffuse. However, we assume that multiple sources of support for a message will summate. Whereas a single shared property will likely yield only a small increment in support for a message describing an associated entity, several shared properties will tend to raise its support sufficiently high as to allow it to have an impact on subsequent processing. If messages representing a possible source analog receive sufficient support, rules for constructing a possible mapping with the target will be invoked.

The summation principle tends to ensure that source analogs sharing multiple properties with the target will be activated. It might seem that situations with many superficial similarities will be retrieved. As we will see, surface similarities *do* play a role in analogical retrieval. However, the retrieval process will tend to be dominated by shared properties that are goal related, since the goal in the target problem will in large part determine which rules are executed, and hence which properties of components of the target will actually be activated. Second, plausible source analogs will be those that are related to multiple components of the target problem. In particular, a situation that is activated by both the initial state and the goal state in the target problem is likely to have associated diachronic rules relevant to transforming a corresponding initial state in the source into a corresponding goal state. In other words, a possible analog has been activated when synchronic rules connect the initial target state to an initial state in a source domain, diachronic rules in the source domain connect its initial state to a subsequent state, and the latter is in turn connected by synchronic rules to the target goal. In terms of the quadrilateral diagram in Fig. 3, at this point the system will have begun to develop the mapping between the source and target and to identify diachronic rules that provide the transition function T'_A for the source.

As the above description suggests, the steps of identifying a source analog and performing a mapping between the target and source actually merge. Once a potential source analog is well supported, it will become the focus of continued processing to extend and refine the mapping. This will set the stage for the fourth step in analogical transfer—generation of new rules for the target by substituting mapped elements in the corresponding source rules. If the entire process is successful, these rules will provide a first approximation to an appropriate transition function T'_B for the target.

C.   SURFACE AND STRUCTURAL SIMILARITIES

Given the above description of retrieval of an analog, we can consider why it often seems so difficult for people to spontaneously access relevant source analogs. The basic problem is that a remote analog by definition shares few of the salient features of the target. To the extent the latter serve as retrieval cues, they will tend to activate competing associations that may block retrieval of more remote analogs. The more the problem solver is able to identify and focus on the aspects of the target problem causally relevant to achieving a solution, the greater the probability that a useful but remote analog will be retrieved.

It is possible, based on the taxonomy of mapping relations discussed earlier, to draw a distinction between *surface* and *structural* similarities and dissimilarities. An identity between two problem situations that plays no causal role in determining the possible solutions to one or the other analog constitutes a surface similarity. Similarly, a structure-preserving difference, as defined earlier, constitutes a surface dissimilarity. In contrast, identities that influence goal attainment constitute structural similarities, and structure-violating differences constitute structural dissimilarities. Note that the distinction between surface and structural similarities, as used here, hinges on the relevance of the property in question to attainment of a successful solution. The distinction thus crucially depends on the goal of the problem solver.

Ideally, a problem solver would use only the structural properties of the target as retrieval cues, thus avoiding activation of superficially similar but unhelpful situations. In reality, however, the problem solver's ability to distinguish structural from surface properties will be at best imperfect, since full knowledge of which properties of the target are structural depends on knowing the possible solutions—information clearly unavailable at the outset of a solution attempt. Consequently, properties that in fact are functionally irrelevant to a solution to the target problem may affect the solution plan indirectly by influencing the selection of a source analog (see Gilovich, 1981).

Once a source analog has been retrieved, surface properties should have less impact on the mapping process than structural ones. In particular, structure-violating differences will necessitate refinement of the initial solution plan generated by the mapping, whereas structure-preserving differences will not. Thus, surface properties will tend to have a relatively greater impact on selection of a source analog than on the subsequent mapping process. For example, it is much easier to learn about atomic structure by mapping it with a solar system than to spontaneously link the two analogs in the first place. In contrast, structure-violating differences will diminish not only the probability of selecting the source analog, but also the probability of using it successfully once mapping is initiated.

Of course, a test of the effects of types of dissimilarity on different steps in the transfer process requires a situation in which subjects in fact sometimes spontaneously notice analogies. As we have seen, there has been little empirical evidence that interdomain analogies are ever spontaneously noticed. However, a recent study by Holyoak and Koh (1985) provides such evidence, setting the stage for investigation of the influence of surface and structural properties on noticing and applying analogies. They investigated transfer between the ray problem and another convergence situation. In the "laser and light bulb" problem, the filament of a light bulb in a physics lab is broken. Because the light bulb is expensive, it would be worthwhile to repair it. A strong laser could be used to fuse the filament; however, it would break the surrounding glass bulb. The convergence solution, of course, is to use several weak lasers focused on the filament.

Relative to the low frequency of spontaneous transfer that Gick and Holyoak (1980, 1983) had found using the military analog described earlier, transfer between the radiation and light bulb problems was excellent. One experiment involved students enrolled in introductory psychology classes. Seventeen experimental subjects were drawn from classes that used a textbook with a detailed discussion of the ray problem, whereas ten control subjects were selected from classes that used texts that did not mention the problem. A few days after the experimental subjects had read about the radiation problem in their textbook as part of a regular assignment, all subjects participated in an experiment (out of class) in which the light bulb problem was presented. About 80% of the subjects who had read about the radiation problem spontaneously generated the convergence solution, as contrasted with a scant 10% of the control subjects who had not. Another experiment revealed that transfer was also good when the light bulb problem was the source and the ray problem the target.

The light bulb analog differs from the military analog described earlier along many dimensions, so it is difficult to determine precisely why the former yields greater transfer. One clear possibility is the difference in the degree of similarity between the instruments of the two analogs and the radiation problem. A laser is obviously far more similar to X rays than an army is, providing a significant additional retrieval cue in the former case. In addition, the deeper structural parallels between the light bulb and radiation analogs make the analogy extremely complete. Both cases involve a target area enclosed within a fragile "container" that is at risk from a high-intensity force. Thus, both a surface similarity of instruments and a structural similarity of problem constraints provide retrieval cues that can connect the light bulb and radiation analogs.

In an attempt to disentangle the contributions of surface and structural similarities as retrieval cues, Holyoak and Koh generated additional variations of the light bulb analog in which these factors were varied. To vary the surface similarity of the instruments to X rays, two of the new stories substituted "ultrasound waves" for lasers. The problem statement was also altered: Instead of the filament being described as broken apart, it was described as having fused together, and the ultrasound waves could repair it by jarring it apart. Thus, in two stories the solution was to use a laser to fuse the filament, and in two it was to use an ultrasound wave to jar apart the filament. To the extent the two types of action differ in their similarity to that required in the radiation problem (destroying a tumor), the latter appears more similar (since "jarring apart" seems more "destructive" than does "fusing together"). However, the more salient difference is that ultrasound waves are far less associated with X rays than are lasers.[4]

Independently of the variation in the instrument, the stories also varied in their structural similarity to the radiation problem. Specifically, the nature of the constraint preventing direct application of a large force was varied. In the versions with relatively complete mappings, the constraint was similar to that in the radiation problem—a high-intensity force would damage the surrounding area (fragile glass). In the versions with less complete mappings, the constraint was simply that no single instrument of sufficient intensity (laser or ultrasound) was available. These latter versions thus removed a structural cue linking them to the radiation problem. Nonetheless, all four of the stories described essentially identical convergence solutions.

These two types of variations—of instruments and constraints—yielded four alternative stories that were used as source analogs for different groups of subjects. A total of 16 subjects served in each of the two fragile-glass conditions and 15 served in each of the insufficient-intensity conditions. As the data in Table III indicate, the versions differed greatly in their subsequent transfer to the target radiation problem. Table IIIA presents the percentage of subjects in each of the four conditions who generated the convergence solution prior to receiving a hint to consider the story. When the source was the "laser and fragile glass" analog, which has both a similar instrument and a complete mapping, 69% of the subjects spontaneously generated the convergence solution. Transfer was significantly impaired if *either* the surface similarity of the instrument *or* the structural constraint similarity was reduced. If both changes were made (the "ultrasound of

---

[4]In a further experiment both the laser and the ultrasound beam were described as being able to "jar apart" a fused filament. The pattern of transfer was the same as in the experiment described here.

TABLE III

Percentage of Subjects Producing Convergence Solution

Structural similarity (constraint)	Surface similarity (instrument)		Mean
	High (laser)	Low (ultrasound)	
A. Prior to hint			
High (fragile glass)	69	38	54
Low (insufficient intensity)	33	13	23
Mean	51	26	
B. Total (before and after hint)			
High (fragile glass)	75	81	78
Low (insufficient intensity)	60	47	54
Mean	68	64	

insufficient intensity'' version), only 13% of the subjects generated the convergence solution. These results indicate that both surface similarities and deeper structural commonalities aid in the retrieval of source analogs, as our earlier account of retrieval mechanisms would predict.

As the data in Table IIIB indicate, a different transfer pattern was observed once a hint to use the story was provided. Structural dissimilarity of the constraint significantly impaired total transfer (78% for the fragile-glass versions vs. 53% for the insufficient-intensity versions), whereas surface dissimilarity of the instruments did not (68% for the laser versions vs. 65% for the ultrasound versions). Thus, although structural and surface similarity had comparable effects on spontaneous transfer, only the former had a significant impact on total analogical transfer once a hint was provided. These results therefore support the prediction that surface similarity will have a greater relative impact on retrieval of a source analog than on application of an analog once it is retrieved.

The results of Holyoak and Koh should not be construed as indicating that surface properties will *never* influence mapping once a source is selected. In the above experiment only a single change was introduced to create a surface dissimilarity. It might well be that introduction of multiple surface dissimilarities would make it more difficult to map the components of the two analogs. In addition, surface differences will continue to impair transfer if the problem solver has difficulty discriminating them from structural differences even after a source analog is provided. In an experiment on analogical transfer performed with 6-year olds, with the ball problem mentioned earlier as the target, Holyoak *et al.* (1984) found that what appeared to be a minor surface dissimilarity between the source and target significantly decreased the percentage of children able to use the analogy. It may be that children, lacking experience with a problem domain, have greater difficulty than adults in analyzing the casually relevant aspects of the source and target problems.

V. Conclusion

Analogical transfer, I have tried to argue, can be best understood within a broad pragmatic framework for induction. The most fundamental questions regarding analogy concern its roles in a goal-directed processing system. When will analogies be noticed? When can they be put to effective use? What information will be transferred from a source analog to a target problem? How does analogy relate to other problem-solving methods? How does it relate to generalization and other inductive mechanisms? Such questions can be fruitfully addressed only by taking account of the goals of the cognitive system and the principles that govern its capacity to draw inferences and to adapt to its environment.

If this characterization is correct, it implies that it would be a mistake to view the study of analogy as an isolated research area or to anticipate development of a theory addressing analogical transfer alone. An adequate theory of analogy will be forced to make commitments regarding a sweeping range of cognitive mechanisms—attention allocation, knowledge representation, memory retrieval, the dynamics of problem solving, and induction. This conclusion, of course, suggests that understanding analogy will remain an elusive goal for some time. It is certainly the case that the present article falls far short of offering a computationally adequate account of how interdomain analogies can be found and effectively used. More optimistically, however, it is likely that what we learn about analogical transfer will impose important constraints on many aspects of cognitive theories. Research on analogy may prove pragmatically central in our attempts to induce the mechanisms of human cognition.

Acknowledgments

This article was prepared while the author held an NIMH Research Scientist Development Award, 1-K02-MH00342-04, and the research described was supported by NSF Grant BNS-8216068. Many of the ideas discussed arose in the course of my collaborations with Mary Gick, John Holland, Richard Nisbett, and Paul Thagard (none of whom should be considered responsible for the vagaries of my exposition). I am grateful for the facilities provided by the Psychology Department of Carnegie-Mellon University, where I was visiting when the article was written. The article benefited from comments on an earlier version provided by Miriam Bassok, Matthew Lewis, Peter Pirolli, and Jeff Shrager, as well as from discussion in John Anderson's research seminar.

REFERENCES

Anderson, J. R., Greeno, J. G., Kline, P. J., & Neves, D. M. (1981). Acquisition of problem-solving skill. In J. R. Anderson (Ed.), *Cognitive skills and their acquisition*. Hillsdale, NJ: Erlbaum.

Carbonell, J. G. (1982). Learning by analogy: Formulating and generalizing plans from past experience. In R. Michalski, J. G. Carbonell, & T. M. Mitchell (Eds.), *Machine learning: An artificial intelligence approach*. Palo Alto, CA: Tioga Press.

Catrambone, R., & Holyoak, K. J. (1985). *The function of schemas in analogical problem solving.* Poster presented at the meeting of the American Psychological Association, Los Angeles, California.

Cheng, P. W., & Holyoak, K. J. (1985). Pragmatic reasoning schemas. *Cognitive Psychology,* in press.

Cheng, P. W., Holyoak, K. J., Nisbett, R. E., & Oliver, L. M. (1985). *Pragmatic versus syntactic approaches to training deductive reasoning.* (in preparation).

Clement, J. (1982). *Spontaneous analogies in problem solving: The progressive construction of mental models.* Paper presented at the meeting of the American Educational Research Association, New York.

Duncker, K. (1945). On problem solving. *Psychological Monographs, 58* (Whole No. 270).

Gentner, D. (1983). Structure-mapping: A theoretical framework for analogy. *Cognitive Science, 7,* 155–170.

Gick, M. L., & Holyoak, K. J. (1980). Analogical problem solving. *Cognitive Psychology, 12,* 306–355.

Gick, M. L., & Holyoak, K. J. (1983). Schema induction and analogical transfer. *Cognitive Psychology, 15,* 1–38.

Gilovich, T. (1981). Seeing the past in the present: The effect of associations to familiar events on judgments and decisions. *Journal of Personality and Social Psychology, 40,* 797–808.

Hayes, J. R., & Simon, H. A. (1977). Psychological differences among problem isomorphs. In N. J. Castellan, Jr., D. B. Pisoni, & G. R. Potts (Eds.), *Cognitive theory.* Hillsdale, NJ: Erlbaum.

Hesse, M. B. (1966). *Models and analogies in science.* Notre Dame, Ind.: Notre Dame Univ. Press.

Holland, J. H. (1975). *Adaptation in natural and artificial systems.* Ann Arbor, Mich.: Univ. of Michigan Press.

Holland, J. H. (in press). Escaping brittleness: The possibilities of general purpose learning algorithms applied to parallel rule-based systems. In R. Michalski, J. G. Carbonell, & T. M. Mitchell (Eds.), *Machine learning: An artificial intelligence approach* (Vol. 2). Palo Alto, CA: Tioga Press.

Holland, J. H., Holyoak, K. J., Nisbett, R. E., & Thagard, P. (1985). *Induction: Processes of inference, learning, and discovery* (in preparation).

Holyoak, K. J. (1982). An analogical framework for literary interpretation. *Poetics, 11,* 105–126.

Holyoak, K. J. (1984a). Mental models in problem solving. In J. R. Anderson & S. M. Kosslyn (Eds.), *Tutorials in learning and memory: Essays in honor of Gordon Bower.* San Francisco: Freeman.

Holyoak, K. J. (1984b). Analogical thinking and human intelligence. In R. J. Sternberg (Ed.), *Advances in the psychology of human intelligence* (Vol. 2). Hillsdale, NJ: Erlbaum.

Holyoak, K. J., Junn, E. N., & Billman, D. O. (1984). Development of analogical problem-solving skill. *Developmental Psychology, 55,* 2042–2055.

Holyoak, K. J., & Koh, K. (1985). *Surface and structural similarity in analogical transfer* (in preparation).

Newell, A., & Simon, H. A. (1972). *Human problem solving.* New York: Prentice-Hall.

Ortony, A. (1979). Beyond literal similarity. *Psychological Review,* **87,** 161–180.

Pirolli, P. L., & Anderson, J. R. (1985). The role of learning from examples in the acquisition of recursive programming skills. *Canadian Journal of Psychology,* in press.

Reed, S. K., Ernst, G. W., & Banerji, R. (1974). The role of analogy in transfer between similar problem states. *Cognitive Psychology,* **6,** 436–450.

Reitman, W. (1964). Heuristic decision procedures, open constraints, and the structure of ill-defined problems. In M. W. Shelley & G. L. Bryan (Eds.), *Human judgments and optimality.* New York: Wiley.

Winston, P. H. (1980). Learning and reasoning by analogy. *Communications of the ACM,* **23,** 689–703.

LEARNING IN COMPLEX DOMAINS: A COGNITIVE ANALYSIS OF COMPUTER PROGRAMMING

Richard E. Mayer

UNIVERSITY OF CALIFORNIA, SANTA BARBARA
SANTA BARBARA, CALIFORNIA

I. Introduction

A. PURPOSE

This article examines how novices learn and use a first programming language. In particular, this article is concerned with the idea that successfully learning a programming language, such as BASIC, includes acquiring a mental model of the underlying system. A goal of this article, then, is to present a formal cognitive analysis of the mental model underlying BASIC statements and to present empirical studies which examine the usefulness of this analysis in explaining how BASIC is learned, used, and comprehended.

B. RATIONALE

The study of human learning and cognition can be based on an attempt to find general principles which apply to a wide range of situations or can be based on an attempt to understand learning and cognition within a much more restricted domain such as a subject matter area. Resnick and Ford (1981) have pointed out that some psychologists ask questions about human learning and cognition in general, whereas other psychologists ask the same questions with a focus on a particular subject matter area. The present article opts for the "subject matter" approach. Thus, to paraphrase Resnick and Ford (1981), instead of asking, "How do people learn and solve problems?", this article asks, "How do people learn and solve problems with a computer programming language?"

The study of computer programming offers a potentially rich subject matter domain, both on practical and theoretical grounds. On practical grounds, there is a need to accomodate the large number of people who will be learning to use computers. On theoretical grounds, programming offers a domain which can be analyzed into well-defined units.

II. A Cognitive Analysis of BASIC

A. MENTAL MODELS

In the course of learning the BASIC programming language, a novice user develops a mental model of the computer system. This hypothesis motivates the present article. In particular, this section summarizes techniques for describing mental models underlying BASIC.

Theoretical and empirical work on how humans learn to interact with machines is emerging as an area of psychological study. A consistent theme of this work concerns the central role of what Young (1981, 1983) calls the user's "mental model" or what Moran (1981a) calls the user's "conceptual model" of the to-be-learned system. For purposes of the present article, a mental model (or conceptual model) of a computer programming system refers to the user's conception of the information-processing transformations and states that occur between input and output. A mental model is a metaphor consisting of components and operating rules which are analogous to the components and operating rules of the system. Thus, a mental model of a BASIC computer system allows the user to conceive of "invisible" transformations (such as replacing a number in memory space A with another number) and "invisible" states (such as waiting for the user to press RETURN) that occur as a program is being executed.

Examples of mental models have been proposed for calculator languages (Bayman & Mayer, 1984; Mayer & Bayman, 1981; Young, 1981, 1983), text editing languages (Card, Moran, & Newell, 1980; Moran, 1981b), file management languages (Mayer, 1980, 1981; Reisner, 1981), LOGO (Duboulay & O'Shea, 1978; DuBoulay, O'Shea, & Monk, 1981), and BASIC (Mayer, 1975, 1976, 1979a, 1979b, 1981). Carroll and Thomas (1982) have argued, for example, that metaphorical models are required to help novices acquire useful cognitive representations of programming languages. Similarly, mental models have been described for a wide variety of complex systems in engineering and the sciences (De Kleer & Brown, 1981, 1983; Gentner & Gentner, 1983; Larkin, 1983; Norman, 1980, 1983; Stevens, Collins, & Goldin, 1979; Williams, Hollan, & Stevens, 1983).

Mental models may vary with respect to usefulness, with more useful models being better able to support sophisticated programming performance by the user. They may vary with respect to completeness, with more complete models specifying more details of the components and operating rules. Mental models may also vary with respect to veridicality, with more veridical models having components which are more closely matched to the physical characteristics of the machine and having operating rules which are more closely matched to the machine language. What is a "good" mental model for elementary BASIC? The present analysis focuses mainly on the dimension of usefulness as a way of defining the "goodness" of a model for BASIC. Thus, for purposes of the present analysis a good model is one that helps novices to successfully perform on programming problems. Du Boulay and O'Shea (1978) offer some advice concerning the construction of "good" mental models, namely, that models should be "visible." By this Du Boulay and O'Shea mean that the internal states and operations of the system should be visible to the user. In attempting to use this advice, we have provided in the present section a cognitive analysis of the states and operations which underlie the execution of BASIC statements.

B. Microstructure Analysis of BASIC

Let us consider the conceptual knowledge (or mental model) required to understand elementary BASIC statements. Two kinds of conceptual knowledge can be identified: (1) microstructure concepts and (2) macrostructure concepts. Microstructure refers to the underlying components which make up any particular BASIC statement. Macrostructure refers to the larger context (e.g., program segment) into which any particular BASIC statement fits. A "mental models" theory of learning BASIC asserts that a user must learn about microstructure and macrostructure concepts in order to successfully use and comprehend BASIC statements.

The formalism used here for describing microstructure concepts is transactional analysis. In transactional analysis, any BASIC statement can be analyzed into a list of transactions. Transactions are not tied to the actual hardware of the computer, but are related to the general functions of the computer. A transaction is a basic unit of programming knowledge which applies some operation on some object at some location in the computer. Thus, a transaction consists of three parts:

> operation—such as MOVE, FIND, CREATE, DESTROY, DECIDE,
>   COMBINE
> object—such as number, program, pointer, program line
> location—such as data stack, memory address, program list, output screen,
>   keyboard, file

An example of a transaction is "move the number that is on the top of the data stack to the finished stack." In the shorthand of transactional analysis, this transaction could be abbreviated as, (OP: MOVE, OB:number, LOC:data stack).

In general, the transactional level of analysis has not been exploited in instruction manuals. A notable exception is that many manuals describe memory as a set of "mailboxes" or "slots." This analogy helps to clarify one of the locations used in many transactions. However, our previous research (Mayer, 1975, 1976, 1979b, 1980, 1981; Bromage & Mayer, 1980) has indicated that knowledge of all of the "locations" in the computer is crucial in enhancing novices' learning of programming. Figure 1 presents a typical analogical model of the functional parts or locations of a computer. This model includes analogies for each of the main locations:

data stack (or ticket window)—Data cards are placed in a pile outside a ticket window and are moved inside, one at a time, as each is processed.

memory scoreboard—Memory is made up of many squares in an erasable chalkboard with a label attached to each.

output screen—Messages are written on successive lines of a scrolling screen.

program list with pointer arrow—The program is like a shopping list or recipe and the pointer arrow points to the current line on the program.

file cabinet—Programs are stored in a file cabinet by name.

run-wait light—When the run light is on, the computer is carrying out the current line of the program; when the wait light is on, the computer is waiting for the user to do something.

scratch pad—An erasable area is available for making arithmetic computations.

In our studies we have used analogies such as those above to describe the

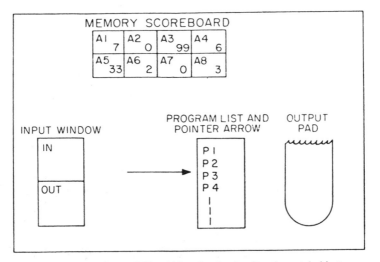

Fig. 1. Model for BASIC machine showing key locations and objects.

locations involved in transactions. It should be noted that comprehension of transactions does not require an understanding of machine-level hardware and operations. Rather, transactions are based on the functional requirements of each statement.

Table I presents a partial list of transactions required for understanding elementary BASIC statements. Since any BASIC statement may be expressed as a list of transactions, a user's ability to use the language may be tied to the user's understanding of the key transactions for each statement. By describing a statement in terms of transactions, in addition to giving the statement a formal definition, we can provide a way of conceptualizing what is going on inside the computer when the statement is executed. In short, the underlying structure of BASIC is made up of transactions. Transactions are powerful units of knowledge because they are few in number and yet can cover all of the elementary BASIC statements.

Table II presents a list of transactions corresponding to each of several BASIC statements. As can be seen, transactional analysis allows for specification of subcategories for statements. These subcategories could be called prestatements because they are more specific than the general category of statements that all share the same name. For example, the LET statement really includes several quite distinct and different types of prestatements, such as to set a counter (LET D = 0), to increment or decrement a counter (LET A = A + 1), to carry out an algebraic formula (LET C = A + B), and so forth.

Each prestatement has its own unique series of transactions; thus, the transactions for a counter set LET are not the same as the series of transactions for a

TABLE I

SOME BASIC TRANSACTIONS

Operation	Object	Location	English translation
FIND	Number	Input stack	Find the next number waiting in the input stack.
FIND	Number	Memory address	Find the number in a particular memory space.
FIND	Number	Keyboard	Find the number just entered in the keyboard.
FIND	Number	Program list	Find the number indicated in a particular place in the program.
FIND	Line	Program list	Find a particular line in the program.
FIND	Program	Program file	Find a particular program in the file.
FIND	Command	Keyboard	Find a particular word just entered in the keyboard.
FIND	Place in line	Input stack	Find the end of line at input stack.
MOVE	Number	Input stack	Move the next number at the input window to the finished pile.
MOVE	Line pointer	Program list	Move the line pointer to a particular line on the program.
MOVE	Program	Program list	Move a particular program to the program space.
MOVE	Printer pointer	Output screen	Move a printer pointer to a particular zone on the output screen.
CREATE	Number	Memory address	Write a number in a particular memory space.
CREATE	Number	Input stack	Put a number in line at the input window.
CREATE	Number	Output screen	Write a number on the output screen.
CREATE	Program	Program list	Write a program into the program space.
CREATE	Word	Output screen	Write a message (such as OUT OF DATA) on output screen.
CREATE	Question mark	Output screen	Write a ? on the output screen.
DESTROY	Number	Memory address	Erase the contents of a particular memory space.
DESTROY	Program	Program list	Destroy a particular program that is in the program space.
DESTROY	Program	Program file	Destroy a particular program that is in the file.
DECIDE	Number	Memory address	Apply a particular logical operation to numbers in memory.
DECIDE	Numbers	Program list	Apply a particular operation to numbers in program.
COMBINE	Number	Memory address	Apply a particular arithmetic operation to numbers in memory.
COMBINE	Numbers	Program list	Apply a particular arithmetic operations to numbers in program.
ALLOW	Command	Keyboard	Execute next statement entered on keyboard.
ALLOW	Command	Program list	Execute next statement pointed to by line pointer.
DISALLOW	Command	Program list	Do not execute next statement pointed to by line pointer.

TABLE II

TRANSACTIONS INVOLVED IN SELECTED PRESTATEMENTS

Prestatement	Operation	Object	Location	English translation
READ address (Single Address READ)	FIND	Number	Input stack	Find the next number waiting at the input stack.
	DECIDE	Number	Input stack	If there are no numbers in the input stack, print "OUT OF DATA" on screen,
	CREATE	Words	Screen	and wait for a new command from the keyboard.
	ALLOW	Command	Keyboard	
	MOVE	Number	Input stock	Otherwise, move the number at the input window to the finished pile.
	FIND	Number	Memory	Find the number in the memory space indicated on the READ statement.
	DESTROY	Number	Memory	Erase that number from the memory space.
	CREATE	Number	Memory	Write the new number into the memory space.
	MOVE	Pointer	Program	Go on to the next statement,
	ALLOW	Command	Program	and do what it says.
Data number (Single Datum DATA)	FIND	Number	Program	Find the number indicated on the DATA statement.
	FIND	Place-in-line	Input stock	Find the end of the line at the input window.
	CREATE	Number	Input stock	Put the number at the end of the line at the input window.
	MOVE	Pointer	Program	Go on to the next statement,
	ALLOW	Command	Program	and do what it says.
PRINT address (Single Address PRINT)	FIND	Number	Memory	Find the number in the memory address indicated.
	CREATE	Number	Screen	Write that number on the next available space on the output screen.
	MOVE	Pointer	Program	Go on to the next statement,
	ALLOW	Command	Program	and do what it says.
END	CREATE	Word (READY)	Screen	Write "READY" on the output screen.
	ALLOW	Command	Keyboard	Wait for a new command from the keyboard.
LET address = number	FIND	Number	Program	Find the number indicated on the right of the equals.

(continued)

TABLE II

(Continued)

Prestatement	Operation	Object	Location	English translation
(Counter Set LET)	FIND	Number	Memory	Find the number in the memory space indicated on the left of the equals.
	DESTROY	Number	Memory	Erase the number in that memory space.
	CREATE	Number	Memory	Write the new number in that memory space.
	MOVE	Pointer	Program	Go on to the next statement,
	ALLOW	Command	Program	and do what it says.
INPUT address (Single Number INPUT)	CREATE	Prompt	Screen	Write a "?" on the output screen.
	ALLOW	Number	Keyboard	Wait for a number to be entered from the keyboard, followed by RETURN.
	CREATE	Number	Screen	Write the entered number on the output screen next to "?".
	FIND	Number	Screen	Find that number that was just entered.
	FIND	Number	Memory	Find the number in the memory space indicated in the input statement.
	DESTROY	Number	Memory	Erase the number in that memory space.
	CREATE	Number	Memory	Write in the new number.
	MOVE	Pointer	Program	Go on to the next statement
	ALLOW	Command	Program	and do what it says.
GO TO line	FIND	Line	Program	Find the line on the program indicated in the GO TO statement.
	MOVE	Pointer	Program	Start working on that statement, ignoring all others in between,
	ALLOW	Command	Program	and do what it says.

96

IF <u>address = number</u> THEN <u>line</u> (Counter Match IF)			
FIND	Number	Program	Find the number indicated to the right of the equals in the IF statement.
FIND	Number	Memory	Find the number stored in the memory space indicated to the left of the equals.
DECIDE	Numbers	Program and memory	If the numbers match,
FIND	Line	Program	find the line that has the number indicated after THEN,
MOVE	Pointer	Program	and start working on that statement, ignoring all
ALLOW	Command	Program	and do what it says.
MOVE	Pointer	Program	Otherwise, go on to the next statement under this IF statement,
ALLOW	Command	Program	and do what it says.
NEW			
FIND	All lines	Program	Find the program that is now in the computer.
DESTROY	All lines	Program	Erase that program.
ALLOW	Commands	Keyboard	Wait for program to be typed in on keyboard.
CREATE	Lines	Program	Copy each line of the program in the space inside the computer,
CREATE	Lines	Screen	and on the screen.
ALLOW	Command	Keyboard	Wait for an operating command.
RUN			
FIND	Top line	Program	Find the first line of the program in the computer.
MOVE	Pointer	Program	Move the pointer arrow to this line.
ALLOW	Command	Program	Execute this statement, and work down from there.
STOP or Control/C			
DISALLOW	Command	Program	Do not execute the next statement in the program.
ALLOW	Command	Keyboard	Wait for an operating command from the keyboard.

TABLE III

Prestatements Involved in Selected Statements

Statement	Type of prestatement	Format of prestatement	Prestatement
LET	Counter set to number	LET address = number	LET X = 2
LET	Counter set to address	LET address = address	LET X = Y
LET	Arithmetic	LET address = number operator number	LET X = 2*4
LET	Formula	LET address = address operator address	LET X = Y*Z
LET	Mixed formula	LET address = address operation number	LET X = Y*4
LET	Increment/decrement	LET address = same address operation number	LET X = X+1
PRINT	Single message	PRINT "message"	PRINT "55"
PRINT	Single address	PRINT address	PRINT A1
PRINT	Multiple address	PRINT address list	PRINT A1, A2, A3
PRINT	Line space	PRINT (blank)	PRINT

counter increment LET. However, for any given prestatement, the list of transactions is the same regardless of specific numbers or memory addresses; thus, the series of transactions is the same for any two counter set LETs such as LET C = 5 or LET X = 999.

One problem facing many novices is that the relationship between statements and prestatements is not made clear from the onset of learning. Each statement—such as LET—may actually be a family of quite different prestatements, and the nature of the prestatements is often not clarified explicitly in instruction. A statement is a class of one or more prestatements all sharing the same key term, such as LET or PRINT. Some of the major prestatements for LET and for PRINT are suggested in Table III.

While statements have traditionally been considered to be the lowest level "building blocks" of a programming language, the foregoing transactional analysis reveals that there are several lower levels of analysis. These include breaking a statement into prestatements, breaking a prestatement into transactions, and breaking transactions into operations and objects and locations.

C.   Macrostructure Analysis of BASIC

The foregoing discussion has shown how transactional analysis can be applied to breaking BASIC statements into more conceptually meaningful units. In addition, a conceptual understanding of BASIC statements requires an understanding of the kinds of contexts into which a statement may fit. A program consists of a list of statements which accomplishes some goal. In addition, a program can often be analyzed into a set of chunks or modules. Each chunk (or module) consists of two or more prestatements and accomplishes some subgoal within the context of the program.

Chunks may be mandatory or nonmandatory. A mandatory chunk is a series of two or more prestatements that must occur in some defined configuration. For example, a READ statement always requires a corresponding DATA statement, or a FOR statement always requires a NEXT statement. Thus, some statements may be learned as parts of a larger "mandatory chunk." A nonmandatory chunk is a series of prestatements that is used in a program to accomplish some specifiable goal. Some nonmandatory chunks may be used widely as components in many different programs. For example, Table IV suggests some very common looping structures which may be used as chunks in many programs. Certainly this listing is not meant to be exhaustive, but rather illustrative of how chunks may be built. Note that each serves as a sort of "superstatement" in the sense that a long list of transactions is called for. As a learner gains more experience, he may acquire a larger store of familiar chunks (or superstatements). This approach, of course, is related to the structured programming revolution—the idea of writing programs that contain clearly recognizable chunks.

III. Users' Misconceptions of BASIC

A. ISSUE

Recent research by McCloskey, Caramazza, and Green (1980) has demonstrated that many students possess "naive conceptions" of science which they use for comprehending and learning about scientific phenomena. This section is concerned with identifying the naive conceptions which beginning programmers possess concerning BASIC. Learning a programming language involves acquiring many types of knowledge—including how to generate a program, correct syntax, and developing a conceptual (or mental) model of the system. The present section explores the question of whether instruction in how to write BASIC programs ensures that students will "automatically" also acquire useful conceptual models (or mental models).

The transactional analysis described in the previous section offers a formalism for specifying mental models associated with elementary BASIC statements. For example, the transactional analysis revealed several different locations in the computer including memory spaces, program list with pointer arrow, wait-run control, data queue (or stack), output screen, and keyboard. A useful mental model might include an understanding of how these locations operate and relate to one another. For any statement, a user would need to understand the key transactions—including what action takes place concerning which object in which location of the computer. Table II lists the transactions for several elementary BASIC statements, with the key transactions marked by an asterisk (*).

TABLE IV

Some Basic Nonmandatory Chunks for Loops

Repeat READ loop

READ	10	READ X
DATA	20	DATA 6, 7, 8, 9, 10

The INITIAL CONDITION is that numbers are waiting at the input window and one is read in.

The EXIT CONDITION is that there are no more numbers at the input window. If the computer tries to read but there are no more numbers left it will end the program and print OUT OF DATA.

(more statements such as	30	LET Y = 612
LET or IF or PRINT)	40	PRINT X, Y

The BODY OF THE LOOP consists of a series of statements such as LET or IF or PRINT which operate on the number that is read in.

GO TO (line with READ)	50	GO TO 10

The RESET statement sends the pointer arrow back to the original state so the next number will be processed in the same loop.

END	60	END

Branch loop

READ	10	READ X
DATA	20	DATA 2, 99, 6, 32, 4

The INITIAL CONDITION is that numbers are waiting at the input window and one is read in.

IF-THEN (Branch 2)	30	IF X > 30 THEN 60

The DECISION CONDITION is whether the number meets some criteria. If so, the pointer shifts to Branch 2; if not, it goes on with Branch 1.

(statements for Branch 1 such as LET and PRINT)	40	PRINT X

The BODY OF THE LOOP has two parts: the body of the loop for Branch 1 and the body of the loop for Branch 2.

GO TO (line with READ)	50	GO TO 10

The RESET sends the pointer arrow back to the same point in the program for both branches.

(statements for Branch 2 such as LET and PRINT)	60	LET X = X/2
	70	PRINT X
GO TO (line with READ)	80	GO TO 10
END	90	END

Wait for a data number

READ	10	READ X
DATA	20	DATA 5, 12, 72, 6, −1
IF-THEN (exit line with END)	30	IF X < 0 THEN 60
(more statements)	40	PRINT X
GO TO (line with READ)	50	GO TO 10
(more statements)	60	END

The INITIAL CONDITION is that numbers are waiting at the input window, and one is read in.

The EXIT CONDITION is that if a certain number (e.g., a negative number) is read in, then the pointer arrow will shift out of the loop.

The BODY OF THE LOOP consists of one or more statements after the EXIT decision but before the RESET.

The RESET puts the pointer arrow back to READ and allows another cycle through the loop.

Wait for a counter

Let C = 0	20	LET C = 1
IF C = _____ THEN (exit line such as END)	30	IF C = 5 THEN 60
(more statements)	40	READ X
	50	DATA 5, 20, 23, 6, 7, 10
	60	PRINT X
LET C = C + 1	70	LET C = C + 1
GO TO (line with IF)	80	GO to 30
	90	END

The INITIAL CONDITION is that the counter is set to zero or one (or some other value).

The EXIT CONDITION is that if the counter meets a certain criteria the pointer arrow will shift down out of the loop.

The BODY OF THE LOOP contains statements such as LET and PRINT.

The RESET involves incrementing the counter and shifting back to the top of the loop.

Research described in this section is aimed at determining whether beginning programmers acquire an understanding of the key transactions during the normal course of learning to program in BASIC. If they do, then explicit instruction in mental models is not needed; if they do not, this implies that users acquire learning outcomes which are severely limited. Research described in this section was carried out by Piraye Bayman.

B.   METHOD

In Study 1, the subjects were 30 undergraduate students at the University of California, Santa Barbara, who had no prior experience with BASIC. The subjects took a self-guided, self-paced, mastery course in BASIC, similar to a course widely taught in the Microcomputer Laboratory at the University of California, Santa Barbara. The instruction involved both a programmed instruction manual and hands-on access to an Apple II computer system. Subjects were required to pass a mastery test over one section before moving on to the next section of the manual. Instruction was carried out over three sessions, with each session lasting about 1 hr.

Following successful completion of the course, the subjects were given a procedure specification test. For each of nine statements that had been covered in the course, subjects were asked to write, in plain English, a list of steps that the computer would carry out. Subjects were instructed to write each step on a separate line of the test sheet. The nine statements are listed on the left side of Table V.

In Study 2, 19 undergraduates from the University of California, Santa Barbara, served as subjects. The method was similar to that used for Study 1, except that the subjects did not have access to a computer, the manuals were modified so that access to a computer was not needed, and the procedure specification test included 10 statements as shown on the left side of Table V.

C.   RESULTS

The data for each subject consisted of the protocol given for each of the statements in the procedure specification test. To score the data, each protocol was broken down into a list of transactions by two scorers. Three types of transactions were observed: (1) correct transactions, for example, the key correct transaction for LET A = B + 1 is "store the value of B plus 1 in memory space A;" (2) incomplete transactions, for example, an incomplete transaction for LET A = B + 1 could be "store the value of B + 1 in memory;" and (3) incorrect transactions, for example, an incorrect transaction for LET A = B + 1 could be "print the value of A on the screen." Examples of correct (marked by asterisks), incomplete, and incorrect transactions for each statement are given in Table V.

The first question addressed in the data analysis concerns the subject's ability

TABLE V

PROPORTION OF USERS GIVING TYPICAL CORRECT AND INCORRECT
TRANSACTIONS FOR EACH OF TEN BASIC STATEMENTS[a]

Transaction	Proportion of users	
	Study 1	Study 2
INPUT A		
**Assign the value typed in by the user to variable A.	.03	.26
**Wait for a value to be entered.	.23	.63
Store A in memory (or in a data list).	.30	.11
READ A		
**Assign next number from DATA to variable A.	.10	.47
Print the value of A on the screen.	.10	.11
DATA 80, 90, 99		
**Put these numbers in input queue.	.27	.47
Put these numbers in memory.	.20	.16
Print numbers on screen.	.13	.05
Put numbers in memory space A.	.07	.00
GOTO 30		
**Move to line 30 in the program, and continue from there.	.37	.32
Find the number 30.	.10	.00
IF A < B GOTO 99		
**If the value of A is less than B, then move to line 99 in the program.	.63	.89
**If the value of A is more than or equal to B, then move on to the next line in the program.	.33	.63
Move to line 99 (without a test).	.10	.00
Print a number on the screen.	.10	.11
Write a number in memory	.10	.00
IF A = B THEN PRINT "THEY ARE EQUAL"		
**If A equals B, then print "they are equal" on the screen.	(na)	1.00
**If A does not equal B, then go on to the next line.	(na)	.42
If A does not equal B, then the computer won't answer.	(na)	.05
LET D = 0		
**Assign the value 0 to variable D.	.47	.74
Write the equation in memory.	.47	.05
Print the equation on the screen.	.07	.05
LET A = B + 1		
**Assign the value of B + 1 to variable A.	.30	.79
Write the equation in memory.	.43	.05
Assign B + 1 to variable A.	.33	.05
Print A or the value of A on the screen.	.23	.16
PRINT C		
**Print the value of C on the screen.	.40	.74
Print the letter C on the screen.	.33	.05
Write a letter or number in memory.	.07	.05
PRINT "C"		
**Print the letter C on the screen.	.83	.68
Print the value of C on the screen.	.07	.00
Print "C" on the screen.	.07	.21

[a]Double asterisk (**) indicates correct key transaction(s).

to correctly specify the key transaction for each statement. Each subject's protocol for each statement was categorized as correct if it contained the key transaction but no incorrect transactions. Table VI shows the percentage of subjects in Study 1 and Study 2 who generated correct conceptions for each of the statements. As can be seen, in spite of several hours of instruction and of being able to pass mastery tests, most subjects failed to be able to express the correct conceptions for many of the statements.

The second question addressed in the data analysis concerns the kinds of misconceptions possessed by the subjects. Table V lists the most common transactions given by subjects for each statement in Study 1 and Study 2, with correct transactions indicated by an asterisk.

D. DISCUSSION

An examination of Tables V and VI reveals that users possess major misconceptions of each of the elementary BASIC statements they learned about. We summarize some of the misconceptions below.

1. Misconceptions concerning INPUT statements: Users have difficulty in conceiving of where the to-be-input data comes from (i.e., entered by user from keyboard) and where it is stored (i.e., in the indicated memory space). Many users fail to understand the concept of executive control, i.e., that the computer

TABLE VI

PERCENTAGE OF USERS WITH CORRECT CONCEPTIONS FOR BASIC STATEMENTS IN TWO STUDIES

	Percentage correct	
Statements	Study 1	Study 2
INPUT A	3	26
READ A	10	47
DATA 80, 90, 99	27	47
GOTO 30	27	32
IF A < B GOTO 99	27	63
IF A = B THEN PRINT "THEY ARE EQUAL"	—	42
LET D = 0	43	74
LET A = B + 1	27	63
PRINT C	33	68
PRINT "C"	80	68

will wait for the user to press the RETURN key. A common misconception is that INPUT A means that the letter A will be stored in memory. Apparently, users who are competent enough to pass mastery tests still have developed inadequate mental models of the role of input devices, wait-run control, and memory spaces.

2. Misconceptions concerning READ and DATA statements: Users have difficulty in conceiving of where the to-be-read data comes from (i.e., the data queue as indicated on the DATA statements) and where it is stored (i.e., in a specified memory space). For example, a common misconception is that READ A means to find the value of A and print that number on the screen. Apparently, users who have "mastered" the material still do not possess useful mental models concerning the operation of the data queue (or data stack) and memory spaces.

3. Misconceptions concerning Conditional and Simple GOTO statements: Users have difficulty in understanding the concept of flow of control such as knowing where to go after moving to the indicated line number on a GOTO statement or knowing where to go when the conditions in an IF statement are false. For example, a common misconception is thinking that IF A<B GOTO 99 means move to line 99, without carrying out a test. Apparently, many users have not developed a correct mental model of the executive control of the order of execution of statements in a program.

4. Misconceptions concerning LET statements: Users have difficulty in understanding that LET involves making an assignment of a value to a particular variable (or memory space). Instead, many users conceive of LET statements as a way of storing formulas in memory. For example, a common misconception is that LET A = B + 1 involves storing the equation A = B + 1 somewhere in the computer's memory. Apparently, many users do not view memory as a set of erasable and assignable address locations but rather see it as a large chalkboard containing a running list of information.

5. Misconceptions concerning PRINT statements: Users seem to confuse the meaning of PRINT C and PRINT "C." Further, some users incorrectly assume that the computer records in memory whatever it prints on the screen. Apparently, users often do not have mental models that correctly relate the operation of the output screen and the memory spaces.

The present studies provide evidence that "hands-on experience" (as in Study 1) and tests of mastery (as in Study 1 and Study 2) do not ensure that students will develop adequate mental models for BASIC. In spite of students' ability to perform on tests of mastery—including the ability to generate code—many users tend to develop conceptions which are incomplete or even incorrect. The foregoing review of users' misconceptions suggests that users often fail to understand the structure and functioning of the main locations of the computer: the memory spaces, the data queue, the wait-run control, the flow of control through the program, the output screen, and the input keyboard. It should be noted that the instructional materials used in these, like most BASIC instruction, did not directly provide a description of a mental model of how the locations of the computer operate. The next section explores several attempts to provide direct instruction concerning mental models for BASIC.

IV. Teaching Mental Models of BASIC

A. ISSUE

The focus of this section is whether mental models can be directly taught to beginning programmers. According to a theory of mental models, users who possess appropriate models should be better able to transfer what they have learned to new situations. This proposition has been tested in a long series of experiments which have been reported elsewhere (Mayer, 1975, 1976, 1979a, 1980, 1981; Mayer & Bromage, 1980). In these studies, novices learned a programming language from a short manual. Before reading the manual, some subjects (before group) were given brief exposure to a model of the computer which explained the main parts—such as memory spaces, program list with pointer arrow, output screen, data stack, and so on. Other subjects (after group) were given the model following instruction, while other subjects did not receive exposure to the model (control group). The results indicated that the before group tended to excel on creative problem solving—generating or interpreting programs that were more complicated than those presented during instruction—and on recall of the main conceptual information in the manuals; in contrast, the after group and the control group tended to excel in generating and interpreting statements and short programs very similar to those presented in the manual and in recall of specific details such as syntactic rules. This pattern was particularly strong for students who scored low in mathematics ability and suggests that direct instruction for mental models is particularly important for students who lack previous experience or expertise in mathematical tasks.

The present study attempts to provide a more detailed analysis of what is learned when students are given "mental models training." In particular, the present section explores several issues concerning the teachability of mental models for BASIC: (1) Does instruction in the transactions underlying each statement affect users' subsequent problem-solving performance in tests of programming? (3) Is the correctness of users' mental models related to programming performance? Research described in this section was carried out by Piraye Bayman.

B. METHOD

The subjects were 95 college students at the University of California, Santa Barbara, who have had no prior exposure to computer programming. Nineteen subjects served in a control group which involved learning BASIC from a standard manual such as described in the previous section. As in the previous studies, the manual covered elementary BASIC statements such as PRINT, LET, IF-THEN, GOTO, IF-GOTO, INPUT, READ, DATA, as well as Apple DOS commands such as NEW, LIST, and RUN. The remaining subjects served in a transactions group which involved learning BASIC from an enhanced version of the manual that included descriptions of the transactions underlying each statement. Nineteen subjects served in each of four subgroups under the transactions group: transactions-1 involved a manual that presented only the major transaction(s) for each statement: transactions-2 involved a manual that presented all of the transactions for each statement; transactions-3 involved a manual that presented the transactions in diagram form by showing the contents of the memory spaces, data stack, wait-go light, program list with pointer arrow, output screen, and scratch pad both before and after execution of the statement; transactions-4 involved both a complete list of transactions for each statement (as in the transactions-2 treatment) and diagrams (as in the transactions-3 treatment). Thus, the transaction manuals were identical to the standard manual used by the Control Group, except that more information about transactions was added to the transactions manuals. Table VII gives examples of corresponding sections of each of the five instruction manuals.

Subjects were randomly assigned to treatment groups (or subgroups). Over the course of two or three sessions, subjects read their manuals at their own pace. After completing each section of the manual subjects were required to pass a mastery test before going on. After successfully completing the manual, including passing the mastery tests, subjects were given several posttests including a programming test and a procedure specification test. The programming test consisted of 18 problems in which the subject had to either write a program, interpret a program, or debug a program. Thus, this test required that the user apply the information in the manual to solving problems. All of the problems involved information that was part of the standard manual. The procedure specification test consisted of 10 sheets of paper with a different statement given at the top of each. The subject's job was to write, in plain English, a list of all of the steps the computer would go through in order to carry out that statement. This test was given in order to determine whether the transactions treatment resulted in the acquisition of more accurate mental models.

C. Results

Since previous studies (Mayer, 1975, 1979b, 1981) had indicated that low-ability students are more strongly affected by mental models training than high-ability students, each treatment group in the present study was divided into low-ability (SAT-quantitative scores below 520) and high-ability (SAT-quantitative scores of 520 or above) subgroups. The programming test was scored by tallying

TABLE VII

Excerpts from Five Versions of a BASIC Manual

Control group

Assume that you type in:

IF 3 < 10 THEN PRINT 10-3 and press the RETURN key.

You will see the result of the computation, i.e., 7, on the screen only if the IF part is true.

Transactions-1 group

Assume that you type in:

IF 3 < 10 THEN PRINT 10-3 and press the RETURN key.

The computer will test the logical relationship between the numbers 3 and 10 and if this test is positive, it will print the result of the computation, i.e., 7. However, if the test is negative, the computer will not print anything on the display screen.

Transactions-2 group

Assume that you type in:

IF 3 < 10 THEN PRINT 10-3 and press the RETURN key.

The steps the computer carries out are:

1. FIND the numbers in the IF part of the statement (i.e., 3 and 10).
2. TEST the logical relationship between those numbers in the workspace (i.e., Is 3 less than 10?).
3. If the test is positive, then SUBTRACT 3 from 10.
4. PRINT the result of the subtract on the display screen.
5. If the test is negative, then DON'T PRINT anything on the display screen. (For this particular example, this step is irrelevant.)
6. WAIT FOR the next statement to be entered from the keyboard.

Transactions-3 group

Assume that you type in:

IF 3 < 10 THEN PRINT 10-3 and press the return key.

Before execution the parts look like this: *After execution* the parts will look like this:

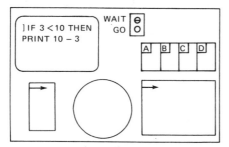
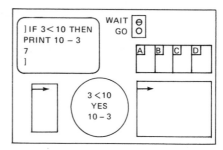

Transactions-4 group

(Contains both Transactions-2 and Transactions-3 material)

the number of correct responses, and the procedure specification test was scored by protocol analysis as summarized in the previous section. For each statement on the procedure specification test, a subject was categorized as having the correct conception if the subject's protocol included the key transaction and no incorrect transactions. The percentage of correct conceptions refers to the proportion of statements on the procedure specification test for which the subject possessed the correct conception.

The first question addressed in the data analysis is whether transactions training affected subjects' conceptions of BASIC, as measured by their performance on the procedure specification test. The top half of Table VIII shows the percentage of correct conceptions of statements for the control group and the transactions group by ability level. For low-ability subjects, transaction training greatly increases knowledge of correct conceptions for each statement, whereas for high-ability subjects knowledge of correct conceptions is equally good for both control and transactions groups. An analysis of variance was conducted on the percentage of correct conceptions data with instructional treatment (control vs. transactions) and ability level (high vs. low) as between subjects factors. The analysis confirmed that high-ability subjects outperformed low-ability subjects, $F(1, 89) = 19.55, p < .001$, and subjects in the transactions group outperformed subjects in the control group, $F(1, 89) = 5.40, p < .02$. In addition, there was a significant ability $\times$ treatment interaction (ATI), $F(1, 89) = 5.15, p < .03$, which is consistent with the observation that the treatment effect was strong only for the low-ability subjects. The observed differential effects of mental model training for different ability levels are consistent with previous results (Mayer, 1975, 1979b, 1981); one explanation of this interaction is that high-ability stu-

TABLE VIII

PERCENTAGE OF CORRECT CONCEPTIONS
FOR CONTROL AND TRANSACTIONS
GROUPS BY ABILITY LEVEL

	Ability level	
	Low	High
Procedural specification		
Control	30	67
Transactions	53	67
Programming test		
Control	48	74
Transactions	58	65

dents may be able to generate appropriate mental models on their own. In summary, these results support the idea that it is possible to directly teach mental models to learners.

The second question addressed in the data analysis is whether mental model training (i.e., training that includes descriptions of underlying transactions) affects students' ability to use the information in the manual to solve programming problems. The bottom half of Table VIII shows the percentage of correct responses on the programming test for the control and transactions groups by ability level. As can be seen, for the low-ability group, training in the underlying transactions tended to result in better problem-solving performance than no training, whereas for the high-ability group, transaction training did not enhance problem-solving performance as compared to the control group. An analysis of variance was carried out on these percentage correct data, with instructional treatment (control vs. transaction) and ability (high vs. low) as between subjects factors. The ANOVA revealed that high-ability students performed better than low-ability students, $F(1, 89) = 3.26, p < .005$, and there was no overall effect due to treatment, $F < 1$. As in the previous analysis, there was also a significant ability by treatment interaction, $F(1, 90) = 3.84, p < .05$. These results are consistent with the idea that mental model training tends to increase problem-solving performance for low-ability subjects but not for high-ability subjects.

The third question addressed in the data analysis concerns the relationship between knowledge of correct conceptions (or mental models) for BASIC and ability to solve programming problems. According to the theory of mental models outlined in the introduction, there should be a strong positive relationship between the correctness of users' mental models of BASIC and their programming performance. In order to address this question, the subjects were divided into groups based on their procedure specification test performance. A total of 24 subjects (good model group) produced correct conceptions for at least 8 out of the 10 statements on the test; 24 subjects (poor model group) produced correct conceptions for 4 or less of the 10 statements on the test. The scores on the programming test were much higher for subjects who possessed good models (75% correct) than subjects who possessed poor models (42%). An analysis of variance revealed that this observed difference was statistically significant, $F(1, 42) = 49.35, p < .001$. In order to further investigate the relation between knowledge of correct mental model and programming performance, a Pearson correlation was computed using data from all subjects. The correlation between percentage of correct conceptions and percentage correct on the programming test was $r = .62$; when the effects of ability were partialled out, the correlation was $r = .56$. These correlations are statistically significant at $p < .01$. These analyses provide support for the idea that having a transaction-based mental model is related to being able to solve programming problems; however, it must be noted that correlational data cannot be successfully used to argue for a causal relationship.

D. Discussion

In summary, the foregoing study provides some detailed evidence that for low-ability students (who presumably lack rich experience with mathematical learning situations) specific kinds of mental models can be successfully taught and that such training tends to enhance students' ability to solve programming problems. Furthermore, there is a strong relationship between the correctness of a user's mental model and the user's programming performance. These results serve to validate the transactional analysis approach as a method of describing users' mental models, but do not preclude the development of other formalisms for describing mental models of BASIC. It should also be pointed out that the foregoing analyses collapsed over all the transactions training subgroups in an effort to provide a straightforward description of the results. Analyses of individual subgroups produce essentially the same conclusions as those expressed above.

V. Users' Comprehension of Procedural Statements

A. Issue

This section is concerned with the comprehension process required for procedural statements which are presented in BASIC and in English. In particular, we are concerned with identifying factors which influence the time needed to comprehend BASIC and English procedural statements. The cognitive task analysis of procedural statements described in a previous section revealed two kinds of factors: microstructure and macrostructure. Microstructure factors include the number and quality of transactions which make up a particular statement. The transactional analysis of BASIC statements described in an earlier section suggests that comprehension of a BASIC statement depends on encoding a list of actions to be carried out. A prediction of this analysis is that statements requiring more transactions (or more complicated transactions) will require more comprehension time. Table IX presents the transactions required for each of several BASIC statements that were used in the present studies. As can be seen, PRINT requires 4 transactions, INPUT requires 9 transactions, and LET requires 10 transactions. Macrostructure factors include the context in which the statement is embedded. Comprehension requires building relations between the target statement and other statements in the same program or module. A prediction of this analysis is that statements embedded in longer programs (or more complicated programs) will require more comprehension time. Research described in this section was carried out by Jennifer L. Dyck.

B. Method

In Study 1, the subjects were 33 college students at the University of California, Santa Barbara, who already knew the BASIC computer programming lan-

TABLE IX

Transactions for PRINT, INPUT, and LET Statements

Transactions			English translation
PRINT A (PRINT1 and PRINT2)			
1. FIND	Number	Memory	Find the number in the memory address indicated.
2. CREATE	Number	Screen	Write that number on the next available space on the output screen.
3. MOVE	Pointer	Program	Go on to the next statement,
4. ALLOW	Command	Program	and do what it says.
INPUT A (INPUT1 and INPUT2)			
1. CREATE	Prompt	Screen	Write a "?" on the output screen.
2. ALLOW	Number	Keyboard	Wait for a number to be entered from the keyboard, followed by RETURN.
3. CREATE	Number	Screen	Write the entered number on the output screen next to "?".
4. FIND	Number	Keyboard	Find the number that was just entered.
5. FIND	Number	Memory	Find the number in the memory space indicated in the INPUT statement.
6. DESTROY	Number	Memory	Erase the number in that memory space.
7. CREATE	Number	Memory	Write in the new number.
8. MOVE	Pointer	Program	Go on to the next statement,
9. ALLOW	Command	Program	and do what it says.
LET A = A + 1 (LET1) OR LET B = A + 1 (LET2)			
1. FIND	Number	Program	Find the number in the mixed formula.

2. CREATE	Number	Scratch Pad	Put that number in the scratch pad.
3. FIND	Number	Memory	Find the number in the memory space indicated in the mixed formula.
4. CREATE	Number	Scratch Pad	Put that number also in the scratch pad.
5. COMBINE	Number	Scratch Pad	Add the two numbers in the scratch pad together.
6. FIND	Number	Memory	Find the number in the memory space indicated to the left of equals.
7. DESTROY	Number	Memory	Erase the number in that memory space.
8. CREATE	Number	Memory	Put the new sum from the scratch pad into this memory space.
9. MOVE	Pointer	Program	Go on to the next statement,
10. ALLOW	Command	Program	and do what it says.

LET A = A + B (LET3) or LET C = A + B (LET4)

1. FIND	Number	Memory	Find the number in the first memory space indicated in the formula.
2. CREATE	Number	Scratch Pad	Put that number in the scratch pad.
3. FIND	Number	Memory	Find the number in the second memory space indicated in the formula.
4. CREATE	Number	Scratch Pad	Put that number also in the scratch pad.
5. COMBINE	Number	Scratch Pad	Add the two numbers in the scratch pad together.
6. FIND	Number	Memory	Find the number in the memory space indicated to the left of equals.
7. DESTROY	Number	Memory	Erase the number in that memory space.
8. CREATE	Number	Memory	Put the new sum from the scratch pad into this memory space.
9. MOVE	Pointer	Program	Go on to the next statement,
10. ALLOW	Command	Program	and do what it says.

guage. The subject was seated in front of an Apple II computer system. On the terminal screen, instructions were presented along with eight practice problems. Then 64 BASIC problems were presented; each problem contained a program and a question about the program. The subject's job was to press a button corresponding to the correct answer. Subjects worked at their own rates, and there was a 2-sec interval after each response before the next problem was presented. The programs were constructed using the statements INPUT, PRINT, and LET, and ranged from two to four lines in length. Table X lists the eight types of programs used; there were eight instances of each program with different variable names and numbers used for each. An example of a problem using the first program form is

10 INPUT B
20 PRINT B

The number for B is 5. What is the output?
(a) 0   (b) 5   (c) 6   (d) 10

The computer stored the subject's response and response time for each problem.

In Study 2, the subjects were 34 students recruited from the same subject pool as Study 1, but who had no previous experience with BASIC. The procedure was identical to that used in Study 1 except that the problems were stated as English procedures. Each English program was a translation of a corresponding BASIC program, with PRINT and INPUT statements requiring seven words and LET statements requiring 14 statements. Table XI shows the English programs corresponding, respectively, to the BASIC programs in Table X. An example problem, corresponding to the BASIC problem given above, is

1. Put the first number shown below in Box A.
2. Write down the first number that is shown in Box A.

The first number is 5. What is the output?
(a) 0   (b) 5   (c) 6   (d) 10

C. RESULTS

Since each subject responded to 64 problems (eight instances for each of eight program types), there were 64 data points for each subject. In order to consolidate these data, a mean response time (RT) was computed for each of the eight types of programs for each subject, using data for correct responses only. Then a subtraction procedure was used to estimate the RT for each of eight target statements for each subject. The mean RT for one problem type was subtracted from the mean RT for another problem type, where the two problems were identical except that the first contained one less statement than the second. For example, to obtain an estimate of the RT to comprehend a PRINT statement, the

TABLE X

Eight BASIC Problem Types

Problem 1	Problem 5
10 INPUT A	10 INPUT A
20 PRINT A	20 LET A = A + 1
Problem 2	30 PRINT A
10 INPUT A	Problem 6
20 INPUT B	10 INPUT A
30 PRINT A	20 LET B = A + 1
Problem 3	30 PRINT B
10 INPUT A	Problem 7
20 PRINT A	10 INPUT A
30 PRINT A	20 INPUT B
Problem 4	30 LET A = A + B
10 INPUT A	40 PRINT A
20 INPUT B	Problem 8
30 PRINT A	10 INPUT A
40 PRINT B	20 INPUT B
	30 LET C = A + B
	40 PRINT C

mean RT for Problem 1 was subtracted from the mean RT for Problem 3. The subtraction procedure for each of the eight target statements is summarized in Table XII. As can be seen, there are two subtraction procedures for PRINT statements—one for PRINT in a four-line program and one for PRINT in a three-line program; there are also two procedures for INPUT statements—one for INPUT in a four-line program and one for INPUT in a three-line program. Finally, it can be observed that this study uses four different kinds of LET statements.

The first question addressed in the data analysis concerns whether the comprehension process for BASIC statements differs from the comprehension process for English statements. Table XIII shows the mean RT on each of the eight target statements for Study 1 (BASIC) and Study 2 (English). As can be seen, the RT for English statements seems to be consistently higher than for corresponding BASIC statements, but the pattern of performance by statement type is remarkably similar for English and BASIC. To examine these observations, an analysis of variance was conducted on the RT data with language (BASIC vs. English) as a between-subjects factor and statement type (eight types) as a within-subjects factor. The ANOVA revealed that the RT for English statements is significantly higher than for BASIC statements, $F(1, 65) = 44.55$, $p < .001$, and identified significant differences in RT among the statement types, $F(7, 455) = 11.11$, $p < .001$, but failed to produce a significant language by statement type interaction, $F(7, 455) = 1.68$, $p > .10$. To examine the relation between the patterns of

TABLE XI

Eight English Problem Types

Problem 1
 1. Put the first number shown below in Box A.
 2. Write down the number that is in Box A.
Problem 2
 1. Put the first number shown below in Box A.
 2. Put the second number shown below in Box B.
 3. Write down the number that is in Box A.
Problem 3
 1. Put the first number shown below in Box A.
 2. Write down the number that is in Box A.
 3. Write down the number that is in Box A.
Problem 4
 1. Put the first number shown below in Box A.
 2. Put the second number shown below in Box B.
 3. Write down the number that is in Box A.
 4. Write down the number that is in Box B.
Problem 5
 1. Put the first number shown below in Box A.
 2. Add the number 1 to the number from Box A,
      and put this new number in Box A.
 3. Write down the number that is in Box A.
Problem 6
 1. Put the first number shown below in Box A.
 2. Add the number 1 to the number from Box A,
      and put this new number in Box B.
 3. Write down the number that is in Box B.
Problem 7
 1. Put the first number shown below in Box A.
 2. Put the second number shown below in Box B.
 3. Add the numbers from Box A and from Box B together,
      and put this new number in Box A.
 4. Write down the number that is in Box A.
Problem 8
 1. Put the first number shown below in Box A.
 2. Put the second number shown below in Box B.
 3. Add the numbers from Box A and from Box B together;
      and put this new number in Box C.
 4. Write down the number that is in Box C.

---

performance for the two languages, a Pearson correlation was computed between the English and BASIC versions on the eight statement types. The resulting correlation was $r = .85$, with a significance level of $p < .01$. Thus, the lack of a language by statement type interaction and the observation of a strong correlation between the two languages are consistent with the hypothesis that similar under-

TABLE XII

SUBTRACTION TECHNIQUE FOR EIGHT PROCEDURAL STATEMENTS

Subtraction technique	BASIC	English translation
PRINT1 = Problem3 − Problem1	PRINT A	Write down the number that is in Box A.
PRINT2 = Problem4 − Problem2	PRINT A	Write down the number that is in Box A.
INPUT1 = Problem2 − Problem1	INPUT A	Put the first number shown below in Box A.
INPUT2 = Problem4 − Problem3	INPUT A	Put the first number shown below in Box A.
LET1 = Problem5 − Problem1	LET A = A + 1	Add the number 1 to the number in Box A, and put this new number in BOX A.
LET2 = Problem6 − Problem1	LET B = A + 1	Add the number 1 to the number in Box A, and put this new number in BOX B.
LET3 = Problem7 − Problem2	LET A = A + B	Add the numbers from BOX A and from Box B together, and put this new number in BOX A.
LET4 = Problem8 − Problem2	LET C = A + B	Add the numbers from BOX A and from Box B together, and put this new number in BOX A.

　　　　　　　　　　　　　Richard E. Mayer

TABLE XIII

RESPONSE TIME (SEC) FOR BASIC AND ENGLISH GROUPS
ON EIGHT TYPES OF STATEMENTS

Group	PRINT1	PRINT2	INPUT1	INPUT2	LET1	LET2	LET3	LET4
Basic	0.3	1.0	1.5	2.3	1.4	2.0	2.2	1.5
English	2.1	2.8	2.7	3.9	3.8	3.6	5.3	3.4

lying comprehension processes are used for English and BASIC procedural statements.

The second question addressed in the data analysis concerns the role of microstructure variables in comprehension of the procedural statements. The second column of Table XIV lists the number of transactions required for each of the eight target statement types, while Table XIII gives the corresponding RTs by statement type for English and BASIC. As can be seen, the number of transactions per statement seems to correspond positively with the time required to comprehend the statement for both English and BASIC. This observation is consistent with the fact that the Pearson correlation between number of transactions per statement and RT on English statements was $r = .68$ (with $p < .05$), and the Pearson correlation between number of transactions and RT on BASIC statements was $r = .75$ (with $p < .02$).

TABLE XIV

MICROSTRUCTURE AND MACROSTRUCTURE FEATURES
OF EIGHT PROCEDURAL STATEMENTS

Procedural statement	Microstructure		Macrostructure
	Total number of transactions (T)	Number of transactions with double-entry variable (Q)	Number of other statements in context (C)
PRINT 1	4	0	2
PRINT 2	4	0	3
INPUT 1	9	0	2
INPUT 2	9	0	3
LET 1	10	1	2
LET 2	10	0	2
LET 3	10	1	3
LET 4	10	0	3

Another microstructure variable, listed in the third column of Table XIV, concerns the type of transactions involved for each statement. For example, some transactions require a "double-entry variable"; that is, some transactions find and use a number in a memory space and substitute a new number in the same memory space. The statements, LET A = A + 1 or LET A = A + B, contain double-entry variable transactions because A is a variable that is used twice—once with its original value and once with its new incremented value. In contrast, LET B = A + 1 or LET C = A + B do not involve double-entry variable transactions. When this variable was added to the number of transactions, the following stepwise regression equations were generated:

English RT = (1.78) + (0.16)T + (0.96)Q
BASIC RT = (0.01) + (0.18)T

T refers to the number of transactions and Q refers to the quality of transactions (i.e., 1 for double entry and 0 for non-double entry). The English regression equation accounts for 66% (adjusted r^2 is .53) of the variance among statement types while the BASIC regression accounts for 56% (adjusted r^2 is .49). Although many other "quality" variables are possible, the present analysis demonstrates that predictions for English RT can be improved by analyzing quality as well as quantity of transactions.

The third question addressed in data analysis concerns the role of macrostructure variables. For example, the fourth column of Table XIV shows that PRINT, INPUT, and LET statements are sometimes presented within the context of a three-line program and other times within the context of a four-line program. For English, when a statement is presented within the context of a three-line program, the mean RT is 3.0 sec while the mean RT for identical statements within a four-line program is 3.8 sec; the corresponding RTs for BASIC are 1.2 and 1.7, respectively. An analysis of variance was conducted on the RT data with language (English vs. BASIC) as a between-subjects factor and context (3-line vs. 4-line program) as a within-subjects factor. As observed above, there was a main effect for context, $F(1, 65) = 5.33$, $p < .05$, in which more time was required when statements were placed in longer programs; but there was no language by context interaction, $F(1, 65) = .11$, $p > .20$, and thus no evidence that context had different effects on English and BASIC languages. When a context variable was added to the number and quality of transactions, the following stepwise regression equations were generated:

English RT = (−0.20) + (0.16)T + (0.96)Q + (0.79)C
BASIC RT = (−1.23) + (0.18)T + (0.50)C

T refers to number of transactions, Q to presence or absence of double-entry variables in the transactions, and C to the number of other statements in the context of the program. All three variables were related to performance in interpreting English procedures while only two of the variables were selected for predicting RTs on BASIC statements. The English equation accounted for 88% (adjusted r^2 of .78) of the variance in RTs, and the BASIC equation accounted for 74% (adjusted r^2 of .63) of the variance.

D. DISCUSSION

These results provide evidence that some microstructure factors (i.e., number of transactions) and some macrostructure factors (i.e., number of other statements in the context) affect comprehension time for BASIC and English procedures in similar ways. The results are most consistent with the theory that BASIC and English procedural statements entail similar underlying comprehension processes such as encoding a list of transactions and building associations with other statements in the program. However, there is also a hint here that the particular formalism used for expressing procedures (or differences in the experience between programmers and nonprogrammers) may affect the relative difficulty of encoding particular types of transactions (such as those with double-entry variables). In the present study, subjects in the BASIC group were not strongly affected by this "quality of transaction" variable while subjects in the English group were. Unfortunately, the present study is unable to determine whether this difference is due to differences between English and BASIC or between subjects who had experience in programming versus those who did not.

VI. Predictors of Success in Learning BASIC

A. ISSUE

The foregoing studies have provided some information concerning the role of existing cognitive skills in learning computer programming. In this section, we report some preliminary studies aimed at determining whether the prerequisite skills for learning BASIC consist mainly of general cognitive skills or more specific ones. General cognitive skills affect performance across a wide range of activities and involve measures such as general intelligence, inductive and deductive reasoning, and spatial visualization. Specific cognitive skills refer to skills that are specifically related to the BASIC language such as the comprehension of a procedure stated as a list of commands or translation of a problem statement into a formal symbol system.

The issue of general versus specific predictors is related to the question of the extent to which learning BASIC depends on relatively fixed versus relatively fluid cognitive abilities. The general cognitive tests used in these studies are designed to tap skills which are relatively resistant to change or difficult to learn because they are related to many different domains; in contrast, the specific cognitive tests are designed to tap more restricted skills which are more readily learnable. It should, of course, be noted that the distinction between general versus specific tests is not identical to the distinction between fixed versus learnable cognitive skills, since the latter distinction must be subjected to empirical verification.

Although these studies are preliminary, they do provide some implications concerning the role of learners' existing cognitive skills. An empiricist theory of learning states that students need appropriate prerequisite experiences in order to develop concepts which are required in BASIC; according to this view, differences among students' ease of learning BASIC may be attributed to differences in the opportunities that students have had to build useful intuitions and conceptions needed for BASIC. The empiricist theory predicts that specific skills will be strong predictors of success in learning BASIC. This finding would encourage the idea that prerequisite instruction could be provided to help beginners develop appropriate preprogramming concepts or intuitions; however, a manipulation of learners' existing skills would be needed to directly test this idea. In contrast, a nativist theory of learning states that students differ inherently in their ability to learn BASIC. The nativist theory predicts that general skills will be strong predictors of success in learning BASIC. This finding implies that selection rather than training is the key to effective learning of BASIC. Thus, these studies determine whether individual differences in learning BASIC are attributable mainly to differences in general (and to some extent, fixed) cognitive skills or to specific (and to some extent, teachable) cognitive skills. Research described in this section was carried out by Jennifer L. Dyck and Bill Vilberg.

B. Method

We designed a battery of pretests aimed at tapping various cognitive skills proported to be related to computer programming. All tests are short, timed paper-and-pencil tests with multiple-choice or constructed answer formats.

Some of the tests deal mainly with the skill of "comprehension of a procedure." For each of four items, the subject had to answer a question about a procedure that was stated in English. For example, one item is

1. Put 5 in Box A.
2. Put 4 in Box B.
3. Add the number in Box A and the number in Box B, put the result in Box C.
4. Add the number in Box A and the number in Box C, put the result in Box A.
5. Write down the numbers from Box A, B, C.

What is the output of this program?
a. 5, 4, 9

b. 14, 4, 9
c. 14, 9, 9
d. 9, 4, 9
e. None of the above

Advanced Procedure Comprehension. For each of four items, the subject had to answer two questions concerning a complex program that was stated in English. For example, one item is

1. Put 1 in Box A.
2. Put 0 in Box B.
3. Add 5 to the number in Box A,
   put the result in Box C.
4. Add the number in Box C to the number in Box B,
   put the result in Box B.
5. Write down the number from Box B.
6. Is Box B greater than 15?
   If yes, stop. If no, go to step 3.

What is the output of this program?
a. 5, 10, 15, 20
b. 6, 11, 16
c. 6, 24
d. 6, 12, 18
e. None of the above

How many times is step 3 done?
a. 1
b. 2
c. 3
d. 4
e. None of the above

Flowchart Comprehension. For each of four items, the subject had to answer a question about how to modify a simple flowchart so that it would deal with a specified situation. For example, the subject was shown a three-operation flowchart that "figures the total cost of some donuts you buy at a bakery, assuming one donut costs 35 cents." Then the subject had to choose, from five alternatives, which steps to add so that "if you buy at least a dozen donuts, each donut will cost 30 cents."

Following Directions. For each of eight items, the subject had to answer a question about an array of letters consisting of five rows as five columns. For example, one item is

	Column				
	1	2	3	4	5
Row 1	A	B	C	D	E
Row 2	B	D	E	A	C
Row 3	C	E	D	A	B
Row 4	B	A	C	E	D
Row 5	A	C	E	B	D

Start in the lower left-hand corner and follow
the letters up column 1, down column 2,
up column 3, and so on, until you reach the
upper right-hand corner. What is the first
letter to appear four times?

A   B   C   D   E

Other tests deal mainly with the skill of "translation from English into a
formal language" as follows.

Algebra Story Problem Translation Test. For each of six items, the subject had
to select the equation which corresponded to a word problem. For example, one
item is

A car rental service charges twenty dollars a day and fifteen cents a mile to
rent a car. Find the expression for total cost, C, in dollars, of renting a car for
D days to travel M miles.

a. $C = 20D + .15M$
b. $C = 15D + .20M$
c. $C = 20D + 15M$
d. $C = .15D + 20M$
e. None of the above

Arithmetic Aptitude Test. For each of nine items, the subject had to select the
correct answer for word problems. For example, one item is

One day Mrs. Arnold worked 3.5 hours in the morning, took a half-hour for
lunch, and worked 4.5 hours in the afternoon. If she began work at 8:30 a.m.,
at what time did she finish?

a. 4:30
b. 5:00
c. 5:30
d. 6:00
e. 6:30

One test deals with a mathematical skill that is not directly related to programming:

Computation Test. For each of 60 items, the subject had to compute an answer. For example, one item is

36
20
+54

The other tests are designed to tap more general cognitive skills:

Inductive Reasoning Test. For each of 10 items, the subject is given five letter sets and has to select the set of letters that did not belong. For example, one item is

BCDE   FGHI   JKLM   PRST   VWXY

Spatial Visualization Test. For each of 10 items, the subjects had to select the correct outcome from a paper-folding sequence.

Deciphering Languages Test. For each of nine items, the subject had to decipher a simple code. For example, one item is

black sheep = dag kip
white dog = tin bud
black cow = dag stam
white sheep =

a. dag kip
b. tin kip
c. stam dag
d. bud tin
e. tin bud

The Procedure Specification Tests are similar to the NCR Flowcharts Test (Luftig, 1972). The Flowchart Comprehension Test is similar to one item from Huber's (1982) Test of Computer Knowledge. The Computation Test, Arithmetic Aptitude Test, Inductive Reasoning Test, Following Directions Test, Spatial Visualization Test, and Deciphering Languages Test were modified from the Kit of Factor-Referenced Cognitive Tests (Ekstrom, French, & Harmon, 1976). The left column of Table XV summarizes the cognitive pretest measures.

Four different studies were conducted using different subject populations, different kinds of instruction in BASIC, and different posttests for measuring learning of BASIC. In all studies, however, the subjects had no prior experience with or knowledge of BASIC. In each study, subjects were given a battery of cognitive pretests, learned BASIC, and then were given a posttest to evaluate learning. Table XVI summarizes the cognitive pretests, instructional, and BASIC posttest as well as the subject population for each of the four studies.

TABLE XV

CORRELATIONS BETWEEN COGNITIVE PREDICTORS AND CRITERION

Predictors	Study 1	Study 2	Study 3	Mayer (1975)
Algebra translation	.28	.64*(r)	.55*(r)	.61*
Procedure	.39*(r)	.28	.44*	na
Advanced procedure	.07	.51*	.14	na
Flowchart	.35*	.44*(r)	.30*	na
Computation	na	.32	.26	na
Arithmetic aptitude	na	.63*	.56*(r)	na
Inductive reasoning	na	.53*(r)	.29*	na
Following directions	na	.46*	.44*(r)	na
Visualization	na	.40	.31*	na
Language	na	.40	.16	na
Multiple correlation	.39*	.82*	.69*	na

[a]Asterisk indicates that correlation is significant at $p < .05$; (r) indicates that this variable was selected for inclusion in a stepwise regression analysis; na indicates test not available.

C. RESULTS

For each subject, the following data were available: number correct on each of the pretests and number correct on the posttest. The right-hand columns of Table XV show the Pearson correlation between each pretest score and the BASIC posttest score. An asterisk indicates that the correlation is statistically significant at $p < .05$. As can be seen, the specific tests tended to be strong predictors of success in learning BASIC—including the Algebra Translation Test and Arithmetic Aptitude Test as measures of how to translate a problem statement into a formal language, and the Procedure Specification Test and Flowchart Test and Following Directions Test as measures of ability to comprehend a procedure. In addition, one of the general tests (Inductive Reasoning) was strongly related to success in learning BASIC.

For each of the first three studies, a stepwise regression analysis was conducted using the pretests as predictors and the posttest score as the criterion. The analysis required $F = 4.00$ to enter or remove a variable. For Study 1, the resulting equation was Posttest Score = 4.1 + 1.5 (Procedure Comprehension). For Study 2, the equation was Posttest Score = −5.9 + 2.9 (Algebra Translation) + 2.1 (Flowchart) + 1.6 (Inductive Reasoning). For Study 3, the best fitting equation required $F = 1.00$ to enter or remove a variable and produced the equation Final Exam Score = 125.3 + 5.7 (Algebra Translation) + 2.8 (Procedure Comprehension) + 2.0 (Flowchart) + 3.2 (Following Directions). The adjusted r^2 values for the equations were, respectively, .13, .63, and .46. In Table XV, the symbol (r) means that the indicated variable was included in the

TABLE XVI

Subject Population, Pretests, Instructional Program, and Criterion Posttest for Four Studies

	Subject population	Pretests (predictors)	Instructional program	Posttest (criterion)
Study 1	35 University of California students, required to learn BASIC as part of a psychology course	Four specific cognitive tests	Unstructured, self-guided study of BASIC	12-item quiz
Study 2	24 University of California students who volunteered to learn BASIC in a noncredit course	Four specific cognitive tests and six general cognitive tests	Two hours of a structured, hands-on, mastery program on BASIC	12-item quiz
Study 3	57 University of Southern Mississippi students who enrolled in a course on BASIC	Four specific cognitive tests and six general cognitive tests	Semester course on BASIC	Final exam
Study 4	80 Indiana University students, recruited from the psychology study pool	One specific cognitive test	Two hours with a 10-page booklet on BASIC	12-item quiz

regression equation; the bottom of Table XV shows the multiple correlation based on the regression equation.

D. DISCUSSION

The four studies provide somewhat consistent results that differences in the learning of BASIC are related to differences in the specific cognitive skills of learners. A cognitive task analysis of generating BASIC programs reveals that two primary underlying skills are the ability to comprehend a procedure and the ability to translate from English into another formal language. Tests that tap these skills were found to be strong predictors of success in learning BASIC.

These results encourage additional research in which some students are given pretraining for specific cognitive skills—such as how to comprehend a procedure or how to translate—while others are not given pretraining. Since the present study is correlational, no conclusions can be drawn concerning whether certain cognitive skills are the cause of better learning of BASIC; only an instructional study as proposed above can directly address this question. However, the present study suggests that procedure comprehension and problem translation are excellent candidates to be included in a training study.

These results also encourage additional refinement of the psychometric measures used for assessing cognitive skills. The failure of some of the general tests to produce significant correlations could be due to poor reliability of the tests, since short versions were used for all tests. The present study suggests how we might begin to design a programmer aptitude battery based on specific cognitive skills. However, since this was not a direct goal of these preliminary studies, additional psychometric work is needed to design tests that are reliable as well as valid.

VII. Summary

This article began by describing a technique, called "transactional analysis," for representing users' conceptual knowledge about BASIC programming statements. Much of the research on mental models has been limited by the lack of a technique for describing users' conceptual knowledge. Transactional analysis was presented as an example of a framework which allows us to describe users' conceptual knowledge underlying BASIC. The remainder of the article summarized empirical studies examining the role of users' conceptual knowledge (or mental models) in learning, understanding, and using BASIC statements. Although there have been many discussions of mental models in person–machine interaction (Carroll & Thomas, 1982; De Kleer & Brown, 1981, 1983; Du Boulay & O'Shea, 1981; Young, 1981, 1983), there has not been a correspondingly rich data base upon which theories may be tested. Thus, the research presented here provides examples from four converging investigations of the role of users' conceptual knowledge in learning BASIC.

At the most general level, we have provided some encouragement that the framework of transactional analysis can be a useful guide to empirical research in person–machine interaction. Similarly, we have provided some encouragement that the "subject matter" approach to the study of human learning and cognition can be a fruitful one.

More specifically, we have presented new information about novices learning BASIC. First, the section on "users' misconceptions of BASIC" provided detailed information concerning the types of incomplete and incorrect conceptual knowledge that novices acquire as they learn BASIC. As in the corresponding research on people's misconceptions of science, the present research suggests that people tend to build mental models which are not always useful. Second, the section on "teaching mental models of BASIC" provided detailed information supporting the idea that conceptual knowledge about BASIC can be directly taught and that such training is related to enhanced problem-solving performance on tests of programming. Third, the section on "users' comprehension of procedural statements" provided an additional line of validation for the transactional analysis framework. In particular, the time to comprehend a procedural statement—expressed in English or in BASIC—was strongly related to the number of transactions that had to be encoded and the number of other statements in the program. Thus, there is some empirical evidence that microstructure and macrostructure variables affect comprehension of procedural statements. Finally, the section on "predictors of success in learning BASIC" showed how underlying conceptual knowledge is related to learning BASIC, even in the context of a semester-long course. The results were consistent with the idea that the learning of BASIC is enhanced when learners possess a rich bank of conceptual knowledge that is specifically relevant to BASIC. In particular, successful learning of BASIC was strongly related to learners' knowledge of how to comprehend procedures stated in English. Since the English procedures tend to require knowledge of the same transactions as BASIC procedures, this result also serves to provide some validation of the transactional analysis framework. In addition, successful learning of BASIC was strongly related to learners' knowledge of how to translate algebra story problems into equations and answers. This is a skill that would be required in translating among problem statements, BASIC programs, and underlying transactions.

ACKNOWLEDGMENTS

This article was written while the author was on sabbatical leave at the Center for the Study of Reading, University of Illinois. The research reported herein was supported in part by the National

Science Foundation under Grant No. MDR-8470248. Piraye Bayman conducted the research described in Sections III and IV, Jennifer Dyck conducted the research described in Sections V and VI, and Bill Vilberg conducted Study 3 described in Section VI.

REFERENCES

Bayman, P., & Mayer, R. E. (1983). A diagnosis of beginning programmers' misconceptions of BASIC programming statements. *Communications of the ACM, 26,* 677–679.

Bayman, P., & Mayer, R. E. (1984). Instructional manipulation of users' mental models for electronic calculators. *International Journal of Man–Machine Studies, 20,* 189–199.

Card, S. K., Moran, T. P., & Newell, A. (1980). Computer text-editing: An information processing analysis of a routine cognitive skill. *Cognitive Psychology, 12,* 32–74.

Carroll, J. M., & Thomas, J. C. (1982). Metaphor and the cognitive representation of computing systems. *IEEE Transactions on Systems, Man, and Cybernerics, 12,* 107–116.

De Kleer, J., & Brown, J. S. (1981). Mental models of physical mechanisms and their acquisition. In J. R. Anderson (Ed.), *Cognitive skills and their acquisition.* Hillsdale, NJ: Erlbaum.

De Kleer, J., & Brown, J. S. (1983). Assumptions and ambiguities in mechanistic mental models. In D. Gentner & A. L. Stevens (Eds.), *Mental models.* Hillsdale, NJ: Erlbaum.

Du Boulay, B., & O'Shea, T. (1981). Teaching novices programming. In M. J. Coombs & J. L. Alty (Eds.), *Computing skills and the user interface.* New York: Academic Press.

Du Boulay, B., O'Shea, T., & Monk, J. (1981). The black box inside the glass box: Presenting computing concepts to novices. *International Journal of Man–Machine Studies, 14,* 237–249.

Gentner, D., & Gentner, D. R. (1983). Flowing water or teeming crowds: Mental models of electricity. In D. Gentner & A. L. Stevens (Eds.), *Mental models.* Hillsdale, NJ: Erlbaum.

Larkin, J. H. (1983). The role of problem representation in physics. In D. Gentner & A. L. Stevens (Eds.), *Mental models.* Hillsdale, NJ: Erlbaum.

Mayer, R. E. (1975). Different problem-solving competencies established in learning computer programming with and without meaningful models. *Journal of Educational Psychology, 67,* 725–734.

Mayer, R. E. (1976). Some conditions of meaningful learning for computer programming: Advance organizers and subject control of frame order. *Journal of Educational Psychology, 68,* 143–150.

Mayer, R. E. (1979a). A psychology of learning BASIC. *Communications of the ACM, 22,* 589–593.

Mayer, R. E. (1979b). Can advance organizers influence meaningful learning? *Review of Educational Research, 49,* 371–383.

Mayer, R. E. (1980). Elaboration techniques for technical text: An experimental test of the learning strategy hypothesis. *Journal of Educational Psychology, 72,* 770–784.

Mayer, R. E. (1981). The psychology of how novices learn computer programming. *Computing Surveys, 13,* 121–141.

Mayer, R. E., & Bayman, P. (1981). Psychology of calculator language: A framework for describing differences in user's knowledge. *Communications of the ACM, 24,* 511–520.

Mayer, R. E., & Bromage, B. (1980). Different recall protocols for technical text due to advance organizers. *Journal of Educational Psychology, 72,* 209–225.

McCloskey, M., Caramazza, A., & Green, B. (1980). Curvilinear motion in the absence of external forces: Naive beliefs about the motion of objects. *Science, 210* (4474), 1139–1141.

Moran, T. P. (1981a). An applied psychology of the user. *Computing Surveys, 13,* 121–141.

Moran, T. P. (1981b) The command language grammar: A representation for user interface of interactive computer systems. *International Journal of Man–Machine Studies. 15,* 3–50.

Norman, D. A. (1983). Some observations on mental models. In D. Gentner & A. L. Stevens (Eds.), *Mental models*. Hillsdale, NJ: Erlbaum.

Reisner, P. (1981). Human factors studies of database query languages: A survey and assessment. *Computing Surveys, 13*, 13–31.

Resnick, L. B., & Ford, W. (1981). *The psychology of mathematics for instruction*. Hillsdale, NJ: Erlbaum.

Stevens, A., Collins, A., & Goldin, S. E. (1979). Misconceptions in students' understanding. *International Journal of Man–Machine Studies, 11*, 145–156.

Williams, M. D., Hollan, J. D., & Stevens, A. L. (1983). Human reasoning about a simple physical system. In D. Gentner & A. L. Stevens (Eds.), *Mental models*. Hillsdale, NJ: Erlbaum.

Young, R. M. (1981). The machine inside the machine: Users' models of pocket calculators. *International Journal of Man–Machine Studies, 15*, 51–85.

Young, R. M. (1983). Surrogates and mappings: Two kinds of conceptual models for pocket calculators. In D. Gentner & A. L. Stevens (Eds.), *Mental models*. Hillsdale, NJ: Erlbaum.

POSTHYPNOTIC AMNESIA AND THE DISSOCIATION
OF MEMORY

John F. Kihlstrom

UNIVERSITY OF WISCONSIN
MADISON, WISCONSIN

Hypnosis may be defined as a social interaction in which one person, designated the subject, responds to suggestions offered by another person, designated the hypnotist, for experiences which involve subjectively compelling alterations in perception, memory, and action. Historically, hypnosis has been of interest to psychologists in part because its phenomena seem to involve a division in consciousness coupled by subconscious mental processing. An example is posthypnotic amnesia: Following an appropriate suggestion, the subject cannot remember the events and experiences that transpired while he or she was hypnotized. Nevertheless, it is easy to demonstrate that these unrecalled memories continue to have an impact on thought and action. For example, subjects can execute posthypnotically some behavior that has been suggested to them during hypnosis, while at the same time showing an inability to report memory for the suggestion itself. Thus, the behavior of these subjects is determined by mental content of which they are not aware. At least since the consolidation of the First Dynamic Psychiatry by Charcot and Janet, hypnosis has been recognized as an important vehicle for studying the relations among conscious, subconscious, and unconscious mental processes (Ellenberger, 1970; Kihlstrom, 1984a).

THE PSYCHOLOGY OF LEARNING
AND MOTIVATION, VOL. 19

131

I. Loss and Recovery of Memory in Hypnosis

Suggestions for posthypnotic amnesia are included in most of the standardized procedures that have been developed to assess individual differences in responsiveness to hypnotic suggestion. These individual differences cannot be predicted with much accuracy by the usual sorts of personality inventories (see reviews by Barber, 1964; Hilgard, 1965, 1975; Kihlstrom, 1985; Shor, Orne, & O'Connell, 1966). Accordingly, investigators of hypnotic phenomena employ work samples of hypnotic response to measure them. These procedures, which include the individually administered Stanford Hypnotic Susceptibility Scales, Forms A, B, and C, and the group-administered Harvard Group Scale of Hypnotic Susceptibility, Form A, present a standardized induction of hypnosis followed by suggestions for a series of representative hypnotic experiences. The final suggestion on these scales is for posthypnotic amnesia. This is tested after hypnosis has been terminated by asking the subject to recall the events and experiences that transpired while he or she was hypnotized. The subject's response to each of these suggestions is scored by means of objective behavioral criteria, and the sum of these dichotomous ratings yields an estimate of his or her hypnotizability. Hypnotizability, so measured, is relatively stable over intervals as long as 10 years (Morgan, Johnson, & Hilgard, 1973) and is a strong predictor of response to a wide variety of hypnotic suggestions including analgesia (Hilgard, 1967), deafness (Crawford, Macdonald, & Hilgard, 1979), and amnesia (Kihlstrom, 1980b).

Through the use of these procedures and variants on them, then, a great deal of descriptive information has accumulated about posthypnotic amnesia (for reviews, see Cooper, 1979; Hilgard, 1965; Kihlstrom, 1977, 1982, 1983; Kihlstrom & Evans, 1979). For example, it is known that amnesia does not occur unless it has been suggested, implicitly or explicitly, to the subject (Hilgard & Cooper, 1965; Young & Cooper, 1972), thus distinguishing posthypnotic amnesia from state-dependent retention.[1] On the standardized scales, the suggestion for amnesia also includes the establishment of a signal, known as the reversibility cue, by which the amnesia suggestion can be canceled. Response to such suggestions, in terms of both initial amnesia (Hilgard, 1965; Kihlstrom & Evans, 1979) and subsequent reversibility (Kihlstrom & Evans, 1976; Kihlstrom &

---

[1]Hypnotic suggestions can also alter memory performance in the absence of specific suggestions for amnesia. For example, Blum and his associates found that distinctive mental contexts suggested to subjects during an encoding phase served as effective memory cues during a retrieval phase, much in the manner of state-dependent retrieval (Blum, 1967; Blum, Graef, & Hauenstein, 1968; Blum, Graef, Hauenstein, & Passini, 1971). More recently, Bower and his colleagues (Bower, 1981; Bower, Gilligan, & Monteiro, 1981; Bower, Monteiro, & Gilligan, 1978) found that hypnotically suggested mood states could, under some conditions, induce similar state-dependent effects on retrieval.

Register, 1984; Nace, Orne, & Hammer, 1974), is positively correlated with hypnotizability.

As observed on the standardized scales of hypnotic susceptibility, posthypnotic amnesia is a phenomenon of incidental memory. The subjects are not specifically instructed to remember the scale items at the time that they are administered, nor is there any formal indication that the subject's memory for the suggestions will be tested subsequently. For these reasons, any effect of the amnesic process is added to the effects of ordinary forgetting, and the two factors are somewhat difficult to disentangle (Cooper, 1979; Kihlstrom & Wilson, 1984; Radtke & Spanos, 1981). Nevertheless, the distinction can be made. The distribution of recall following an amnesia suggestion is not the same as that observed when it is deleted from the procedure (Cooper, 1979). Furthermore, the occurrence of amnesia does not appear to be related to individual differences in memory measured in the normal waking state (Kihlstrom & Twersky, 1978).

Although posthypnotic amnesia is reversible, some degree of residual amnesia may persist, at least for a time, in hypnotizable subjects (Kihlstrom & Evans, 1977). The amnesia is not reversed simply by the reinduction of hypnosis (Kihlstrom, Brenneman, Pistole, & Shor, 1985), again distinguishing it from state-dependent retrieval. However, subjects who manifest amnesia on an initial posthypnotic test of recall show some recovery of memory when retested (Kihlstrom, Evans, Orne, & Orne, 1980; Kihlstrom, Easton, & Shor, 1983). Suggested amnesia is densest when tested by free recall; as might be expected, recognition testing typically yields higher levels of retention (Kihlstrom & Shor, 1978; McConkey & Sheehan, 1981; McConkey, Sheehan, & Cross, 1980; Shechan & McConkey, 1982).

As noted, the extent of amnesia is correlated with hypnotizability, with the most hypnotizable subjects showing a complete, or virtually complete, inability to recall the target events. Among subjects of more moderate hypnotizability, the partial effects of the amnesia suggestion may be observed in the vague and fragmentary manner in which they reconstruct those items that they are able to successfully remember (Evans, Kihlstrom, & Orne, 1973; Kihlstrom & Evans, 1978). Although they remember too many items on an initial memory test to meet the standardized criterion for posthypnotic amnesia, they nevertheless may show a further recovery of memory (Kihlstrom & Evans, 1976), and some residual amnesia (Kihlstrom & Evans, 1977), after the reversibility cue has been given. Even insusceptible subjects generally fail to recall a few of their hypnotic experiences, presumably due to ordinary forgetting (Cooper, 1979). In insusceptible, nonamnesic subjects, recall tends to favor those suggestions that were successfully experienced; the more hypnotizable partially amnesic subjects, by contrast, tend not to show this imbalance (Hilgard & Hommel, 1961; O'Connell, 1966; Pettinati & Evans, 1978; Pettinati, Evans, Orne, & Orne, 1981; but see Coe, Baugher, Krimm, & Smith, 1976).

Many of the features of amnesia on the standardized scales also can be observed in more familiar laboratory situations involving intentional verbal learning. Consider, for example, an experiment in which hypnotized subjects memorized a list of 15 unrelated words to a criterion of two successive perfect repetitions before receiving a suggestion for temporary, reversible amnesia covering both the word list and the study phase itself (Kihlstrom, 1980b, Experiment 1). Figure 1 presents data from 40 subjects stratified into categories of hypnotizability according to their scores on the 12-point Stanford Hypnotic Susceptibility Scale, Form C: low, 0–4; medium, 5–7; high, 8–10; and virtuoso, 11–12. Hypnotic virtuosos, who respond positively to virtually all the suggestions offered to them, comprise approximately 5–10% of an unselected sample (Hilgard, 1965). Because of the intentional learning procedure that was employed, all subjects showed perfect acquisition of the word list, as measured by recall on the final trial of the study phase. The filled bars indicate the average number of items recalled by each of the groups on the initial test of posthypnotic amnesia: Memory is virtually perfect among the insusceptible subjects, while the amnesia is virtually complete among the virtuosos. The open bars show the average number of additional items recalled after administration of the reversibility cue: The pattern for recovery is the mirror image of that observed for initial amnesia.

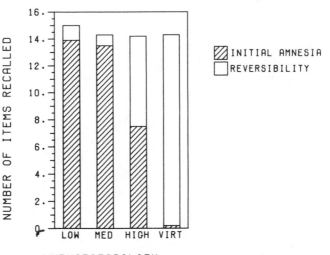

Fig. 1. Average number of words recalled (out of a total pool of 15) on an initial amnesia test and on a test of reversibility following suggestions for posthypnotic amnesia. Subjects have been classified as low, medium, high, or virtuoso in hypnotic susceptibility (Kihlstrom, 1980b).

II. Theoretical Controversy Concerning Amnesia

While there is little disagreement about these observations, there is considerable controversy concerning how to explain them. Broadly speaking, two classes of theoretical approaches currently guide research, social and cognitive (Hilgard, 1966; Kihlstrom, 1977, 1985). A third class, based on the psychoanalytic notion of repression, is no longer popular (for examples, see Clemes, 1964; Levitt, Persky, & Brady, 1964; Reyher, 1967).

A. Amnesia as Strategically Motivated Behavior

In general, the social point of view construes amnesia as a phenomenon of behavioral compliance—a motivated failure to report items that the subject actually remembers perfectly well. Actually, there are several variants of the social–psychological approach. Coe (1978; Sarbin & Coe, 1979), for example, argues that the memories covered by amnesia are analogous to secrets and has emphasized the features of the social context which determine whether the subject will keep or reveal them. Spanos and Radtke (1980, 1982), on the other hand, argue that amnesia is an instance of strategic social enactment, and have emphasized the contextual cues that determine the subject's interpretation of the suggestion and the cognitive strategies that he or she deploys in order to conform to it. Both versions place heavy reliance on processes of causal attribution and self-perception by which compliant subjects may deceive themselves into thinking that they actually cannot remember the critical material.

Evidence bearing on the social–psychological point of view comes from a variety of experiments. For example, it has been shown that appropriately motivated but unhypnotized subjects often perform on memory tasks in a manner similar to that observed in hypnotic subjects (e.g., Barber & Calverley, 1966). Furthermore, it has been shown that response to amnesia suggestions is affected by subjects' expectations concerning hypnosis, as manipulated by preexperimental instructions (e.g., Gandolfo, 1971; Spanos, Stam, D'Eon, Pawlak, & Radtke-Bodorik, 1980c). Finally, hypnotized subjects who have received amnesia suggestions sometimes report deliberately withholding information during subsequent memory testing or engaging in self-distraction or other strategies that would serve to impair their performance (e.g., Spanos & Bodorik, 1977; Spanos & Ham, 1973).

At the same time, there are a number of anomalies in these experiments, indicating that an exclusively social–psychological analysis of amnesia is incomplete (Kihlstrom, 1977, 1978). For example, insusceptible subjects who have been instructed to simulate hypnosis are extraordinarily sensitive to the demand characteristics of the testing situation (Orne, 1979). Simulators are able

to mimic the behavior of real hypnotic subjects in many instances, indicating—
though not *proving*—that the behavior of the reals may be an artifact of demand
characteristics. On the other hand, differences between reals and simulators
indicate that the behavior of the reals is, in these respects, *not* an artifact of
demand characteristics. In this respect, it is interesting to note that simulators
typically present different patterns of performance on tests of recall (Bowers,
1966), source amnesia (Evans, 1979), disorganized recall (Spanos, Radtke,
Bertrand, Addie, & Drummond, 1982a; Spanos, Radtke-Bodorik, & Stam,
1980b), and recognition (McConkey *et al.*, 1980; Williamsen, Johnson, &
Eriksen, 1965) compared to hypnotized subjects. These effects, at least, do not
appear to be due to the demand characteristics of the hypnotic situation and
require explanation in other, presumably cognitive terms.

Similarly, the amnesia observed in the hypnotic context differs in several ways
from that which is observed after subjects have received suggestions to imagine
themselves to be amnesic (McConkey, 1980). And certain effects are not consistently obtained in nonhypnotic subjects who are strongly motivated to forget
the critical material (Radtke-Bodorik, Planas, & Spanos, 1980; Radtke-Bodorik,
Spanos, & Haddad, 1979; Spanos & Bodorik, 1977; Spanos *et al.*, 1980c).

In addition, subjects' preexisting expectations concerning their hypnotic behavior are not particularly powerful determinants of their actual response to
amnesia suggestions (Ashford & Hammer, 1978; Shor, 1971; Shor, Pistole,
Easton, & Kihlstrom, 1984; Young & Cooper, 1972). Furthermore, the deliberate suppression of memory reports is rather rare. While disattention and self-
distraction can produce recall deficits similar to posthypnotic amnesia (Spanos &
D'Eon, 1980), the relationship between self-distraction and other sorts of strategic helping and the actual occurrence of amnesia in the hypnotic setting has been
found to be weak (Kihlstrom, 1977; Kihlstrom *et al.*, 1983; Spanos & Bodorik,
1977; Spanos *et al.*, 1980b, 1980c).

Additional relevant evidence is provided by experiments which vary the instructional demands placed on subjects during the time the amnesia suggestion is
tested. In one experiment, subjects of moderate and high hypnotizability who
met a criterion for initial amnesia did not respond differentially to the various
instructions for effort, honesty, organization, or repeated recall. All conditions
showed an increase in memory from the first to the second test of amnesia,
however, an effect that may reflect the dissipation of the amnesic process over
time (Kihlstrom *et al.*, 1983). Subsequent research by Coe and his colleagues
found that insertion of a putative lie detector test or strong honesty demands
could affect the memory reports of hypnotizable, amnesic subjects (Coe &
Yashinski, 1985; Howard & Coe, 1980; Schuyler & Coe, 1981; but see Spanos,
Radtke, & Bertrand, 1984). However, these effects were found in those subjects
who reported that their amnesic behavior was under voluntary control. In the
absence of strong honesty demands, the amount of spontaneous recovery ob-

served during amnesia is unrelated to reports of either subjective conviction or strategic helping (Kihlstrom *et al.*, 1983).

B.   AMNESIA AS DISRUPTED MEMORY PROCESSING

By contrast, the cognitive point of view construes amnesia as a phenomenon of memory analogous to ordinary forgetting and clinical amnesia—a genuine inability to remember memorable events (Hilgard, 1977; Kihlstrom, 1978, 1979; Kihlstrom & Evans, 1979). At the same time, it must be recognized that this amnesia is not monolithic. Amnesia suggestions disrupt some aspects of memory functioning, but not others. In an early case study of amnesia, for example, Bitterman and Marcuse (1945) presented a word to a hypnotized subject, followed by an amnesia suggestion. Upon termination of hypnosis, the subject showed neither recall nor recognition for the critical word. Nevertheless, in a lie detector situation she gave differential autonomic responses to critical and neutral words such that the targets were identifiable by experienced polygraphers on five of eight trials (or on all eight trials, if second guesses were counted).

Such differential effects might be called the "paradox" of posthypnotic amnesia (Kihlstrom, 1977; Kihlstrom & Evans, 1979). The paradox consists of the apparent contradiction between the hypnotic subject's assertion that he or she cannot remember some item of information and objective evidence of the presence of the target information in memory storage as well as its dynamic impact on ongoing thought and action. On occasion, the paradoxical behavior of the amnesic subject has led some to dismiss posthypnotic amnesia as a genuine phenomenon of memory and to attribute the subject's behavior to a motivated neglect of memories that have been adequately preserved (e.g., Coe, 1978; Spanos & Radtke-Bodorik, 1980). However, as will be noted below, similar paradoxes can be observed in the memory performance of clinical patients whose amnesia is not in question as well as normal subjects whose motivation is to remember rather than to forget. In this light, the paradoxes of amnesia may be taken as clues as to the precise nature of the memory deficit induced by hypnotic suggestion.

1.   Encoding, Storage, and Retrieval

Almost since the beginning of memory research, investigators have been concerned with specifying the locus of memory deficits induced by natural, laboratory, and pathological conditions. In contemporary memory research, it has been popular to cite three sources of forgetting: poor encoding, loss from storage, and failure of retrieval (Crowder, 1976). However, this analytic scheme has been muddied somewhat by the encoding specificity principle (Tulving & Thomson, 1973; Watkins & Tulving, 1975) and the application of levels of processing theory to the encoding of the retrieval cue as well as the original event itself (Jacoby & Craik, 1979; Lockhart, Craik, & Jacoby, 1976). The nature of the encoding received by a trace determines whether a particular retrieval cue will be effective, and some cue conditions can compensate for originally poor encodings.

Nevertheless, the three-stage model of memory has proved to be an extraordinarily valuable heuristic—as demonstrated, for example, in research concerned with the pathologies of memory. For example, a number of clinical and experimental amnesias, once commonly regarded as failures of encoding or storage, are now thought to involve the interaction between encoding and retrieval deficits (Craik, 1977; Craik & Simon, 1980; Crowder, 1982; Jacoby, 1982; Kinsbourne & Wood, 1982; Moscovitch, 1982; Rozin, 1976; Schachter & Tulving, 1982; Schonfield & Stones, 1979). In other cases, amnesias once classified as relatively pure instances of encoding or storage deficit are now known to reflect largely retrieval deficits (Miller & Marlin, 1979; Miller & Springer, 1973).

From the perspective of stage analysis, it appears that reversibility is the most important property of posthypnotic amnesia. The fact that the memories forgotten during amnesia can be recovered indicates that amnesia represents a disruption in memory retrieval rather than in the encoding or storage of the target items (Kihlstrom & Evans, 1976; Nace *et al.*, 1974). The importance of accessibility can also be seen in the fact that different measures of memory performance typically yield different estimates of the extent of amnesia. For example, recognition is usually superior to free recall (Barber & Calverley, 1966; Kihlstrom & Shor, 1978; St. Jean & Coe, 1981), although Wells (1932, 1940) found a strong effect on recognition when the subjects were given an amnesia suggestion that explicitly mentioned recognition failure. In other words, amnesic subjects fail to gain access to memories that are actually available to them (Tulving & Pearlstone, 1966). The notion of retrieval failure is the starting point for studies that attempt to reveal the memory mechanisms underlying posthypnotic amnesia.

2. *Declarative vs. Procedural Memory*

Memory contains stored representations of knowledge. In classifying the contents of the memory system, many contemporary memory theories find it convenient to distinguish between those memories that are declarative in form and those that are procedural (Anderson, 1976, 1983; Hastie & Carlston, 1980; Tulving, 1983; Winograd, 1975). Declarative memories represent factual knowledge concerning the nature of the physical and social world. They include information concerning what words, numbers, and other symbols mean, what attributes objects possess, and to which categories they belong. They represent the conceptual relationships among objects as well as the spatial and temporal relationships among events. Declarative knowledge has truth value—it is either correct or incorrect—and may be represented in the form of propositions in which concepts stand as subjects, predicates, relations, and arguments. By contrast, procedural knowledge represents the cognitive processes by which declarative knowledge is manipulated and transformed. It includes the person's knowledge of mathematical operations and linguistic syntax as well as the rules by which he or she can make inferences and arrive at judgments. It also includes a variety of motoric abilities as well as the strategies by which the person acquires, stores, and retrieves memory. Procedural knowledge does not have truth value—it simply yields an output given particular inputs, regardless of whether that output is accurate—and can be represented in the form of production systems linking certain goals, conditions, and actions.

Here again, there is abundant evidence of the selectivity of memory deficits in a variety of clinical amnesias. For example, patients with the amnesic syndrome are frequently able to acquire new perceptual, cognitive, and motoric skills through training and practice, although they typically fail to display any memory for having learned the relevant task or any feelings of familiarity with it (Kinsbourne & Wood, 1982; Moscovitch, 1982). Unfortunately, only two studies of amnesia employed tasks that qualify as procedural in nature. Patten (1932) gave subjects practice in complex mental addition—adding the digits 6, 7, 8, and 9 serially to a two-digit seed number. Subjects practiced for 10 30-sec trials on each of 18 days, showing a progressive decline in errors with practice. On the first 6 days the practice was carried out in the normal waking state; on the second 6, practice was in hypnosis, covered by posthypnotic amnesia; the final 6 days were again in the waking state. A control group carried out all trials in the normal waking state. Examination of the practice curves revealed (a) a progressive decline in errors throughout the six hypnotic sessions, even though each ended with posthypnotic amnesia; and (b) the practice curve for the second waking session was continuous with that for the hypnotic session, again even though the series was covered by posthypnotic amnesia. Similarly, Life (1929) examined practice effects in learning paired associates consisting of a geometrical figure and a nonsense syllable, using a design parallel to Coors'. Hull (1933) reports that posthypnotic amnesia had no effect on the practice curve, either during the hypnotic series or in the carry-over from hypnosis to the normal waking state.

A problematic aspect of the experiments performed in Hull's laboratory is that no explicit suggestions of amnesia were given to the hypnotic subjects. However, Hull (1933) makes it clear that the subjects selected for the experimental groups had all demonstrated dense amnesia after previous hypnotic sessions (whether with or without suggestions it is not clear), and that all demonstrated amnesia for the acquisition trials during the formal experiments, as tested by free recall. In both experiments, then, posthypnotic amnesia affected the subjects' memory for declarative knowledge, as indicated by their inability to remember what they did while they were hypnotized; but it had no affect on memory for procedural knowledge, as indicated by their display of skills practiced during hypnosis.

3. Episodic vs. Semantic Memory

Within the domain of declarative knowledge, many theorists maintain a further distinction between episodic and semantic memory (e.g., Tulving, 1972, 1983). Episodic memory is one's knowledge of one's own personal experiences—what he or she has done, where, and when. Taken as a whole, the organized network of episodic memories comprises the person's record of autobiographical memory (Kihlstrom, 1980a; Kihlstrom & Cantor, 1984). Semantic memories, by contrast, may be thought of as the person's "mental lexicon," consisting of categorical knowledge (including both abstract concepts and particular instances of them) which has been stored without reference to the episodic context in which it has been acquired and used. Semantic memory contains world knowledge in addition to lexical knowledge, which is why some theorists prefer the term *generic* to *semantic* (e.g., Hastie & Carlston, 1980; Schonfield & Stones, 1979). Both the episodic and semantic forms of declarative memory can be represented propositionally. For example, an episodic memory consists of a proposition describing the event in question, plus other propositions representing the self as agent or experiencer, and the spatial and temporal context in which the event occurred (Kihlstrom, 1984a).

As with the declarative–procedural distinction, the difference between episodic and semantic memories helps organize a large part of the literature on the selectivity of posthypnotic amnesia. In experiments employing conventional verbal learning paradigms, for example, subjects who cannot remember the words memorized during the study phase do not thereby lose these words from their vocabularies. Specifically, the items remain available for use as word associations or category instances (Kihlstrom, 1980b; Spanos, Radtke, & Dubreuil, 1982b; Williamsen *et al.*, 1965). Perhaps the most compelling demonstration of the sparing of semantic memory is the phenomenon of posthypnotic source amnesia (Cooper, 1966; Evans, 1979; Evans & Thorn, 1966; Gheorghiu, 1967). In this instance, amnesic subjects retain access to factual information acquired during hypnosis, but cannot reconstruct the (hypnotic) source of that information. Instead, they may confabulate, attributing the memory to some other plausible context. In both cases, episodic memory is impaired while semantic memory is spared. This dissociation between episodic and semantic memory is a feature shared by posthypnotic amnesia with certain pathologies of memory observed clinically, such as the amnesic (Korsakoff's) syndrome (Jacoby, 1982; Moscovitch, 1982; Schachter & Tulving, 1982).

4. A Note on Hypnotic Agnosia

It is the case, however, that hypnotic suggestions can also disrupt the functioning of the semantic memory system, as represented by a disruption in word association performance as well, resulting in a kind of *agnosia* instead of amnesia (Spanos *et al.*, 1982b). Hypnotic agnosia has often been observed in the standardized scales of hypnotic susceptibility as an inadvertent consequence of suggestions for nominal aphasia (Hilgard, 1965, 1977). For example, the Stanford Profile Scales of Hypnotic Susceptibility, Forms I and II, contain suggestions of nominal aphasia for the words *house* and *scissors,* respectively. In hypnotizable subjects, this suggestion results in an inability to pronounce the target words, to understand the word when used by the experimenter, or to use it in the naming of objects. Occasionally, however, the suggestion also results in an inability to understand the meaning of a related word such as *home,* or to demonstrate the proper use of a pair of scissors. What is intended by the hypnotist to be a form of aphasia then, often turns into a difficulty in assessing categorical knowledge about familiar objects—in other words, an agnosia.

Hypnotic agnosia has also been demonstrated in more formal experimental contexts. For example, Evans (1972) showed that a suggestion that the integer "6" had disappeared from subjects' number system led to computation errors when they were subsequently confronted with problems that contained that number in the problem, solution, or intermediate step. In general, these subjects treated the digit as if it were not present or not meaningful—a pattern of performance that distinguished them from simulators, who tended to operate on the offending digit in a logical, mathematically acceptable manner. An analogous suggestion was employed in the verbal domain by Spanos *et al.* (1982b), in a replication and extension of the experiment by Kihlstrom (1980b). Subjects mastered a list of words and then were divided into two groups. One received a standard amnesia suggestion, while the other was additionally told that they would be unable *to think of them in any way.* Both groups were unable to recall the stimuli that they had memorized earlier in the experiment. However, the former group was able to use these items appropriately as responses in a word association test, while the former showed significant disruptions in word association performace.

These experiments indicate that appropriately worded suggestions can disrupt semantic as well as episodic aspects of memory processing. Just as research on posthypnotic amnesia has made effective use of methodologies developed for the study of episodic memory, so too research on hypnotic agnosia may profitably draw on paradigms developed in the clinical study of aphasia (especially receptive aphasia) and the laboratory study of semantic memory.

5. Optional vs. Obligatory Memory

Just as a distinction can be drawn between episodic and semantic memory in the declarative domain, differences can be discerned in the procedural domain between optional and obligatory memory processes (Cofer, 1976; Gregg, 1979, 1980). Obligatory processes are those which occur automatically, without any conscious control of the subject. Processes are obligatory either because they have been built into the system by virtue of the individual's genetic endowment, or because they have been routinized through repeated exercise. Optional processes, by contrast, are those whose deployment and operation can be deliberately controlled by the individual.

There is a large body of research indicating that posthypnotic amnesia has differential effects on those memory phenomena that possess optional rather than obligatory qualities (Gregg, 1979, 1980). A case in point is the psychophysiological study of Bitterman and Marcuse (1945), discussed earlier. Presumably the respiratory and cardiovascular responses measured by the polygraph were at least to some degree obligatory. A later study by Stern, Edmonston, Ulett, and Levitsky (1963) did find that amnesia suggestions produced a lifting of habituation to a tone stimulus, as measured by the electrodermal orienting response. And an earlier study by Scott (1930) found that conditioned hand-withdrawal and respiratory responses acquired during hypnosis were reduced considerably during subsequent waking test trials. Presumably autonomic and skeletal responses of this sort are also obligatory, so these would seem to constitute counterexamples. In the Stern *et al.* (1963) experiment, however, six of seven subjects in the experimental condition reported that they distorted either their memory of the stimulus presented during habituation trials or their perception of the stimulus presented during amnesia—for example, by changing the tone into a buzzer. In itself, this change would be sufficient to lift habituation, regardless of the effects of the suggestion. Similarly, in Scott's (1930) experiment the waking tests of the conditioned response followed the hypnotic tests, and thus were confounded with extinction.

Obligatory memory processes are perhaps best represented by the sorts of interference, savings, and transfer effects familiar from the literature on paired associate learning (Crowder, 1976). For example, two studies from Hull's (1933) laboratory examined savings in relearning material covered by the amnesia suggestion (Coors, 1928, cited in Hull, 1933; Strickler, 1929). In the experiment by Strickler (1929), subjects learned paired associate lists consisting of a simple line drawing and a nonsense syllable to a strict criterion. For half the trials, the learning took place during hypnosis and was covered by suggestions for posthypnotic amnesia; for the remainder it occurred in the normal waking state. When cued by the drawings, the subjects failed to recall an average of 97% of the nonsense syllables in the amnesia condition, compared to only 16% in the waking control condition. When required to relearn the response terms, however, they showed considerably more savings in amnesia (52%) compared to control (2%). Thus, while savings in relearning were significantly diminished in amnesia, they were not abolished entirely (though see Wells, 1932, 1940).

Somewhat different findings have been obtained in studies on proactive and retroactive inhibition effects (e.g., Coe, Basden, Basden, & Graham, 1976; Coe,

Taul, Basen, & Basden, 1973; Dillon & Spanos, 1983; Graham & Patton, 1968; Mitchell, 1932; Nagge, 1935; Stevenson, Stoyva, & Beach, 1962; Takahashi, 1958). In the experiment by Graham and Patton, highly hypnotizable subjects learned a list of adjectives to a rigorous criterion in the normal waking state; they then learned a second list of adjectives in one of three conditions: waking, hypnosis followed by suggestions for amnesia, hypnosis followed by suggestions for recall; a fourth group served as a resting control. Compared to the control group, all groups who received the interpolated learning task showed retroactive inhibition by diminished savings in relearning the original list. Although the subjects in the amnesia group showed a very dense amnesia for the interpolated list (mean recall = 0.6 out of 12), retroactive inhibition in this group did not differ from that displayed in the waking and hypnotic recall groups, who recalled the interpolated list almost perfectly (mean recall = 11.9 and 11.2, respectively). Similar results were obtained more recently by Coe *et al.* (1976). Thus, amnesia suggestions affect recall but not retroactive inhibition.

A number of other studies, while not employing relearning or retroactive inhibition paradigms, have found conceptually similar effects (Goldstein & Sipprelle, 1970; Kihlstrom, 1980b; Norris, 1973; Spanos *et al.*, 1982b; Stewart & Dunlap, 1976; Thorne, 1969; Thorne & Hall, 1974). For example, Kihlstrom (1980b) taught hypnotized subjects a list of words, followed by suggestions for posthypnotic amnesia. As noted earlier, even those subjects who showed a dense amnesia for the learning experience were not thereby prevented from using the list items appropriately as word associations or category instances. In fact, the production of these critical items was *facilitated,* compared to neutral items that had not been previously learned; more important, the magnitude of this priming effect did not differ in amnesic and nonamnesic subjects. Similar findings were obtained by Spanos *et al.* (1982b); interestingly, the priming effect was eliminated in subjects who received suggestions for agnosia as well as amnesia. According to most network models of memory (e.g., Anderson, 1983), the spread of activation from one item to another in memory occurs automatically. Thus, the persistence of priming effects in the face of a failure of free recall seems to indicate that amnesia affects the optional, but not the obligatory aspects of memory functioning.

Selective effects such as these are commonly used to impeach the memory reports of hypnotic subjects. From this point of view, it appears that the ostensibly amnesic subject remembers the critical material perfectly well, but is suppressing these memories in order to conform to the explicit and implicit demands presented by the hypnotic situation (e.g., Coe, 1978; Sarbin & Coe, 1979). This inference is consistent with the optional–obligatory distinction—insofar as optional memory processes, but not obligatory ones, are held to be affected by voluntary mechanisms such as response suppression and self-distraction (Spanos & Radtke, 1980, 1982). However, the inference is inconsistent with recent evidence that such ostensibly obligatory phenomena as priming and relearning are essentially independent of recall and recognition (Jacoby & Dallas, 1981; Nelson, Fehling, & Moore-Glascock, 1979). Normal subjects show facilitation in perceptual recognition and savings in relearning that reflect their prior experiences, even though they cannot gain conscious access to memory traces of these experiences. Patients with Korsakoff syndrome commonly show memory for their past experiences when they are tested by indirect means, but nobody would suggest that they are faking their amnesia in response to situational demands.

Moreover, it should be pointed out that the optional–obligatory distinction does not completely organize the results of experiments on posthypnotic amnesia. For example, recognition—in the sense of indicating by a check mark or keypress that some items are old rather than new—is no less optional than free recall; yet hypnotic subjects commonly show more memory on recognition tests than on recall tests (Barber & Calverley, 1966; Kihlstrom & Shor, 1978; Williamsen et al., 1965). Similarly, the spread of activation throughout a memory network may be obligatory; but word associations—in the sense of giving one response rather than another to a stimulus word—are surely optional, and these are not affected negatively by posthypnotic amnesia. Highly motivated, compliant subjects—which is what hypnotizable subjects are held to be by the social–psychological view—are surely capable of evaluating the implications of their behavior and of shaping their responses accordingly. In the final analysis then, the optional–obligatory distinction seems to be inappropriate, if not misleading. A more relevant distinction, however, is suggested by the sorts of tasks that are unaffected by amnesia: those requiring some sort of perceptual, cognitive, or motoric skill; those requiring only semantic or generic knowledge; and those involving transfer, savings, and interference. None of these requires that episodic memories be brought into the subject's phenomenal awareness.

C. TOWARD A RAPPROCHEMENT

It should be underscored that the cognitive perspective does not by any means offer a complete account of amnesia. It does not deny the impact of social–psychological factors on amnesia, or for that matter on any other aspect of hypnotic experience. After all, hypnosis is fundamentally an interpersonal phenomenon which transpires in a situation defined by certain social roles, and little occurs in hypnosis in the absence of explicit or implicit suggestions. Rather, it accepts the amnesia displayed by hypnotic virtuosos as a genuine impairment of memory—albeit one whose specific manifestation can be influenced by features of the social context in which the amnesia suggestion is offered and evaluated. Thus, as demonstrated by Spanos et al. (1982), a feature of the social context— the specific wording of the suggestion—is an important determinant of whether hypnotized subjects will display impairments of episodic or semantic memory.

And, as demonstrated much earlier by Wells (1932, 1940), the way in which an amnesia suggestion is worded will determine whether subjects show impairments in recognition or relearning. In both cases, however, the mechanism of the effect itself must be understood in terms of the principles of memory structure and process. In the final analysis, amnesia must be viewed in terms of both its underlying cognitive processes and the social context in which this change in memory functioning takes place (Kihlstrom *et al.,* 1980; Laurence, Perry, & Kihlstrom, 1983).

A variety of approaches may be taken toward the goal of integration. One possibility would be to determine the proportion of variance in amnesic response which may be attributable to cognitive changes and social demands, respectively. For example, Young and Cooper (1972) found that subjects' differential expectations accounted for about 10% of the variance in observed amnesia; by contrast, individual differences in hypnotizability, presumably tapping underlying cognitive processes, accounted for considerably more. Another possibility would be to divide the pool of amnesic subjects into those whose behavior may be accounted for by deliberate response to social demands ("doings"; Sarbin & Coe, 1979) and those whose behavior reflects a kind of temporary psychological deficit ("happenings"; Sarbin & Coe, 1979). For example, Coe and his co-workers (Howard & Coe, 1980; Schuyler & Coe, 1981) found a significant effect of contextual change on the memory reports of subjects who reported that they retained voluntary control over their memories; no effect of context, however, was found in those subjects who reported that their loss of memory occurred involuntarily. Most likely, the most satisfactory solution will take an interactionist form. For example, social demands may have little impact on the responses of hypnotic virtuosos who possess a high capacity for dissociation; however, they may have correspondingly greater impact on the vast majority of the population who lack these skills and must construct their response to hypnosis by other means.

Both proposals have an unpalatable flavor of monolithicity, however. In the first place, investigators engage in a battle of the correlation coefficients similar to that which has consumed the psychology of personality (e.g., Bowers, 1973; Mischel, 1968; Sarason, Smith, & Diener, 1975). In the other case, the behavior of one group of subjects is accounted for in exclusively social–psychological terms, while that of the other group is accounted for in exclusively cognitive terms. What appears to be required is a comprehensive theoretical point of view which considers both the interpersonal processes which shape subjects' interpretations of the hypnotist's suggestions and the cognitive structures and processes which mediate the subjects' responses. It is too soon, however, to attempt a meaningful integration of the social and cognitive viewpoints on posthypnotic amnesia. Accordingly, investigators of the phenomenon, each more or less cognizant of the liabilities of theoretical monolithicity, have focused on either social or cognitive processes. This article, which focuses on the memory structures and processes involved in amnesia, is no exception.

III.   Memory Structures, Memory Processes, and Posthypnotic Amnesia

A previous review of cognitive processes involved in posthypnotic amnesia (Kihlstrom & Evans, 1979) focused on research employing the standardized scales of hypnotic susceptibility and relied heavily on the two-process theories (e.g., Anderson & Bower, 1972, 1973, 1974) that dominated research on memory retrieval in the early 1970s. Since that time, researchers have adopted more conventional experimental paradigms, and the nature of memory theory has changed greatly. The remainder of this article, then, provides an update of the earlier account by viewing the more recent empirical literature from the perspective of currently popular network theories of memory (e.g., Anderson, 1976, 1983).

A.   DISORGANIZED RETRIEVAL IN POSTHYPNOTIC AMNESIA

One of the major operating principles of the memory system is organization. Regardless of whether the stimulus material has any intrinsic structure, the perceiver imposes some organization on it at the time of encoding, and this framework, once established, is followed at the time of retrieval (Bousfield, 1953; Bower, 1970; Mandler, 1967; Tulving, 1962). Such organizational activity is held to underlie successful retrieval. Thus, Evans and Kihlstrom (1973; Kihlstrom & Evans, 1979) suggested that the retrieval deficit observed in posthypnotic amnesia might be mediated by a disruption in the organization of memory. A series of investigations then sought evidence of disorganized retrieval during posthypnotic amnesia.

It is difficult, of course, to study the organization of recall in densely amnesic subjects precisely because they do not remember much of what they did while they were hypnotized. Accordingly, in these investigations subjects who recalled little or none of the target material were eliminated from analysis. Among those subjects who recalled at least some of the critical material, despite the suggestion for complete amnesia, various indices of organization were compared in hypnotizable and insusceptible subjects. The logic of the paradigm is that the average hypnotizable subject is likely to experience at least a partial effect of the amnesia suggestion, while the average insusceptible subject is unlikely to experience anything beyond ordinary forgetting.

In posthypnotic amnesia the target memories describe events that have occurred during hypnosis. Thus, the memories classify as declarative (Anderson, 1976) and episodic (Tulving, 1972, 1983). Declarative memories can be thought of as bundles of features describing concepts, objects, and events, and the characteristic feature of an episodic memory is some representation of the personal and spatiotemporal context in which the event occurred. It is known that seriation—following the temporal sequence in which events occurred—is the preferred method of organizing both word lists and stories, even when other organizational rubrics are available (Mandler & Dean, 1969). Thus, the primary focus of the earliest studies was on temporal organization.

1. Temporal Organization

The initial experiments focused on subjects' recall of the test suggestions administered during the standardized scales of hypnotic susceptibility, such as HGSHS:A and SHSS:C, where the overarching structure of the hypnotic experience is explicitly temporal. When recall was examined during the time that the amnesia suggestion was in effect, it was found that hypnotizable subjects were less likely than their insusceptible counterparts to follow the order in which the suggestions had been given (Evans & Kihlstrom, 1973; Kihlstrom & Evans, 1979). Although some investigators have reported failures to replicate the disorganization phenomenon (Radtke & Spanos, 1981; St. Jean & Coe, 1981), successful replications have been reported by Geiselman and his associates (Geiselman, Fishman, Jaenicke, Larner, MacKinnon, Shoenberg, & Swartz, 1983). However, no such difference was observed when the amnesia suggestion was deleted from the standardized scale (Kihlstrom & Evans, 1979). Thus, the temporal disorganization effect appeared to be specifically related to the amnesia suggestion rather than some state-specific effect of the induction of hypnosis or some cognitive style characteristic of hypnotizable individuals.[2]

As noted by Radtke and Spanos (1981), use of the standardized scales to study the mechanisms of posthypnotic amnesia is not optimal because they involve incidental memory for test items that may confound the effects of the amnesia suggestion with ordinary forgetting (Cooper, 1979), Zeigarnik and VonRestorff

[2]The conclusion that the temporal disorganization effect is specifically related to the amnesia suggestion rather than to hypnosis or hypnotizability has been called into question by Schwartz (1978, 1980), who has found temporal disorganization in hypnotizable subjects tested during hypnosis, but before the amnesia suggestion was administered. However, Kihlstrom and Evans (1979) found no relation between hypnotizability and temporal organization in recall after the amnesia suggestion was canceled; and Kihlstrom and Wilson (1984) found no relation between hypnotizability and seriation either during hypnosis, before amnesia was suggested, or posthypnotically, after amnesia was canceled. The reasons for the discrepancy are unclear, but there is no evidence of any relation between hypnotizability and memory performance in the normal waking state (Kihlstrom & Twersky, 1978).

effects (Pettinati & Evans, 1978; Pettinati *et al.*, 1981), and other factors. Accordingly, attention has turned to more conventional verbal learning paradigms involving memory for word lists deliberately memorized during hypnosis (e.g., Coe *et al.*, 1973; Spanos & Bodorik, 1977).

A recent study has confirmed the temporal disorganization effect within the verbal learning paradigm (Kihlstrom & Wilson, 1984). In this study, 35 subjects classified as low, medium, or high in hypnotizability were hypnotized and asked to memorize a list of 16 unrelated words. The items were presented for study by an incremental learning procedure that guarantees both efficient learning and serial organization (Mandler & Dean, 1969). After reaching a criterion of two successive perfect repetitions, the subjects received a suggestion of amnesia for the list items followed by the termination of hypnosis. Figure 2 presents trial means for temporal organization, as indexed by unidirectional intertrial repetitions (ITR; Sternberg & Tulving, 1977). This measure compares the order of recall during testing with the order of presentation during acquisition and is adjusted to reflect the ratio of the observed ITR to the maximum value obtainable, given the number of items recalled (Pellegrino & Huber, 1982). Clearly, temporal organization diminishes substantially during amnesia, and the extent of this loss is greatest in the hypnotizable subjects; seriation is restored to baseline levels when the amnesia suggestion is canceled by the reversibility cue.

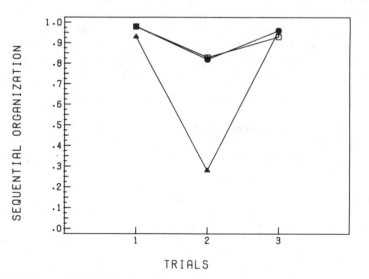

Fig. 2. Unidirectional ITR index of serial organization on three tests of posthypnotic memory. Subjects have been classified as low (□), medium (●), or high (▲) in hypnotic susceptibility. Test 1: Final trial of the study phase; Test 2: test of posthypnotic amnesia; Test 3: test of reversibility (Kihlstrom & Wilson, 1984).

2. Linguistic Organization

A number of conceptual replications of the seriation studies have investigated the fate of other forms of organization during amnesia. Thus, Radtke, Spanos, and their colleagues have found a significant loss of category clustering during amnesia (Radtke-Bodorik *et al.*, 1979, 1980; Spanos & Bodorik, 1977; Spanos *et al.*, 1980b). Coe *et al.* (1973) failed to find the clustering effect, and Spanos and his colleagues (Spanos *et al.*, 1980a) failed to obtain an analogous effect on subjective organization of a list of unrelated words. However, both failures appear to have been due to poor initial acquisition of the list, resulting in low baseline levels of organization (Radtke-Bodorik *et al.*, 1980; Tkachyk, Spanos, & Bertrand, 1984).

However, two recent experiments appear to set some limits on the generalization of the effect across modes of organization (Wilson & Kihlstrom, 1985). Figure 3 presents results from an experiment in which hypnotized subjects memorized a list of 20 unrelated words presented in varying orders during study trials. Amnesia was suggested, and hypnosis terminated, after subjects reached a criterion of two successive perfect repetitions. Organizational activity was measured by bidirectional pair frequencies (PF; Sternberg & Tulving, 1977), expressed as a ratio of observed to maximum PF. The effects of amnesia on subjective organization were considerably smaller than those observed in the seriation study.

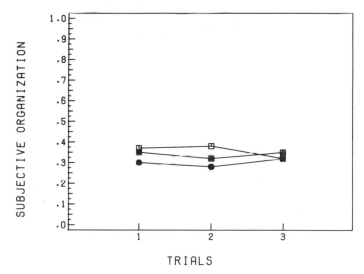

Fig. 3. Number of items recalled and bidirectional PF index of subjective organization on three tests of posthypnotic memory (Wilson & Kihlstrom, 1985, Experiment 1). Classification of subjects and label of each test same as in Fig. 2.

Figure 4 presents results from yet another experiment (Wilson & Kihlstrom, 1985) in which hypnotized subjects memorized a list of 16 related words, four from each of four taxonomic categories, to a strict criterion of mastery. In this case, organizational activity was measured by the adjusted ratio of clustering (ARC; Roenker, Thompson, & Brown, 1971), which is comparable to the adjusted PF. Again, the effect of the amnesia suggestion is small.

In some respects, the discrepancy between the seriation study and the studies of subjective organization and category clustering is more apparent than real. In the first place, there is an important methodological difference between the studies by Radtke and Spanos (e.g., Spanos & Bodorik, 1977), which have obtained reliable effects on both category clustering and subjective organization, and the studies by Wilson and Kihlstrom (1985), which failed to do so. Whereas Kihlstrom and Wilson eliminate from the analysis of organization only those subjects who respond to the amnesia suggestion with an almost total recall failure, Radtke and Spanos also exclude those subjects who show perfect recall during amnesia. The procedure of Kihlstrom and Wilson, which was also followed in the earlier studies by Kihlstrom and Evans (1979), is based on the assumption that subjects who manage to recall the entire word list may still have difficulty doing so because of the partial effects of the amnesia suggestion. It offers a more conservative test of the disorganization hypothesis. When the subjects are selected according to the procedure of Radtke and Spanos, a signifi-

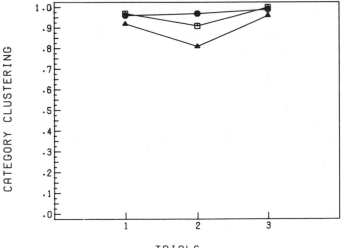

TRIALS

Fig. 4. Number of items recalled and ARC index of category clustering on three tests of posthypnotic memory (Wilson & Kihlstrom, 1985, Experiment 2). Classification of subjects and label of each test same as in Fig. 2.

cant disorganization effect is observed in subjects with partial, but not full, recall. There are also differences in the amount of baseline organizational activity displayed by the subjects in the various experiments. In the seriation and clustering studies, recall was perfectly organized, or virtually so, on the final trial of the acquisition phase. In the subjective organization study, however, the subjects showed relatively low baseline levels of organization, even though their mastery of the list met the same criterion imposed in the other two experiments. This situation, of course, places a floor on the amount of (dis)organization that could be shown during amnesia. When Tkachyk *et al.* (1984) gave subjects overlearning trials that increased their baseline levels of organization, the predicted decrement in subjective organization was observed. Similarly, in the present experiment those subjects above the median in baseline PF showed the disorganization effect of amnesia, while those below the median did not.

However, the differences between the seriation experiment on the one hand, and the clustering and subjective organization experiments on the other, may not be due entirely to methodological factors. While it is easy to think of ITR, ARC, and PF as alternative measures of a single psychological process, organizational activity, it is also possible that these measures map onto *different forms* of organizational activity. It should be noted, for example, that seriation reflects only the chronological order in which the list items occurred, while category clustering and subjective organization are based on the conceptual relationships among list items. Recently, J. Mandler (1979) has suggested that schematic (temporal) and taxonomic (linguistic) organization are qualitatively different (see also G. Mandler, 1979). In much the same way, Anderson (1983) has argued that temporal strings underlying seriation may be a different form of memory representation than the abstract propositions that presumably underlie category clustering and subjective organization (and that these two, in turn, are different from spatial images and kinesthetic motor codes). If these arguments are correct, then we would not necessarily expect the amnesic process to exert equivalent effects on all forms of organizational activity. Clearly then, further research comparing the fates of the various organizational forms in amnesia is in order.

B.   RECOGNITION DURING POSTHYPNOTIC AMNESIA

Another fundamental operating principle of the memory system is that retrieval is *cue dependent* (Tulving, 1974). Memories that are available in the memory system may not be accessible unless sufficient retrieval cues are supplied by the query or generated by the rememberer. The principle of cue dependency is illustrated in the familiar finding that recognition is superior to free recall, with cued recall lying somewhere in between. Amnesia is typically tested by means of free recall, a procedure that provides only very impoverished retrieval cues to the subject. Accordingly, a number of studies have compared the various measures of retention in order to determine the effect of richer, more informative retrieval queries (e.g., Kihlstrom & Shor, 1978; St. Jean & Coe, 1981; Williamsen *et al.*, 1965). Regardless of whether they employed the standardized scales or conventional verbal learning procedures, the studies have found recognition to be superior to recall (for exceptions, see Wells, 1932, 1940). However, recognition does not necessarily abolish the amnesia observed on free recall tests.

1. Free Recall, Cued Recall, and Recognition

A recent study in our laboratory included a test of cued recall as well as free recall and recognition (Kihlstrom, 1984b). In the first experiment, a group of virtuoso subjects studies a list of 16 categorized words (four items from each of four categories) while hypnotized. After reaching a criterion of mastery, they were given an amnesia suggestion and hypnosis was terminated. A comparison group of unselected subjects memorized the list in the normal waking state. Figure 5 presents the results of a series of four memory tests administered to these subjects. (a) As might be expected, the control subjects showed perfect performance on an initial free recall test, while the hypnotic subjects showed a very dense amnesia. (b) The subjects were then presented with the names of the four target categories contained on the list, plus four neutral categories that were

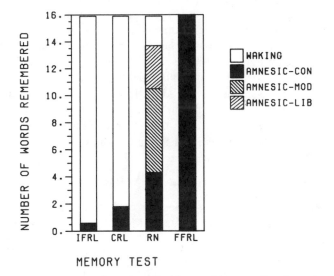

Fig. 5. Comparison of free recall, cued recall, and recognition tests of posthypnotic amnesia for a word list memorized during hypnosis. Also shown are comparable results for subjects who memorized the list and performed the memory tests in the normal waking state. Recognition results are presented separately for conservative, moderate, and liberal criteria for retention.

matched to the targets. After a test of category recognition, the subjects were asked again to recall the items that they had memorized. The hypnotic subjects showed a nonsignificant improvement in memory on this test of cued recall. (c) Next, the subjects were presented with a list consisting of the 16 target items that they had memorized, 16 matched lures drawn from the same critical categories, and 32 items drawn from the neutral categories, half matched to the critical targets and the remainder matched to the critical lures. The subjects were asked to rate, on a 1–4 scale, their confidence that each item had appeared on their lists. The results for item recognition depend on the criterion that is selected: under a very strict criterion, recognition is not significantly better than cued recall; under a very loose criterion, recognition by the hypnotic subjects was slightly (but significantly) inferior to that of the waking controls. (d) Finally, after the amnesia suggestion was canceled, the hypnotic and waking groups showed identical levels of free recall.

Another perspective on these data is provided by the mean confidence ratings assigned to the various categories and items on the recognition tests. On the category recognition test (Fig. 6), the waking control subjects, as might be expected, made a perfect discrimination between the critical and neutral categories. However, the hypnotic subjects apparently found it more difficult to distinguish between categories that had been included on their list and those that had not. The item recognition test (Fig. 7) occurred a few minutes later, after the test of cued recall. Again, the control subjects performed perfectly, recognizing the critical targets with a high degree of confidence and rejecting all the critical lures

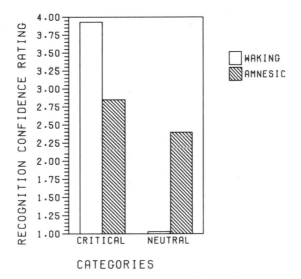

Fig. 6. Confidence ratings in category recognition test for amnesic and nonamnesic subjects.

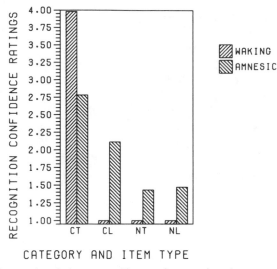

Fig. 7. Confidence ratings in item recognition test for amnesic and nonamnesic subjects.

as well as the items drawn from the neutral categories. The hypnotic subjects made a clearer distinction between the critical and neutral categories on this test than they had on the earlier category recognition test; however, within the critical categories they did not make a reliable distinction between targets and lures.

The findings of this experiment are consistent with those of earlier studies and with the cue-dependency principle of memory (Tulving, 1974). Free recall, cued recall, and recognition supply increasing amounts of information to the subject concerning the items that are to be remembered. Accordingly, it is not surprising that items forgotten in a free recall test are recovered in one or more of the other conditions. Earlier research on posthypnotic amnesia by Kihlstrom and Evans (1979; Evans & Kihlstrom, 1973) was guided by two-process theories of recall popular at the time (e.g., Anderson & Bower, 1972, 1973, 1974). The finding that recognition was superior to recall was interpreted at that time as indicating that the locus of memory deficit in amnesia was in the generation process, which was necessary to recall but not to recognition (e.g., Kihlstrom & Shor, 1978; St. Jean & Coe, 1981). However, other findings, from conventional memory research as well as hypnosis, have undercut this interpretation.

For example, observation of the recognition failure of recallable words casts doubt on the two-process theory as an adequate conceptualization of memory retrieval (Tulving & Thomson, 1973; Watkins & Tulving, 1975). This should not occur if recognition is a subprocess in recall, as two-process theory proposes. Rather, it appears that recall and recognition differ only quantitatively, in terms of the amount of cue information supplied by the query unique to recall (Tulving,

1976). Even so, provision of extra retrieval cues should facilitate rather than impair remembering; yet just such an impairment is found in the recognition failure of recallable words. The implication of this effect then, is that retention is not merely a function of the quantity of information contained in the retrieval query. According to the encoding specificity principle (Tulving & Thomson, 1973), retrieval is best when the information supplied by the query matches the information encoded with the item at the time of acquisition. This principle is illustrated in the phenomenon of state-dependent retrieval in which retention is best when there is congruence between the subject's organismic state at the time of encoding and at the time of retrieval.

Analogous effects have been observed in posthypnotic amnesia. In the first place, it should be noted that recognition testing does not abolish amnesia entirely, even though memory does typically improve in this condition. Recognition failure during amnesia is not merely an artifact of ordinary forgetting, however, for the simple reason that it is *inferior* to free recall after the amnesia suggestion has been canceled—a finding similar to Tulving's recognition failure of recallable words. What is critical, then, is not merely the amount of retrieval cues provided by the query, but rather the nature of the cues: Something is missing during the recognition test that is present during the subsequent free recall test.

That something, of course, is the prearranged reversibility cue. Apparently, the reversibility cue is encoded with the target memories at the time the amnesia suggestion is administered. This cue information is not presented to the subject, of course, during the time that the amnesia suggestion is in effect; but it is supplied as part of the prearranged signal by which the amnesia suggestion is canceled. The reversibility signal has more value as a retrieval cue than the hypnotic state itself, even though state cues related to being hypnotized are also available to be encoded as part of the subject's memory trace (Kihlstrom et al., 1984). The role of the reversibility cue is consistent with the encoding specificity principle, and a proper understanding of its mechanisms is likely to shed a great deal of light on the cognitive processes involved in posthypnotic amnesia.

2. The Basis of Recognition in Amnesia

The encoding specificity principle notwithstanding, recognition is still superior to recall during posthypnotic amnesia, and this effect deserves some extended consideration. Recently, a number of investigators have suggested that recognition can be mediated by two different processes: (a) the reconstruction of the context in which the item was originally encoded; and (b) a feeling that the item is familiar (Atkinson & Juola, 1974; Jacoby & Dallas, 1981; Mandler, 1980). The former process, which is close to the ordinary meaning of the term remembering (Bergson, 1896; Claparede, 1911; Piaget & Inhelder, 1973; Reiff &

Scheerer, 1959), involves retrieving the spatiotemporal context in which the remembered event took place as well as some recollection of the self as agent or experiencer (Kihlstrom, 1984a). The second process, which is closer to inference, involves a judgment, in the absence of such episodic information, that an event has occurred before. One basis of this "recognition by inference" is perceptual fluency: The item "rings a bell" with the subject, even though he or she cannot remember the circumstances under which the event occurred.

The phenomenon of perceptual fluency has been observed in patients suffering from the organic amnesic syndrome, indicating that these patients do in fact encode some aspects of their postmorbid experiences, although they are not aware of these memories or of their impact on ongoing behavior and experience (Jacoby, 1982; Moscovitch, 1982; Schachter & Tulving, 1982). The phenomenon has been demonstrated in posthypnotic amnesia as well. Williamsen *et al.* (1965) presented subjects with degraded copies of familiar words and asked the subjects to identify them. Hypnotic subjects were better able to identify those items that they had memorized in an earlier verbal learning experiment than those that had not been memorized—even though they were amnesic for those same words.

A more recent study using a priming methodology has demonstrated an analogous verbal fluency effect in retrieval from semantic memory (Kihlstrom, 1980b). In the first experiment, subjects memorized a list of 15 unrelated words while hypnotized. After reaching criterion, they received an amnesia suggestion and hypnosis was terminated. Then, an attempt was made to elicit the items that had been memorized during hypnosis as word associates. A list of words was prepared, consisting of two kinds of items, carefully matched: critical stimuli, for which the most probable response was one of the items in the acquisition set, and neutral stimuli, which targeted some word that had not been memorized. The second experiment followed the same methodology, except that the subjects memorized a list of 16 related words, four items from each of four taxonomic categories. In this case, an attempt was made to elicit these critical items, and their matched neutral counterparts, as category instances.

The virtuoso subjects showed a very dense amnesia on an initial test of free recall, while the insusceptible subjects showed virtually no impairment in memory. Nevertheless, in both experiments the probability of eliciting the intended targets was significantly greater for critical than for neutral stimuli, and the difference between critical and neutral stimuli was the same for the densely amnesic hypnotic virtuosos as it was for the insusceptible, nonamnesic subjects. A similar difference between critical and neutral targets was obtained by Spanos *et al.* (1982b) in that portion of their experiment which replicated Kihlstrom's (1980b) word association task. The differential performance favoring the production of critical items in the semantic memory tasks is a priming effect (McKoon & Ratcliff, 1979; Meyer & Schvaneveldt, 1971; Neely, 1977). This priming effect is apparently unaffected by posthypnotic amnesia.

The priming effects on semantic memory observed in this experiment are analogous to the perceptual fluency effects observed by Jacoby and Dallas (1981) and in the amnesic syndrome (Schachter & Tulving, 1982). Presumably, both effects reflect the activation received by underlying semantic representations (Anderson, 1983) of target items during the acquisition phase of the experiment. Given a model of memory in which retrieval is based at least partly on activation (Anderson, 1983), it is possible that this persisting activation could form the basis for a judgment of familiarity, and thus for accurate recognition, even though the subjects cannot remember the episodic context in which the item occurred.

Accordingly, a replication of the earlier experiment was conducted, with the difference that the subjects learned *two* lists of words. Each list contained 16 words, four items from each of four taxonomic categories. Moreover, the two lists learned by each subject were drawn from the *same* categories, with the exemplars carefully matched in terms of frequency. A group of hypnotic virtuosos learned the lists while hypnotized, followed by a suggestion for posthypnotic amnesia; a comparison group of unselected subjects memorized the lists in the normal waking state. For subjects in both groups, study trials for the second list began immediately after reaching a criterion of mastery on the first one. In this experiment there were no tests of category recognition or item recall cued by category names.

As might be expected, the hypnotic subjects showed a very dense amnesia on the initial test of free recall. For the recognition test, a computer presented the subjects with the 32 critical targets (16 from each list), 32 matched lures drawn from the critical categories, and 64 words from neutral categories, matched to the critical items. For each item, the subjects were asked to rate their confidence, on a 1–4 scale, that they had learned the item earlier in the experiment. Recognition was perfect for the control subjects, of course. For the hypnotic subjects, recognition depended on the criterion employed. With a strict criterion, there was a significant but incomplete improvement in retention; with the loose criterion, the amnesia was abolished entirely.

Following the recognition procedure, the subjects completed a test of list differentiation. The 32 critical targets were again presented, one at a time, on the computer screen. The subjects were informed (or reminded, in the case of the waking controls) that these items were in fact the ones that they had memorized and were instructed to indicate the list to which they belonged. The waking controls were extremely confident in their responses, which were accurate as well. The hypnotic subjects, by contrast, were both significantly less confident and significantly less accurate in their decisions—however, they were more confident, and accurate, than chance. The relative inability of amnesic subjects to assign items correctly to their proper lists in the list differentiation portion of the experiment indicates that at least some of their recognition performance was mediated by judgments of familiarity rather than the reconstruction of the episodic context. (It may be that *all* of their recognition performance was mediated by familiarity, if it can be demonstrated that nonepisodic cues such as perceptual fluency can contribute to list differentiation as well as recognition.)

IV. A Model for Posthypnotic Amnesia

Posthypnotic amnesia may be characterized as dissociative in nature in that it involves a disruption in both the monitoring and controlling functions of consciousness (Hilgard, 1977; Kihlstrom, 1984a). Amnesic subjects show a lack of awareness of their prior experiences, and they also show a lack of strategic control over the process of memory retrieval. The amnesia reflects a division rather than a loss of consciousness: The subject is aware of the events at the time that they occur, and the material covered by the amnesia continues to affect ongoing experience, thought, and action. And the memories are subconscious rather than unconscious: They can be retrieved under certain circumstances and brought into introspective awareness.

In order to encompass posthypnotic amnesia and other dissociative phenomena, as observed in hypnosis and related states, Hilgard (1977, 1979) has proposed a neodissociation theory of divided consciousness. The theory states that under some circumstances consciousness can be divided so that two or more streams of cognitive activity run simultaneously, and that under some circumstances one or more of these streams of consciousness can be rendered subconscious, outside of phenomenal awareness, and perceived as involuntary. Neodissociation theory offers a perspective on nonconscious mental processes that differs from that of the classical accounts offered by both psychoanalytic and information-processing theory (Bowers & Meichenbaum, 1984; Ellenberger, 1970). For this reason, it seems important to attempt to represent dissociations such as amnesia within contemporary models of the cognitive system. Posthypnotic amnesia, as a disruption in memory retrieval, may be viewed from the perspective of a generic network model of memory similar to HAM (Anderson & Bower, 1973), ACT (Anderson, 1976, 1983), or similar approaches developed by others (e.g., Collins & Loftus, 1975; Kintsch, 1974; Quillian, 1968; Rummelhart, Lindsay, & Norman, 1972; for reviews, see Anderson, 1976; Johnson-Laird, Herrmann, & Chaffin, 1984).

A. MEMORY STRUCTURES AND PROCESSES

As described by Anderson, the basic architecture of the cognitive system involves three components: a sensory–perceptual system, which processes inputs from the external and internal environment and encodes a memory trace of the input in permanent memory; a declarative memory store, consisting of factual and categorical knowledge; and a procedural memory store, consisting of rules and skills by which declarative knowledge can be manipulated and transformed. The sensory–perceptual system and procedural memory are both unconscious in principle in that their operations and contents are not accessible to introspection and can be known only by inference. By contrast, the contents of declarative memory are available to consciousness in that they can be accessed and brought into awareness by appropriate retrieval cues provided by the external environment or generated internally by a deliberate act of thought. In these terms, the dissociation of posthypnotic amnesia, which primarily affects declarative episodic memory, would seem to involve a division within the declarative memory store such that available memories are inaccessible to retrieval, although they can still affect other cognitive processes.

1. Representational Assumptions

According to ACT and other network models, the declarative memory store can be represented as a graph structure with nodes representing concepts and associative links representing relationships between them. In this way, the factual knowledge comprising declarative memory is represented as propositions consisting of subjects and predicates, relations and arguments. As in the arguments of Tulving (1972, 1983), two types of propositions can be distinguished (Kihlstrom, 1984a). Some propositions are semantic in nature, representing the features characteristic of the constituent concepts (e.g., *Birds have wings*), the hierarchical relations among concepts (e.g., *A robin is a type of bird*), and part-of relationships (e.g., *The arm is a part of the body*). These kinds of propositions form the mental lexicon. Other propositions are episodic in nature, forming the record of autobiographical memory. These link factual descriptions of specific events to propositions representing the spatiotemporal context in which the events occurred and the self as the agent or experiencer of the event (e.g., *I learned about robins in the sixth grade; I saw the hippie touch the debutante in the park last Thursday*).

In a similar manner, the procedural memory store can be represented as a set of nodes representing goals, conditions, and actions that can be taken to achieve a particular goal if certain conditions are in force, linked to form a production. A production is applied if the nodes representing its goals and conditions are activated in working memory (i.e., that portion of the declarative memory system which is active at any particular time). Execution of a production leads automatically to the outcome represented by the action node: an inference or some behavior, for example. At the same time, execution of a production encodes this inference or behavior into declarative memory as a new fact. For example, if a production has been employed to make an inference about a target's personality, this inference is now stored in semantic memory independent of the preexisting knowledge on which it was based (Hastie, 1981; Smith, 1984). Alternatively, if a production has been employed to generate some behavior, this act is now stored in episodic memory as a new piece of autobiographical memory (Kihlstrom, 1980a).

2. Processing Assumptions

According to ACT, a new event is encoded in memory in terms of preexisting knowledge. Nodes representing the features of the event are activated by the perceptual process, and links representing the relations among perceived features are formed—resulting in a new proposition. Once a node is activated by the encoding process, activation can spread from the source node to related concepts along the associative links that comprise the network. The speed of spreading activation depends on the strength of the various links. Activation decays and spreading ceases when a node ceases to be a source. Once a cognitive unit (a proposition, or part thereof) has been encoded, there is some probability that it will become a permanent structure in declarative memory, a residue persisting after its transient activation has decayed. While single events are represented as propositions, a sequence of events is represented as a temporal string that preserves ordinal but not interval information. Long sequences of events are encoded as a hierarchy of such strings.

According to ACT, retrieval of a memory is chiefly a function of activation. Encoding of a retrieval query activates nodes in the memory network that correspond to information supplied by (or inferred from) the cue. Activation then spreads through the network along the established associative pathways. When these activated pathways intersect, the corresponding proposition, or fragment thereof, is checked against the specifications of the query. If there is a match between the query and the trace, then a production generates a memory report. Retrieval failure occurs when a corresponding trace is not located within some period of time or if insufficient activation converges on the trace. The only constraints on retrieval are shortness of time and the requirement that the trace cross some threshold of activation. Thus, assuming that the source nodes remain active, allowing activation to spread throughout the network, every fact represented by a permanent trace would be retrieved by this process. When a sequence of items is encoded as a temporal string, the first item in the string typically serves as a source node, and activation spreads according to ordinal position.

In contrast to earlier two-process theories, ACT assumes that recall and recognition are both the product of a single process, activation. However, there remain important task differences between the two types of retention tests; in addition, there are important task differences between tests of episodic and semantic memory. For purposes of illustration, assume that a subject has memorized a list of familiar words. As a result, nodes corresponding to each word are activated in the memory network, and each of these is linked to a node specifying the context in which the learning occurred. In a *semantic recognition* test (e.g., lexical decision), a test word is presented. If a corresponding node in the network is activated, a production generates a report that the item is, in fact, a word. In a *semantic recall* test (e.g., word association), a test word is presented. When activation spreads from the source node to some other node, a production generates a report of the word corresponding to the second node. In these cases, task performance will be facilitated by virtue of the fact that the words retain some activation from the prior study phase—a priming effect (Meyer & Schvanaveldt, 1971). In an *episodic recognition* test, a test word is presented. If superthreshold activation spreads from the word node to the context node, a production generates a report that the item is old rather than new. In a *episodic recall* test, a description of the context is presented. If superthreshold activation spreads from the context node to a word node, a production generates a report of a word from the list.

Of course, as noted earlier, episodic memory is not entirely determined by retrieval of the context (e.g., Jacoby & Dallas, 1979; Mandler, 1979). In the absence of context retrieval, recall and recognition can be mediated solely by activation. Consider, for example, a recall test employing the simplest form of retrieval query: *Remember something*. If the subjects take the task seriously, they are likely to report the first thing that occurs to them—and this, according to ACT, will be whatever fragment of the memory network possesses the most residual activation. Given the prior study phase, items retrieved in this manner are highly likely to have been on the list. However, the subjects will be uncertain whether they are meeting the task demands—and, if asked, they will be uncertain that the item was, in fact, one that they studied. As another example, consider a recognition test in which for some reason activation does not spread to the context node. In this case, activation from the retrieval cue may be added to residual activation from the study phase, resulting in a very strongly activated fragment of the memory network. Under these circumstances, subjects might well make the inference that the item is old rather than new. Again, however, such an item may not be recognized confidently. Moreover, recognition based on such a judgment of familiarity would seem to have a different phenomenological character from recognition based on retrieval of context. Unless the context and (especially) self-reference are retrieved, a memory will lack the character of personal recollection.

B. APPLICATION TO POSTHYPNOTIC AMNESIA

From a cognitive point of view, a satisfactory account of posthypnotic amnesia must include some assumptions concerning the representation of memories. According to the ACT model of memory (Anderson, 1983), the subject encodes a set of propositions describing the hypnotic events and experiences. In the process, several types of nodes are linked with the propositions representing factual descriptions of the events and experiences. Some of these nodes are semantic in nature, representing concepts related to those contained in the propositions; others are episodic in nature, representing self-reference and spatiotemporal context. Figure 8 shows a specimen propositional representation of a garden-variety hypnotic experience.

Figure 9 shows a simplified network representation of a series of typical hypnotic experiences, such as those suggested on one of the standardized scales of hypnotic susceptibility, that includes a verbal learning procedure—memorizing a list of categorized words. As in Fig. 8, the proposition representing each suggestion is linked to other propositions representing episodic information. Each event is linked sequentially to others that occurred immediately before and afterward, forming a temporal string. Finally, the list items are linked to semantically related concepts as well as to episodic concepts.

Figure 10 shows an extremely simplified representation of an episodic memory for one item on a word list memorized during hypnosis according to the method of serial learning. The node representing the word is linked to other nodes representing temporally and semantically related concepts. It is also linked propositionally to nodes representing the self and the spatiotemporal context of the event, and in a temporal string to the words immediately preceding and

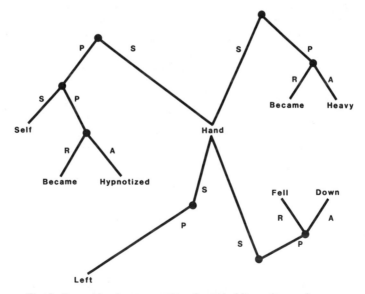

Fig. 8. Propositional representation of a typical hypnotic experience.

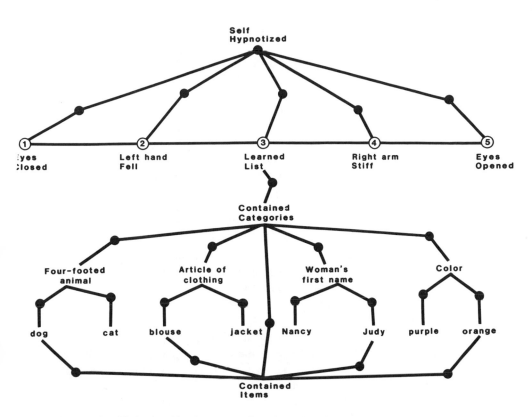

Fig. 9. Simplified propositional representation of a series of hypnotic experiences, including a verbal learning procedure.

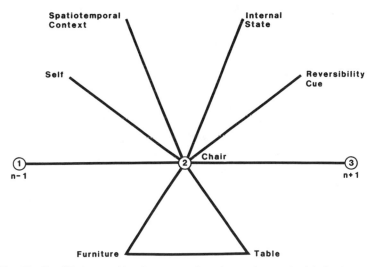

Fig. 10. Simplified propositional representation of a word memorized during hypnosis.

following it in the study list. It is these links that are disrupted during posthypnotic amnesia.

1. Episodic Memory

In the context of such a network model, the amnesic process can be represented as breaks in two types of associative links: (a) those connecting the node representing the hypnotic event with those describing the episodic context in which the event occurred, and (b) those linking the event node to nodes representing the immediately preceding and following events. Such a situation will result in a major disruption of episodic memory retrieval.

Consider, for example, a subject who has memorized a list of categorized words according to the method of free recall. The resulting memory trace of each word will consist of a node representing the item linked to nodes representing the self and the learning context; in addition, the item node will also be linked to nodes representing the superordinate category of which the word is a member and—by virtue of spreading activation—at least some other members of that category. In a free recall test, the retrieval query ("What did you just learn during hypnosis?") contains information pertaining to the episodic context in which the word was studied. Processing of the query then activates the corresponding nodes in the memory network. However, activation cannot spread to the item node, and recall fails. In cued recall, the query supplies information related to the target ("Were there any articles of furniture on the list? Does *chair* remind you of anything that you learned?"). Processing these sorts of retrieval cues will activate both episodic and semantic nodes. Activation may spread from nodes representing semantically related traces to the node representing the item; however, there will be no intersection between activated pathways emanating from the episodic nodes and activated pathways from the item node, again resulting in recall failure. Finally, in recognition the query supplies information pertaining to both the word and the episodic context ("Was *table* on the list that you learned?"); but again the activated pathways do not intersect, and recognition fails. In this way, hypnotic subjects will display retrieval failure on tests of free recall, cued recall, and recognition (Kihlstrom, 1984b).

This model, as described, will result in a complete failure of episodic recall. However, cases of partial amnesia are also observed, typically among subjects who classify as highly hypnotizable but not hypnotic virtuosos. In partial amnesia some episodic memories but not others, or perhaps only fragments of such memories, are successfully recalled. If continuity between partial and complete posthypnotic amnesia is assumed, the model as outlined must be modified to account for the fact that posthypnotic amnesia is not an all-or-none case of retrieval failure. One mechanism for partial amnesia is suggested by the assumption that episodic links are weakened rather than broken, with the degree of amnesia corresponding to the degree of loss of strength. In fact, ACT does allow for a continuous distribution of associative strength, thus permitting such a state of affairs. This situation would permit activation to spread out from source nodes activated by the retrieval cue. If the source nodes are assumed to remain activated long enough, then, activation would eventually reach the item node, and the target would be retrieved. In this manner, items forgotten on one recall trial could be retrieved on a subsequent one. In fact, such a spontaneous recovery of memory is observed during posthypnotic amnesia (Kihlstrom et al., 1980, 1983).

A complementary approach is based on the assumption in ACT that retrieval is a function of the degree of activation received by the trace. After encoding, some critical propositions or parts thereof may remain activated above the threshold for retrieval. Assume that retrieval is typically controlled by a production which matches episodic information specified in the query to episodic information stored in memory. For reasons noted above, such a production will not retrieve the target item itself. However, retrieval could also be controlled by another production which searches the network for any fragment that is above a certain threshold of activation. The application of such a procedure would be expected to retrieve all or part of at least some relevant memory traces, even under free recall conditions. Cued recall queries may increase the probability of retrieval because activation spreading from semantic nodes to item nodes may bring more of these item nodes above the threshold for retrieval. A similar argument would apply to item nodes activated in the course of recognition testing. In these cases, however, retrieval may well be incomplete. For example, the subject may not retrieve a full description of the event, as found in the phenomenon of generic recall (Evans et al., 1973; Kihlstrom & Evans, 1978). In addition, successful recognition will be accompanied by a failure to access and reconstruct the specifically episodic features of the event, as required by list differentiation and similar tasks (Kihlstrom, 1984a).

Thus, by virtue of activation spreading slowly along weakened episodic links or the application of productions geared to make inferences about likely target memories, or both, subjects may well be able to retrieve at least some of their hypnotic experiences. However, the strategic organization that ordinarily characterizes retrieval will be disrupted. Consider, for example, a subject who has memorized a list of unrelated words according to the method of serial recall. In the absence of amnesia, retrieval would ordinarily begin with the first item in the list and proceed in order, as activation spread from one node to the next in the temporal string. In the case of amnesia, however, even if some event is successfully retrieved, activation will not necessarily spread to adjacent events. This state of affairs will result in a disruption of serial organization (Evans & Kihlstrom, 1973; Kihlstrom & Evans, 1979; Kihlstrom & Wilson, 1984).

It is possible for linguistic forms of organization to be disrupted by this process. Consider, for example, the subjective organization which is built up during free recall learning of a list of unrelated words. Even when there is no inherent structure in the list items presented for study, subjects will eventually impose some consistent, if idiosyncratic, order on recall. For example, subjects frequently use the list items to construct a narrative description of one or more scenes or events. This organization is based primarily on semantic and syntactic relationships among these list items; yet disruptions of subjective organization have been observed during posthypnotic amnesia, provided that subjects build up appropriately high levels of subjective organization during the acquisition phase (Kihlstrom & Wilson, 1984b; Tkachyk *et al.*, 1984). However, it should be noted that high levels of subjective organization are only achieved if subjects recall the list items in a consistent sequence (Sternberg & Tulving, 1977). Thus, serial organization is superimposed on linguistic organization. Similarly, Anderson (1983) notes that phrase structure relationships may also be represented in temporal strings preserving word order. If subjects impose subjective organization on material during acquisition in a manner that preserves ordinal information, then a disruption of seriation might lead to an apparent disruption of the other, more linguistic modes of organization as well.

2. Recovery of Memory

In the case of an amnesia produced by the weakening or breaking of episodic links between stored items, instructions for honesty or effort will not be expected to lead to improvements in memory. Such instructions (e.g., "Be honest in reporting what happened during hypnosis," or "Try very hard to remember everything") do not provide any relevant retrieval information that is not specified in the standard query. Therefore, activation will not spread in a manner differently than obtains with the standard query, and retrieval failure will persist. If the honesty or effort instructions accompany a retest of memory, following an initial test with the standard query, some improvement in memory would be expected. However, the extent of improvement would not differ from what occurs spontaneously on an uninstructed retest (Kihlstrom *et al.*, 1980). Similar considerations apply to the reinduction of hypnosis. During encoding, it is possible that nodes representing the subjective experience of hypnosis are linked to the item nodes. If so, then reinstatement of hypnosis during posthypnotic amnesia might be expected to improve memory, after the manner of state-dependent retrieval effects observed in drug and mood states. Note, however, that the induction procedure itself does not provide any way for activation from the episodic nodes to spread to the item nodes. Thus, the reinduction of hypnosis would not be expected to lead to any improvement in memory over and above what is observed on a simple retest in the normal waking state (Kihlstrom *et al.*, 1985).

Obviously, administration of the prearranged reversibility cue is the most effective and efficient way to restore access to the items covered by posthypnotic amnesia. In order to account for the effect of the reversibility cue, it is necessary to assume that the encoding of an event can be revised by subsequent events. Thus, during the acquisition phase, links are forged between item and episodic nodes in the usual manner. However, when the amnesia suggestion is administered, a new link is encoded alongside the old one. This link connects a node representing the reversibility cue to *both* the item node and the episodic node: It is this link that is broken or weakened by the amnesic process. Presentation of the reversibility cue activates the corresponding node in the memory network, activation spreads to the episodic and item nodes, restoring the link between them, and the episodic memory is retrieved as a personal recollection.

3. Semantic and Procedural Memory

It should be clear that the breaking or weakening of episodic links poses no difficulty for semantic retrieval. Such tasks do not require retrieval of episodic information and therefore will be unimpaired. Subjects who forget words memorized during hypnosis will have no difficulty in defining these words, using them in sentences, and the like. Similarly, they will have no difficulty in retrieving factual information acquired during hypnosis (Evans, 1979). In fact, performance on such tasks may well be facilitated by the activation received by event nodes and corresponding semantic nodes during encoding. This facilitation would result in the kinds of perceptual fluency, transfer, and priming effects that are displayed by amnesic subects (e.g., Kihlstrom, 1980b; Williamsen et al., 1965).

In a similar manner, there is nothing about this state of affairs that would prevent declarative knowledge covered by the amnesia from being employed in some skilled perceptual, cognitive, or motoric task. According to ACT, productions are applied if structures representing their goals and conditions are activated in the declarative memory network. Assuming that a production (or the beginnings of one) has been acquired in hypnosis, there is nothing about the amnesic process that will prevent goal and condition nodes from being activated by the processing of task demands. If this occurs, the production will generate the desired outcome, although the subjects will not be able to retrieve the fact that they possess this skill. This situation will result in the sparing of acquired skills in amnesic subjects, despite their inability to remember the practice session in which they acquired these skills (Life, 1929; Patten, 1932).

4. Difficulties for the Model

The model described here can account for many findings in the literature on posthypnotic amnesia, but certain results pose problems for it. For example, it has difficulty dealing with the documented disruptions in category clustering (e.g., Spanos & Bodorik, 1977), where linguistic organization is rarely compounded by seriation. Another problem is presented by data indicating that amnesia may not dissipate progressively over time, as would be predicted by an account of the spontaneous recovery effects in terms of weakened episodic links and spreading activation (Spanos *et al.*, 1982a). Neither of these findings represents a fatal challenge to the model, but they do indicate that a number of details remain to be worked out.

A major task for the immediate future is to work out how the amnesia suggestion works to break the episodic links, thus denying access to memories, and how the reversibility cue operates to restore them, resulting in the retrieval of a personal recollection. Some hints along these lines are to be found in ACT, which departs from traditional associative theories of memory by permitting the strategic control of memory by means of production systems. In addition, ACT assumes that several productions can be applied simultaneously. Thus, just as retrieval is controlled by a set of productions that search memory for patterns matching cue information, so amnesia may be produced by a set of opposing productions that control the spread of activation between nodes in the memory network.

Perhaps the biggest difficulty posed for the model is the extensive literature documenting the effect of situational factors, such as expectations and the wording of suggestions, on response to suggestions for posthypnotic amnesia. Such results are outside the scope of models such as ACT and will require the addition of another set of concepts and principles before a complete theory of posthypnotic amnesia will have been achieved. Moreover, it is possible that a theory based exclusively on social–psychological principles will prove to be better than one which has both cognitive and interpersonal components—although this seems unlikely in view of the evidence reviewed earlier, not to mention the nature of human mental life. In that case, it is possible that some of the principles outlined here will prove useful in understanding some other nonhypnotic form of memory pathology. After all, this is the wider goal of hypnosis research: to suggest ways of conceptualizing a wider set of psychological phenomena (Kihlstrom, 1979).

V. Amnesic Processes and a General Model of Dissociation

Assuming that a cognitive model is found appropriate for at least some aspects of posthypnotic amnesia, it may be possible to use the model as the basis for understanding other dissociative phenomena in hypnosis.

Consider, first, the phenomenon of posthypnotic suggestion. In this phenomenon, the hypnotist suggests that when a signal is given after hypnosis is terminated, the subject will perform some action. For example, on the Stanford

Hypnotic Susceptibility Scale, Form A, it is suggested that the subject will change chairs when the experimenter raps a pencil on the desk. It is also suggested that the subject will not be able to remember that the experimenter gave this suggestion until the reversibility cue is given to cancel the suggestion for posthypnotic amnesia. In the classic case, response to posthypnotic suggestions has a quasiautomatic, compulsive quality in which the subjects experience themselves as responding involuntarily and are not aware of the motivation for their action—if indeed they are aware of their action at all. From a cognitive point of view, the posthypnotic suggestion can be viewed as possessing two components: (a) the encoding of a production which will produce a response if certain conditions are met, and (b) the establishment of amnesia covering the event of the suggestion itself. Given this situation, the production will be applied if the signal is processed, even though the subjects will not remember the source of their behavior.

A similar analysis may be offered for analgesia, blindness, deafness, and other negative hallucinations experienced in hypnosis. In these phenomena, the person appears to be unaware of perceptible stimuli available in his or her perceptual field. Despite this lack of awareness, however, it is easy to demonstrate that these stimuli have been registered by the perceptual apparatus and exert an impact on ongoing experience, thought, and action. Thus, the negative hallucinations involve paradoxes much like those observed in posthypnotic amnesia. A substantial empirical literature exists concerning these effects (e.g., Hilgard, 1965, 1975, 1977; Kihlstrom, 1984a, 1985). To date, however, these studies have sought, and largely failed to find, evidence for alterations in the perceptual processing of the stimuli. In conceptualizing analgesia and other negative hallucinations, Hilgard (1977, 1979) has referred to an "amnesic barrier" that prevents awareness of percepts that are fully and accurately represented in the cognitive system. The ACT model provides a way of thinking about these *post*perceptual effects. For example, the perceptual apparatus may encode a propositional (or imagistic; see Anderson, 1983) representation of the stimulus in declarative memory. Activation can spread from this memory fragment to other portions of the memory network, and the activated elements can serve as conditions for the application of production systems. However, if there is no link between the source node and nodes in "working memory" (Hastie & Carlston, 1980) representing the contents of the subject's current phenomenal awareness, these percepts and their influence will remain subconscious.

This is not to argue that all hypnotic phenomena are dissociative in nature or even that memory models like ACT can account for all the aspects of divided consciousness and subconscious processing observed there. However, a number of phenomena in hypnosis as well as other observations in the laboratory, clinic, and everyday life seem to invite a concept of dissociation; and given the metaphor of an "amnesic barrier," it would seem that memory structures and processes are central features of whatever it is that dissociation entails (Kihlstrom, 1984a). Network models such as ACT seem able, at least in principle, to account for many of the paradoxes observed in posthypnotic amnesia; at least, these models generate experiments of a sort that would not be performed if they did not exist. At the same time, it is possible that posthypnotic amnesia and other pathologies of memory—both functional and organic—may serve as a sort of proving ground for the models themselves. The happy prospect of such a symbiotic relation between fields seems reason enough to continue to investigate hypnotic phenomena from a cognitive standpoint.

Acknowledgments

Preparation of this article was supported in part by Grant MH-35856 from the National Institute of Mental Health and an H. I. Romnes Faculty Fellowship from the University of Wisconsin. I thank Nancy Cantor, Reid Hastie, William C. Heindel, Irene P. Hoyt, Larry Jacoby, Mary A. Peterson, Patricia A. Register, and Endel Tulving for their helpful comments at various stages in the writing.

References

Anderson, J. R. (1976). *Language, memory, and thought.* Hillsdale, NJ: Erlbaum.
Anderson, J. R. (1983). *The architecture of cognition.* Cambridge, MA: Harvard Univ. Press.
Anderson, J. R., & Bower, G. H. (1972). Recognition and retrieval processes in free recall. *Psychological Review, 79,* 97–123.
Anderson, J. R., & Bower, G. H. (1973). *Human associative memory.* Hillsdale, NJ: Erlbaum.
Anderson, J. R., & Bower, G. H. (1974). A propositional theory of recognition memory. *Memory and Cognition, 2,* 406–412.
Ashford, B., & Hammer, A. G. (1978). The role of expectancies in the occurrence of posthypnotic amnesia. *International Journal of Clinical and Experimental Hypnosis, 26,* 281–291.
Atkinson, R. C., & Juola, J. F. (1974). Search and decision processes in recognition memory. In D. H. Krantz, R. C. Atkinson, R. D. Luce, & P. Suppes (Eds.), *Contemporary developments in mathematical psychology: Vol. 1. Learning, memory, and thinking.* San Francisco: Freeman.
Barber, T. X. (1964). Hypnotizability, suggestibility, and personality: V. A critical review of research findings. *Psychological Reports, 14,* 299–320.
Barber, T. X., & Calverley, D. S. (1966). Toward a theory of "hypnotic" behavior: Experimental analyses of suggested amnesia. *Journal of Abnormal Psychology, 71,* 95–107.
Bergson, H. (1896). *Matter and memory.* London: Allen, 1911. (Originally published, 1896.)
Bertrand, L. D., Spanos, N. P., & Parkinson, B. (1983). A test of the dissipation hypothesis of hypnotic amnesia. *Psychological Reports, 52,* 667–671.
Bitterman, M. E., & Marcuse, F. L. (1945). Autonomic response in posthypnotic amnesia. *Journal of Experimental Psychology, 35,* 248–252.
Blum, G. S. (1967). Experimental observations on the contextual nature of hypnosis. *International Journal of Clinical and Experimental Hypnosis, 15,* 160–171.
Blum, G. S., Graef, J. R., & Hauenstein, L. S. (1968). Overcoming interference in short-term memory through distinctive mental contexts. *Psychonomic Science, 11,* 73–74. (b)
Blum, G. S., Graef, J. R., Hauenstein, L. S., & Passini, F. T. (1971). Distinctive mental contexts in long-term memory. *International Journal of Clinical and Experimental Hypnosis, 19,* 117–133.

Bousfield, W. A. (1953). The occurrence of clustering in the recall of randomly arranged associates. *Journal of General Psychology, 49,* 229–240.

Bower, G. H. (1970). Organizational factors in memory. *Cognitive Psychology, 1,* 18–46.

Bower, G. H. (1981). Mood and memory. *American Psychologist, 36,* 129–138.

Bower, G. H., Gilligan, S. G., & Monteiro, K. P. (1981). Selectivity of learning caused by affective state. *Journal of Experimental Psychology: General, 110,* 451–473.

Bower, G. H., Monteiro, K. P., & Gilligan, S. G. (1978). Emotional mood as a context for learning and recall. *Journal of Verbal Learning and Verbal Behavior, 17,* 573–585.

Bowers, K. S. (1966). Hypnotic behavior: the differentiation of trance and demand characteristic variables. *Journal of Abnormal Psychology, 71,* 42–51.

Bowers, K. S. (1973). Situationism in psychology: An analysis and a critique. *Psychological Review, 80,* 307–336.

Bowers, K. S., & Meichenbaum, D. (Eds.). (1984). *The unconscious reconsidered.* New York: Wiley.

Claparede. (1911). Recognition et moiite. *Archives de Psychologie, 11,* 79–90.

Clemes, S. (1964). Repression and hypnotic amnesia. *Journal of Abnormal Psychology, 69,* 62–69.

Coe, W. C. (1978). The credibility of posthypnotic amnesia: A contextualist's view. *International Journal of Clinical and Experimental Hypnosis, 26,* 218–245.

Coe, W. C., Basden, B., Basden, D., & Graham, C. (1976). Posthypnotic amnesia: Suggestions of an active process in dissociative phenomena. *Journal of Abnormal Psychology, 85,* 455–458.

Coe, W. C., Baugher, R. J., Krimm, W. R., & Smith, J. A. (1976). A further examination of selective recall following hypnosis. *International Journal of Clinical and Experimental Hypnosis, 22,* 13–21.

Coe, W. C., Taul, J. H., Basden, D., & Basden, B. (1973). Investigation of the dissociation hypothesis and disorganized retrieval in posthypnotic amnesia with retroactive inhibition in free-recall learning. *Proceedings of the 81st Annual Convention of the American Psychological Association, 8,* 1081–1082.

Coe, W. C., & Yashinski, E. (1985). Volitional expericnces associated with breaching amnesia. *Journal of Personality and Social Psychology.*

Cofer, C. N. (Ed.). (1976). *The structure of human memory.* San Francisco: Freeman.

Collins, A. M., & Loftus, E. F. (1975). A spreading-activation theory of semantic processing. *Psychological Review, 82,* 407–428.

Cooper, L. M. (1966). Spontaneous and suggested posthypnotic source amnesia. *International Journal of Clinical and Experimental Hypnosis, 14,* 180–193.

Cooper. L. M. (1979). Hypnotic amnesia. In E. Fromm & R. E. Shor (Eds.), *Hypnosis: Developments in research and new perspectives.* New York: Aldine.

Coors, D. (1928). *A determination of the density of posthypnotic amnesia for the stylus maze.* Unpublished bachelor's thesis. University of Wisconsin.

Craik, F. I. M. (1977). Age differences in human memory. In J. E. Birren & K. W. Schaie (Eds.), *Handbook of the psychology of aging.* New York: Van Nostrand-Reinhold.

Craik, F. I. M , & Simon, E. (1980). Age differences in memory: The roles of attention and depth of processing. In L. W. Poon, J. L. Fozard, L. S. Cermak, D. Arenberg, & L. W. Thompson (Eds.), *New directions in memory and aging: Proceedings of the George A. Talland Memorial Conference.* Hillsdale, NJ: Erlbaum.

Crawford, H. J., Macdonald, H., & Hilgard, E. R. (1979). Hypnotic deafness: A psychophysical study of responses to tone intensity as modified by hypnosis. *American Journal of Psychology, 92,* 193–214.

Crowder, R. G. (1976). *Principles of learning and memory.* Hillsdale, NJ: Erlbaum.

Crowder, R. G. (1982). General forgetting theory and the locus of amnesia. In L. S. Cermak (Ed.), *Human memory and amnesia.* Hillsdale, NJ: Erlbaum.

Dillon, R. F., & Spanos, N. P. (1983). Proactive interference and the functional ablation hypothesis: More disconfirmatory data. *International Journal of Clinical and Experimental Hypnosis*, **31**, 47–56.

Ellenberger, H. F. (1970). *The discovery of the unconscious: The history and evolution of dynamic psychiatry*. New York: Basic Books.

Evans, F. J. (1972). *Posthypnotic amnesia and the temporary disruption of retrieval processes*. Paper presented at the 80th annual meeting of the American Psychological Association, Honolulu.

Evans, F. J. (1979). Contextual forgetting: posthypnotic source amnesia. *Journal of Abnormal Psychology*, **88**, 556–563.

Evans, F. J., & Kihlstrom, J. F. (1973). Posthypnotic amnesia as disrupted retrieval. *Journal of Abnormal Psychology*, **82**, 317–323.

Evans, F. J., & Kihlstrom, J. F., & Orne, E. C. (1973). Quantifying subjective reports during posthypnotic amnesia. *Proceedings of the 81st Annual Convention of the American Psychological Association*, **8**, 1077–1078.

Evans, F. J., & Thorn, W. A. F. (1966). Two types of posthypnotic amnesia: Recall amnesia and source amnesia. *International Journal of Clinical and Experimental Hypnosis*, **14**, 333–343.

Gandolfo, R. L. (1971). Role of expectancy, amnesia, and hypnotic induction in the performance of posthypnotic behavior. *Journal of Abnormal Psychology*, **77**, 324–328.

Geiselman, R. E., Fishman, D. L., Jaenicke, C., Larner, B. R., MacKinnon, D. P., Shoenberg, S., & Swartz, S. (1983). Mechanisms of hypnotic and nonhypnotic forgetting. *Journal of Experimental Psychology: Learning, Memory, and Cognition*, **9**, 626–635.

Gheorghiu, V. (1967). Some peculiarities of posthypnotic source amnesia of information. In L. Chertok (Ed.), *Psychophysiological mechanisms of hypnosis*. New York: Springer.

Goldstein, M. S., & Sipprelle, C. N. (1970). Hypnotically induced amnesia versus ablation of memory. *International Journal of Clinical and Experimental Hypnosis*, **18**, 211–216.

Graham, K. R., & Patton, A. (1968). Retroactive inhibition, hypnosis, and hypnotic amnesia. *International Journal of Clinical and Experimental Hypnosis*, **16**, 68–74.

Gregg, V. H. (1979). Posthypnotic amnesia and general memory theory. *Bulletin of the British Society of Experimental and Clinical Hypnosis*, (2), 11–14.

Gregg, V. H. (1980). Posthypnotic amnesia for recently learned material: A comment on the paper by J. F. Kihlstrom (1980). *Bulletin of the British Society of Experimental and Clinical Hypnosis*, (2), 11–14.

Hastie, R. (1980). Memory for behavioral information that confirms or contradicts a personality impression. In R. Hastie, T. M. Ostrom, E. B. Ebbesen, R. S. Wyer, D. L. Hamilton, & D. E. Carlston (Eds.), *Person memory: The cognitive basis of social perception*. Hillsdale, NJ: Erlbaum.

Hastie, R., & Carlston, D. (1980). Theoretical issues in person memory. In R. Hastie, T. M. Ostrom, E. B. Ebbesen, R. S. Wyer, D. L. Hamilton, & D. E. Carlston (Eds.), *Person memory: The cognitive basis of social perception*. Hillsdale, NJ: Erlbaum.

Hilgard, E. R. (1965). *Hypnotic susceptibility*. New York: Harcourt.

Hilgard, E. R. (1966). Posthypnotic amnesia: Experiments and theory. *International Journal of Clinical and Experimental Hypnosis*, **14**, 104–111.

Hilgard, E. R. (1967). A quantitative study of pain and its reduction through hypnotic suggestion. *Proceedings of the National Academy of Sciences of the U.S.A.*, **57**, 1581–1586.

Hilgard, E. R. (1975). Hypnosis. *Annual Review of Psychology*, **26**, 1944.

Hilgard, E. R. (1977). *Divided consciousness: Multiple controls in human thought and action*. New York: Wiley (Interscience).

Hilgard, E. R. (1979). Divided consciousness in hypnosis: The implications of the hidden observer.

In E. Fromm & R. E. Shor (Eds.), *Hypnosis: Developments in research and new perspectives.* New York: Aldine.

Hilgard, E. R., & Cooper, L. M. (1965). Spontaneous and suggested posthypnotic amnesia. *International Journal of Clinical and Experimental Hypnosis, 13*, 261–273.

Hilgard, E. R., & Hommel, L. S. (1961). Selective amnesia for events within hypnosis in relation to repression. *Journal of Personality, 29*, 205–216.

Howard, M. L., & Coe, W. C. (1980). The effect of context and subjects' perceived control in breaching posthypnotic amnesia. *Journal of Personality, 48*, 342–359.

Hull, C. L. (1933). *Hypnosis and suggestibility: An experimental approach.* New York: Appleton.

Jacoby, L. L. (1982). Knowing and remembering: Some parallels in the behavior of Korsakoff patients and normals. In L. S. Cermak (Ed.), *Human memory and amnesia.* Hillsdale, NJ: Erlbaum.

Jacoby, L. L., & Craik, F. I. M. (1979). Effects of elaboration of processing at encoding and retrieval: Trace distinctiveness and recovery of initial context. In L. S. Cermak & F. I. M. Craik (Eds.), *Levels of processing and human memory.* Hillsdale, NJ: Erlbaum.

Jacoby, L. L., & Dallas, M. (1981). On the relationship between autobiographical memory and perceptual learning. *Journal of Experimental Psychology: General, 110*, 306–340.

Johnson-Laird, P. N., Herrmann, D. J., & Chaffin, R. (1984). Only connections: A critique of semantic networks. *Psychological Bulletin, 96*, 292–315.

Kihlstrom, J. F. (1977). Models of posthypnotic amnesia. In W. E. Edmonston (Ed.), Conceptual and investigative approaches to hypnosis and hypnotic phenomena. *Annals of the New York Academy of Sciences, 296*, 284–301.

Kihlstrom, J. F. (1978). Context and cognition in posthypnotic amnesia. *International Journal of Clinical and Experimental Hypnosis, 26*, 246–267.

Kihlstrom, J. F. (1979). Hypnosis and psychopathology: Retrospect and prospect. *Journal of Abnormal Psychology, 88*, 459–473.

Kihlstrom, J. F. (1980a). On personality and memory. In N. Cantor & J. F. Kihlstrom (Eds.), *Personality, cognition, and social interaction.* Hillsdale, NJ: Erlbaum.

Kihlstrom, J. F. (1980b). Posthypnotic amnesia for recently learned material: Interactions with "episodic" and "semantic" memory. *Cognitive Psychology, 12*, 227–251.

Kihlstrom, J. F. (1982). Hypnosis and the dissociation of memory, with special reference to posthypnotic amnesia. *Research Communications in Psychology, Psychiatry, and Behavior, 7*, 181–197.

Kihlstrom, J. F. (1983). Instructed forgetting: Hypnotic and nonhypnotic. *Journal of Experimental Psychology: General, 112*, 73–79.

Kihlstrom, J. F. (1984a). Conscious, subconscious, unconscious: A cognitive view. In K. S. Bowers & D. Meichenbaum (Eds.), *The unconscious reconsidered.* New York: Wiley.

Kihlstrom, J. F. (1984b). *Recognition processes in posthypnotic amnesia.* Unpublished manuscript, University of Wisconsin.

Kihlstrom, J. F. (1985). Hypnosis. *Annual Review of Psychology, 36*, 385 418.

Kihlstrom, J. F., Brenneman, H. A., Pistole, D. D., & Shor, R. E. (1985). *Hypnosis as a retrieval cue in posthypnotic amnesia. Journal of Abnormal Psychology*, in press.

Kihlstrom, J. F., & Cantor, N. (1984). Mental representations of the self. In L. Berkowitz (Eds.), *Advances in experimental social psychology* (Vol. 19). New York: Academic Press.

Kihlstrom, J. F., Easton, R. D., & Shor, R. E. (1983). Spontaneous recovery of memory during posthypnotic amnesia. *International Journal of Clinical and Experimental Hypnosis, 31*, 309–323.

Kihlstrom, J. F., & Evans, F. J. (1976). Recovery of memory after posthypnotic amnesia. *Journal of Abnormal Psychology, 85*, 564–569.

Kihlstrom, J. F., & Evans, F. J. (1977). Residual effect of suggestions for posthypnotic amnesia: A reexamination. *Journal of Abnormal Psychology, 86,* 327–333.

Kihlstrom, J. F., & Evans, F. J. (1978). Generic recall during posthypnotic amnesia. *Bulletin of the Psychonomic Society, 12,* 57–60.

Kihlstrom, J. F., & Evans, F. J. (1979). Memory retrieval processes during posthypnotic amnesia. In J. F. Kihlstrom & F. J. Evans (Eds.), *Functional disorders of memory.* Hillsdale, NJ: Erlbaum.

Kihlstrom, J. F., Evans, F. J., Orne, E. C., & Orne, M. T. (1980). Attempting to breach posthypnotic amnesia. *Journal of Abnormal Psychology, 89,* 603–616.

Kihlstrom, J. F., & Register, P. A. (1984). Optimal scoring of amnesia on the Harvard Group Scale of Hypnotic Susceptibility, Form A. *International Journal of Clinical and Experimental Hypnosis, 32,* 51–57.

Kihlstrom, J. F., & Shor, R. E. (1978). Recall and recognition during posthypnotic amnesia. *International Journal of Clinical and Experimental Hypnosis, 26,* 330–349.

Kihlstrom, J. F., & Twersky, M. (1978). Relationship of posthypnotic amnesia to aspects of waking memory. *International Journal of Clinical and Experimental Hypnosis, 26,* 330–335.

Kihlstrom, J. F., & Wilson, L. (1984). Temporal organization of recall during posthypnotic amnesia. *Journal of Abnormal Psychology, 93,* 200–206.

Kintsch, W. (1974). *The representation of meaning in memory.* Hillsdale, NJ: Erlbaum.

Kinsbourne, M., & Wood, F. (1982). Theoretical considerations regarding the episodic-semantic memory distinction. In L. S. Cermak (Ed.), *Human memory and amnesia.* Hillsdale, NJ: Erlbaum.

Laurence, J.-R., Perry, C., & Kihlstrom, J. F. (1983). "Hidden observer" phenomena in hypnosis: An experimental creation? *Journal of Personality and Social Psychology, 44,* 163–169.

Levitt, E. E., Persky, H., & Brady, J. P. (1964). *Hypnotic induction of anxiety: A psychoendocrine investigation.* Springfield, IL: Thomas.

Life, C. (1929). *The effects of practice in the trance upon learning in the normal waking state.* Unpublished bachelor's thesis, University of Wisconsin.

Lockhart, R. S., Craik, F. I. M., & Jacoby, L. L. (1976). Depth of processing, recognition, and recall. In J. Brown (Ed.), *Recall and recognition.* New York: Wiley.

Mandler, G. (1967). Organization and memory. In K. W. Spence & J. T. Spence (Eds.), *The psychology of learning and motivation* (Vol. 1). New York: Academic Press.

Mandler, G. (1979). Organization, memory, and mental structures. In C. R. Puff (Ed.), *Memory organization and structure.* New York: Academic Press.

Mandler, G. (1980). Recognizing: The judgment of previous occurrence. *Psychological Review, 87,* 252–271.

Mandler, G., & Dean, P. J. (1969). Seriation: The development of serial order in free recall. *Journal of Experimental Psychology 81,* 207–215.

Mandler, J. (1979). Categorical and schematic organization in memory. In C. R. Puff (Ed.), *Memory organization and structure.* New York: Academic Press.

McConkey, K. M. (1980). Creatively imagined "amnesia." *American Journal of Clinical Hypnosis, 22,* 197–205.

McConkey, K. M., & Sheehan, P. W. (1981). The impact of videotape playback of hypnotic events on posthypnotic amnesia. *Journal of Abnormal Psychology, 90,* 46–54.

McConkey, K. M., Sheehan, P. W., & Cross, D. G. (1980). Posthypnotic amnesia: Seeing is not remembering. *British Journal of Social and Clinical Psychology, 19,* 99–107.

McKoon, G., & Ratcliff, R. (1979). Priming in episodic and semantic memory. *Journal of Verbal Learning and Verbal Behavior, 18,* 463–480.

Meyer, D. E., & Schvaneveldt, R. W. (1971). Facilitation in recognizing pairs of words: Evidence of a dependence between retrieval operations. *Journal of Experimental Psychology, 90,* 227–234.

Miller, R. R., & Marlin, N. A. (1979). Amnesia following electroconvulsive shock. In J. F. Kihlstrom & F. J. Evans (Eds.), *Functional disorders of memory.* Hillsdale, NJ: Erlbaum.

Miller, R. R., & Springer, A. D. (1973). Amnesia, consolidation, and retrieval. *Psychological Review,* **80,** 69–79.

Mischel, W. (1968). *Personality and assessment.* New York: Wiley.

Mitchell, M. B. (1932). Retroactive inhibition and hypnosis. *Journal of General Psychology,* **7,** 343–358.

Morgan, A. H., Johnson, D. L., & Hilgard, E. R. (1973). The stability of hypnotic susceptibility: A longitudinal study. *International Journal of Clinical and Experimental Hypnosis,* **22,** 249–257.

Moscovitch, M. (1982). Multiple dissociations of function in amnesia. In L. S. Cermak (Ed.), *Human memory and amnesia.* Hillsdale, NJ: Erlbaum.

Nace, E. P., Orne, M. T., & Hammer, A. G. (1974). Posthypnotic amnesia as an active psychic process: The reversibility of amnesia. *Archives of General Psychiatry,* **31,** 257–260.

Nagge, J. W. (1935). An experimental test of the theory of associative interference. *Journal of Experimental Psychology,* **18,** 663–682.

Neeley, J. H. (1977). Semantic priming and retrieval from lexical memory: Roles of inhibitionless spreading activation and limited-capacity attention. *Journal of Experimental Psychology: General,* **106,** 226–254.

Nelson, T. O., Fehling, M. R., & Moore-Glascock, J. (1979). The nature of semantic savings for items forgotten from long-term memory. *Journal of Experimental Psychology: General,* **108,** 225–250.

Norris, D. L. (1973). Barber's task-motivational theory and posthypnotic amnesia. *American Journal of Clinical Hypnosis,* **15,** 181–190.

O'Connell, D. N. (1966). Selective recall of hypnotic susceptibility items: Evidence for repression or enhancement? *International Journal of Clinical and Experimental Hypnosis,* **14,** 150–161.

Orne, M. T. (1979). On the simulating subject as a quasi-control group in hypnosis research: What, why, and how. In E. Fromm & R. E. Shor (Eds.), *Hypnosis: Developments in research and new perspectives.* New York: Aldine.

Patten, E. F. (1932). Does posthypnotic amnesia apply to practice effects? *Journal of General Psychology,* **7,** 196–201.

Pellegrino, J. W., & Huber, L. J. (1982). The analysis of organization and structure in free recall. In C. R. Puff (Ed.), *Handbook of research methods in memory and cognition.* New York: Academic Press.

Pettinati, H. M., & Evans, F. J. (1978). Posthypnotic amnesia: Evaluation of selective recall of successful experiences. *International Journal of Clinical and Experimental Hypnosis,* **26,** 317–329.

Pettinati, H. M., Evans, F. J., Orne, E. C., & Orne, M. T. (1981). Restricted use of success cues in retrieval during posthypnotic amnesia. *Journal of Abnormal Psychology,* **90,** 345–353.

Piaget, J., & Inhelder, B. (1973). *Memory and intelligence.* London: Routledge & Keegan Paul.

Quillian, M. R. (1968). Semantic memory. In M. L. Minsky (Ed.), *Semantic information processing.* Cambridge, MA: MIT Press.

Radtke, H. L., & Spanos, N. P. (1981). Temporal sequencing during posthypnotic amnesia: A methodological critique. *Journal of Abnormal Psychology,* **90,** 476–485.

Radtke-Bodorik, H. L., Planas, M., & Spanos, N. P. (1980). Suggested amnesia, verbal inhibition, and disorganized recall for a long word list. *Canadian Journal of Behavioral Science,* **12,** 87–97.

Radtke-Bodorik, H. L., Spanos, N. P., & Haddad, M. (1979). The effects of spoken versus written recall on suggested amnesia in hypnotic and task-motivated subjects. *American Journal of Clinical Hypnosis,* **22,** 8–16.

Reiff, R., & Scheerer, M. (1959). *Memory and hypnotic age regression: Developmental aspects of cognitive function explored through hypnosis.* New York: International Universities Press.

Reyher, J. (1967). Hypnosis in research on psychopathology. In J. E. Gordon (Ed.), *Handbook of clinical and experimental hypnosis.* New York: Macmillan.

Roenker, D. L., Thompson, C. P., & Brown, S. C. (1971). Comparison of measures for the estimation of clustering in free recall. *Psychological Bulletin,* **76,** 45–48.

Rozin, P. (1976). The psychobiological approach to human memory. In M. R. Rosenzweig & E. L. Bennett (Eds.), *Neural mechanisms of learning and memory.* Cambridge, MA: MIT Press.

Rummelhart, D. E., Lindsay, P. H., & Norman, D. A. (1972). A process model for long-term memory. In E. Tulving & W. Donaldson (Eds.), *Organization and memory.* New York: Academic Press.

Sarason, I. G., Smith, R. E., & Diener, E. (1975). Personality research: Components of variance attributable to the person and the situation. *Journal of Personality and Social Psychology,* **32,** 199–204.

Sarbin, T. R., & Coe, W. C. (1979). Hypnosis and psychopathology: Replacing old myths with fresh metaphors. *Journal of Abnormal Psychology,* **88,** 506–526.

Schachter, D. L., & Tulving, E. (1982). Amnesia and memory research. In L. S. Cermak (Ed.), *Human memory and amnesia.* Hillsdale, NJ: Erlbaum.

Schonfield, D., & Stones, M. J. (1979). Remembering and aging. In J. F. Kihlstrom & F. J. Evans (Eds.), *Functional disorders of memory.* Hillsdale, NJ: Erlbaum.

Schuyler, B. A., & Coe, W. C. (1981). A physiological investigation of volitional and nonvolitional experience during posthypnotic amnesia. *Journal of Personality and Social Psychology,* **40,** 1160–1169.

Schwartz, W. S. (1978). Time and context during hypnotic involvement. *International Journal of Clinical and Experimental Hypnosis,* **26,** 307–316.

Schwartz, W. S. (1980). Hypnosis and episodic memory. *International Journal of Clinical and Experimental Hypnosis,* **28,** 375–385.

Scott, H. D. (1930). Hypnosis and the conditioned reflex. *Journal of General Psychology,* **4,** 113–130.

Sheehan, P. W., & McConkey, K. M. (1982). *Hypnosis and experience: the exploration of phenomena and process.* Hillsdale, NJ: Erlbaum.

Shor, R. E. (1971). Expectancies of being influenced and hypnotic performance. *International Journal of Clinical and Experimental Hypnosis,* **19,** 154–166.

Shor, R. E., Orne, M. T., & O'Connell, D. N. (1966). Psychological correlates of plateau hypnotizability in a special volunteer sample, *Journal of Personality and Social Psychology,* **3,** 80–95.

Shor, R. E., Pistole, D. D., Easton, R. D., & Kihlstrom, J. F. (1984). Relation of predicted to actual hypnotic responsiveness, with special reference to posthypnotic amnesia. *International Journal of Clinical and Experimental Hypnosis,* **32,** 376–387.

Spanos, N. P., & Bodorik, H. L. (1977). Suggested amnesia and disorganized recall in hypnotic and task-motivated subjects. *Journal of Abnormal Psychology,* **86,** 295–305.

Spanos, N. P., & D'Eon, J. L. (1980). Hypnotic amnesia, disorganized recall, and disattention. *Journal of Abnormal Psychology,* **89,** 744–750.

Spanos, N. P., & Ham, M. L. (1973). Cognitive activity in response to hypnotic suggestion: Goal-directed fantasy and selective amnesia. *American Journal of Clinical Hypnosis,* **15,** 191–198.

Spanos, N. P., & Radtke, H. L. (1982). Hypnotic amnesia as strategic enactment: A cognitive social–psychological perspective. *Research Communications in Psychology, Psychiatry, and Behavior,* **7,** 215–231.

Spanos, N. P., Radtke, H. L., & Bertrand, L. D. (1984). Hypnotic amnesia as a strategic enactment: Breaching amnesia in highly susceptible subjects. *Journal of Personality and Social Psychology,* **47,** 1155–1169.

Spanos, N. P., Radtke, H. L., Bertrand, L. D., Addie, L. D., & Drummond, J. (1982a). Disorganized recall, hypnotic amnesia and subject faking: More disconfirmatory data. *Psychological Reports*, **50**, 383–389.

Spanos, N. P., Radtke, H. L., & Dubreuil, D. L. (1982b). Episodic and semantic memory in posthypnotic amnesia: A reevaluation. *Journal of Personality and Social Psychology*, **43**, 565–573.

Spanos, N. P., & Radtke-Bodorik, H. L. (1980). Integrating hypnotic phenomena with cognitive psychology: An illustration using suggested amnesia. *Bulletin of the British Society of Experimental and Clinical Hypnosis*, **3**, 4–7.

Spanos, N. P., Radtke-Bodorik, H. L., & Shabinsky, M. A. (1980a). Amnesia, subjective organization, and learning of a list of unrelated words in hypnotic and task-motivated subjects. *International Journal of Clinical and Experimental Hypnosis*, **28**, 126–139.

Spanos, N. P., Radtke-Bodorik, H. L., & Stam, H. J. (1980b). Disorganized recall during suggested amnesia: Fact not artifact. *Journal of Abnormal Psychology*, **89**, 1–19.

Spanos, N. P., Stam, H. J., D'Eon, J. L., Pawlak, A. E., & Radtke-Bodorik, H. L. (1980c). The effects of social psychological variables on hypnotic amnesia. *Journal of Personality and Social Psychology*, **39**, 737–750.

St. Jean, R., & Coe, W. C. (1981). Recall and recognition memory during posthypnotic amnesia: A failure to confirm the disrupted-search hypothesis and the memory disorganization hypothesis. *Journal of Abnormal Psychology*, **90**, 231–241.

Stern, J. A., Edmonston, W. E., Ulett, G. A., & Levitsky, A. (1963). Electrodermal measures in experimental amnesia. *Journal of Abnormal and Social Psychology*, **67**, 397–401.

Sternberg, R. J., & Tulving, E. (1977). The measurement of subjective organization in free recall. *Psychological Bulletin*, **84**, 539–556.

Stevenson, D. R., Stoyva, J., & Beach, H. D. (1962). Retroactive inhibition and hypnosis. *Bulletin of the Maritime Psychological Association*, **11**, 11–15.

Stewart, C. G., & Dunlap, W. P. (1976). Functional isolation of associations during suggested posthypnotic amnesia. *International Journal of Clinical and Experimental Hypnosis*, **24**, 426–434.

Strickler, C. B. (1929). A quantitative study of posthypnotic amnesia. *Journal of Abnormal and Social Psychology*, **24**, 108–119.

Takahashi, R. (1958). An experimental examination of the dissociation hypothesis in hypnosis. *Journal of Clinical and Experimental Hypnosis*, **6**, 139–151.

Thorne, D. E. (1969). Amnesia and hypnosis. *International Journal of Clinical and Experimental Hypnosis*, **17**, 225–241.

Thorne, D. E., & Hall, M. V. (1974). Hypnotic amnesia revisited. *International Journal of Clinical and Experimental Hypnosis*, **22**, 167–178.

Tkachyk, M. E., Spanos, N. P., & Bertrand, L. D. (1984). *Variables affecting subjective organization during posthypnotic amnesia*. Unpublished manuscript, Carleton University.

Tulving, E. (1962). Subjective organization in free recall of "unrelated" words. *Psychological Review*, **69**, 344–354.

Tulving, E. (1972). Episodic and semantic memory. In E. Tulving & W. Donaldson (Eds.), *Organization of memory*. New York: Academic Press.

Tulving, E. (1974). Cue-dependent forgetting. *American Scientist*, **62**, 74–82.

Tulving, E. (1976). Ecphoric processes in recall and recognition. In J. Brown (Ed.), *Recall and recognition*. New York: Wiley.

Tulving, E. (1983). *Elements of episodic memory*. London and New York: Oxford Univ. Press.

Tulving, E., & Pearlstone, Z. (1966). Availability and accessibility of information in memory for words. *Journal of Verbal Learning and Verbal Behavior*, **5**, 381–391.

Tulving, E., & Thomson, D. M. (1973). Encoding specificity and retrieval processes in episodic memory. *Psychological Review,* **80,** 352–373.

Watkins, M. J., & Tulving, E. (1975). Episodic memory: When recognition fails. *Journal of Experimental Psychology: General,* **104,** 5–29.

Wells, W. R. (1932). The extent and duration of experimentally induced amnesia. *Psychological Bulletin,* **28,** 690–691.

Wells, W. R. (1940). The extent and duration of posthypnotic amnesia. *Journal of Psychology,* **2,** 137–151.

Williamsen, J. A., Johnson, H. J., & Eriksen, C. W. (1965). Some characteristics of posthypnotic amnesia. *Journal of Abnormal Psychology,* **70,** 123–131.

Wilson, L., & Kihlstrom, J. F. (1985). Linguistic organization of recall during posthypnotic amnesia. Unpublished manuscript, University of Wisconsin.

Winograd, T. (1975). Computer memories: A metaphor for memory organization. In C. N. Cofer (Ed.), *The structure of human memory.* San Francisco: Freeman.

Young, J., & Cooper, L. M. (1972). Hypnotic recall amnesia as a function of manipulated expectancy. *Proceedings of the 80th Annual Convention of the American Psychological Association,* **7,** 857–858.

UNIT FORMATION IN PERCEPTION AND MEMORY

John Ceraso

RUTGERS UNIVERSITY
NEWARK, NEW JERSEY

I. Introduction

Repetition and reinforcement as the major factors in memory have gradually given way in current thinking to more internal processes. The hypotheses of encoding specificity (Tulving & Thomson, 1973) and levels of processing (Craik & Lockhart, 1972) stand as perhaps the main examples. This article also deals with the initial apprehension of a stimulus and its representation in memory. Specifically, I will focus on the assumption that the perceived unitariness of an array is causally related to the way in which that array is structured in memory.

By perceptual unity I refer to the fact that in our experience of the visual world we perceive objects, and we perceive these objects in relation to each other. For example, when seeing two people standing together we apprehend the individual person as a different sort of entity than the two taken together. For one thing, we are prepared to see one person next to someone new, but we are not prepared to see half of one person's face conjoined with half of someone else's face. Objects preserve themselves under a wide range of conditions, while relational structures are much more labile. Also, while we could count the set of two people as one thing or one event, it would only be under an unusual set of circumstances that we would do so. Two units in relation do not become one unit, and one object, such as a face, though containing many features, is still counted as one thing. It has even been suggested (Hogben, 1951) that the distinction between unitary and relational structures is reflected in the way in which numbers are used. Numbers applied within units are understood to be approximations. When we say a person is 5 feet tall we understand that the number could be refined by more precise measurement. Numbers applied to collections of units, however, are intended to be more exact. When we say that there are five people standing in line we would not admit that there could be 4.9 or 5.1 people involved.

In the conceptualization of learning as the formation of associative structures there is again a distinction made between units (ideas, objects, nonsense syllables, numbers, words, nodes, etc.) and the relations between them (associations, pathways, bonds, labeled relations, etc.). So, for example, in studying the learning of paired words one could study recall of the words themselves, or one could study recall for how the words were paired (Underwood & Schulz, 1960).

It is almost a truism to say that the units we find in memory reflect the units apprehended in our initial perception of the stimulus. After all, it would be quite strange if memory represented the world in a way other than the way in which it was initially perceived. What is perhaps more questionable is the assumption that there are two kinds of structures in memory. While most psychologists acknowledge the unitary/relational distinction, they are inclined to view one or the other as more fundamental. Holistic psychologists tend to regard relational structures as "weak" units, while associationists tend to regard units as "strong" associations. I am happy when I can divide things into two categories. so I will examine the idea that there is a basic difference in the way events are represented in memory, which derives from whether they are initially perceived as unitary structures or as relational structures. I want to first review a few early studies and then turn to the research my students and I have done on this problem.

II. Earlier Studies of Grouping and Unit Formation

Woodworth (1938) has described some very elegant studies done in 1894 and 1900 by Müller and Schumann and Müller and Pilzecker, respectively. In one procedure, for example, subjects were asked to read a list of nonsense syllables in rhythm. They were instructed to accent the odd-numbered items in the series, which resulted in a list of rhythmically grouped pairs (1 2, 3 4, 5 6, . . . , etc.). After the list had been learned subjects were tested for recall in a number of ways, all of which showed that within-group associations (i.e., 1 to 2 or 3 to 4) were easier to recall than between-group associations (i.e., 2 to 3 or 4 to 5). These studies also demonstrate an important point about the grouping effect in memory; that is, since the same items participate in within-group and between-group pairs, it is clear that the effect works on the pairing between items rather than on item learning itself. These grouping effects are very reliable and have been demonstrated in some widely cited, more recent studies by Johnson (1972) and Bower and Winsenz (1969), among others.

Another early study of grouping is the surprising "belongingness" study of Thorndike (1931), which was far in advance of its time, since it dealt with the effect of sentence structure on memory. Thorndike presented a series of 10 sentences 10 times each. Examples are, "Lincoln Blake and his uncle listened gladly," "Jackson Craig and his son struggled often," and so on. The subjects were then presented with various words or phrases and were asked to recall the subsequent word. So, for example, they might be asked to recall what came after "gladly" or what came after "Lincoln." Based on several experiments of this kind, Thorndike came to the conclusion that within-sentence associations (i.e., from the first to the second word of a sentence) were much easier to recall than between-sentence associations (i.e., from the last word of a sentence to the first word of the following sentence). In fact, Thorndike's data suggested that between-sentence associations were at chance level. This result meant to Thorndike that temporal contiguity per se does not lead to the formation of an association. He wrote, "Repetition of a connection in the sense of the mere sequence of two things in time has then very, very little power, perhaps none as a cause of learning. Belongingness is necessary." It should be pointed out that these studies used an incidental learning procedure. Subjects were told, "Listen to what I read just attentively enough so that you can say that you have heard it and understood it." His data showed that within-sentence sequences were formed without the intention to learn, but that without intention, between-sentence associations were not formed.

The experiments which first involved me with the within- versus between-unit distinction were the studies of Asch, Ceraso, and Heimer (1960) on the effects of perceptual organization on memory. A typical experiment in this series involved two properties which were joined together as the attributes of a unit or as the components of separate units (see Fig. 1). There were 10 pairs of properties in each series. In the unitary condition each pair had a unique shape and a unique line (the mode) which delineated the shape, while in the separate condition each shape was drawn in a continuous black line, and each mode described a straight line. Therefore, each card in the unitary condition displayed one unit with two properties, and in the separate condition those same two properties were distributed over two units. The tasks for the subjects can be described as the acquisition of a within-unit association in the first case and a between-unit

Condition	Pair Recall	Item Recall
 UNITARY	39	51
 SEPARATE	24	49

Fig. 1. Percentage pair recall and item recall for unitary and separate stimuli.

association in the second case. In most of these studies learning was under conditions of intentional learning.

Results for a typical experiment, in this case using free recall of pairs, are given in Fig. 1. Before discussing the within/between pairing difference, I would like to focus on the fact that the total number of items recalled (total forms and modes) is about the same in the two conditions. It seems to me that this finding indicates that within/between unit differences are not due to a difference in chunking (Miller, 1956). If they were, one should expect to find greater item recall in the unitary condition, since chunking is associated with greater item recall. The differences could, however, be attributed to an elegant hypothesis devised by Begg (1978) to account for recall differences produced by interactive as against separate imagery (see also Bower, 1970). Begg's hypothesis is that interactive imagery produces fewer but larger traces than does separate imagery; that is, the traces of the interactive condition are more likely to contain both members of the pair. The hypothesis accounts for the fact that the same number of items are recalled in the two imagery conditions and that superior pairing of items is found in interactive imagery. Can this hypothesis be applied to our within/between results? I do not believe that it can. Begg's hypothesis appeals to a difference in the probability of formation of a large trace under the two conditions, while I believe that within and between associations are different kinds of structures. At any rate, the most important finding in Fig. 1 is that there are more within pairs recalled than between pairs.

What does the Asch *et al.* (1960) study add to earlier findings such as those of Müller or Thorndike? One important difference, in my opinion, is that the earlier investigators used grouping to define within and between associations, while Asch used unitization. It is my feeling that two nonsense syllables rhythmically grouped make a looser and perhaps a different sort of combination than, for example, form and mode when they are grouped as units. In any case, the distinction between grouping and unitization is one which can be put to empirical test.

A second difference between the Asch study and the earlier studies has to do with the intention to learn. In the Müller *et al.* (Woodworth, 1938) experiments, for example, subjects are given a list which has both between-group and within-group associations to be learned. It could be the case that subjects follow a strategy of trying to learn within-group pairs, and only then attempt to learn between-group pairs. That strategy could account for the superiority of the within-group pairs. In the Asch *et al.* (1960) procedure, however, subjects are instructed to form within-unit associations in the unitary case and between-unit associations in the separate case. If the subjects could make the between-unit associations the first order of priority, then they should do as well with the separate as with the unitary stimuli. The results make it clear that when the intention to learn these two types of pairs is equated, the unitary association is still better learned. Another finding in the Asch *et al.* (1960) paper leads to a similar conclusion. Subjects were shown unitary or separate stimuli under conditions of incidental learning. The result of that procedure was that the recall superiority of the unitary to the separate condition was even greater than that found with intentional learning. Taken together, these results seem to argue against the idea that the superiority of within-unit to between-unit associations can be accounted for in terms of a deliberate strategy to process the former before the latter. If there is such a priority in processing, it would have to occur at a level beyond conscious control.

III. Further Studies of Grouping and Unit Formation in Memory

A. INTENTION AND THE LEARNING OF GROUPED AND
UNITARY ATTRIBUTES

As part of her dissertation, Patricia Heindel (1985), of the Institute for Cognitive Studies, has been investigating both the difference between grouping and unit formation and the role of intention in the learning of within- and between-unit structures.

One study dealt with the effect on memory of the three perceptual arrangements illustrated in Fig. 2. The grouped condition had two shapes in black outline and two color patches. Each shape was grouped by spatial proximity with a color patch, making two form/color groups. In previous studies, color and

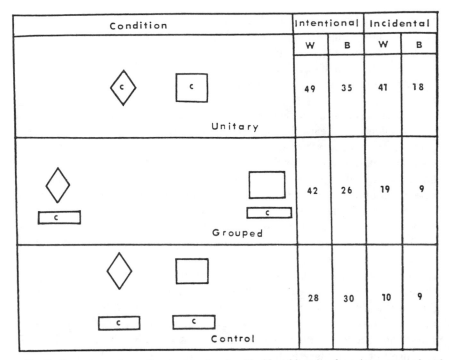

Condition	Intentional		Incidental	
	W	B	W	B
Unitary	49	35	41	18
Grouped	42	26	19	9
Control	28	30	10	9

Fig. 2. Percentage pair recall under intentional and incidental learning for unitary, grouped, and control conditions.

shape had been presented as separate entities, as in Fig. 4, where each group was presented on a separate card and was, therefore, temporally segregated from the rest of the series. We believe that stronger grouping is produced by the relative spatial proximity which creates the two form/color pairs, as in Fig. 2. The control condition had the same shapes and color patches as the grouped condition, but these were spaced equidistantly, so that no spatial grouping occurred. In the unitary condition the shapes and colors were conjoined to form two unitary colored shapes. The main question of this experiment was whether the association between forms and colors which are part of the same group is as strong as the association between forms and colors which are part of the same unit.

In each of the three conditions there were five cards, each with two forms and two colors, arranged as shown in Fig. 2. The cards were shown for 5 sec, and after all had been seen there was a 3-min distractor task followed by a recall test. The test required subjects to produce the contents of each card on a separate sheet of the recall booklet. When complete recall of a card was not possible, subjects were encouraged to recall whatever portion was available to them. Subjects drew the forms and wrote the names of the colors. The recall booklets were scored for the number of correct within (group or unit) pairings as well as for the number of correct between (group or unit) pairings. For the within pairings only form/color combinations are possible, while for the between pairings, form/color, color/color, and form/form pairings are possible. Since the control condition had neither groups nor units as defined for the other conditions, vertical pairs were designated as within associations, while horizontal pairs were designated as between associations.

The results of the experiment are given in Fig. 2. With regard to the within pairings the data show very little difference between the unitary and grouped conditions, and both are clearly superior to the control condition. I will not discuss the between-group pairings other than to note that within and between pairs are recalled at about the same level for the control group stimuli, the stimuli with no imposed grouping.

The results suggest that unitization and spatial grouping have equivalent effects on association in memory. One could regard unitization as another form of grouping and argue that the basic phenomenon is that whatever conditions serve to group items perceptually also result in their coherence in memory. Before accepting this conclusion, however, Heindel ran another experiment in which she examined the role of intention in the learning of unitary and grouped material. If the memory effects of grouping and unitization are both the aftermath of perceptual organization, then the same superiority of these conditions to the control condition should be found as with intentional learning.

The material and procedures of the incidental experiment were generally the same as those described for the intentional experiment. The main difference was in the way the purpose of the experiment was described to the subjects. They were told that the experimenter was interested in their ability to reproduce material immediately after it had been seen. Each card was shown for 5 sec (as in the previous experiment), after which it was removed and the subjects attempted to reproduce its contents. When all the cards had been seen, there was again a 3-min distractor task, after which subjects were given an unexpected recall task, which was otherwise identical to that given in the previous experiment.

The results of the experiment are shown in Fig. 2. Before discussing those results, I should mention that there was little difference between the conditions with respect to the immediate reproduction score. The groups do differ substantially, however, in the final recall test; recall of within-unit pairs is clearly better than recall of within-group pairs, and the within-group pairs are not significantly better than the control group within pairs. An interesting result is that there is little difference in the recall of the within-unit pairs under intentional and incidental procedures. It is the grouped and control conditions which are adversely affected by the switch to an incidental procedure. In interpreting this result, however, we must keep in mind that the incidental group subjects had the potential advantage of reproducing each figure immediately after it had been seen. Therefore, for the unitary group the benefit of intention could have been balanced by the extra recall test.

The results indicate that the effect of unitization on memory is different than is the effect of grouping. Grouping had a facilitative effect on memory pairing only under conditions of intentional learning. This finding is congruent with the hypothesis suggested earlier—grouping operates by establishing a priority in learning; that is, the subjects may learn groups first, and then turn their attention to the relations between groups. The facilitative effect of unitization, however, is not contingent on intentional learning, but also occurs with incidental learning. The finding can be taken to mean that one does not need a learning strategy to acquire unitized pairs; rather, unitization is a perceptual operation which leads directly to learning. In what follows, I will pursue that idea by exploring the relation between the initial perceptual processing of a display and the memory for that display.

B. RETRIEVAL AND UNITARY STIMULI

Before proceeding with that project, however, I want to discuss some other differences between unitary and separate stimuli. One hypothesis has been that they are recalled in a different way. For example, to quote Asch *et al.* (1960), "When part of a unitary stimulus is recognized the missing part will be invariably completed; in contrast, one of the members of a nonunitary pair may be recognized without producing completion of the other member." Horowitz and Prytulak (1969) resurrected Sir William Hamilton's term "redintegration" to express the idea that a whole can be reinstated by a part, in contrast to associative recall where part retrieves part. They presented evidence which showed that for well-integrated verbal phrases such as "chocolate cake" the most effective retrieval cue would be the most "important" or "salient" aspect of the unit (in this case, "cake"), that is, the aspect which most characterized the phrase as a whole. Bower and Glass (1976) have presented similar evidence for visual materials. For poorly integrated pairs, for example, "foz"-"cake," recall occurs in two steps: The nonsense syllable arouses its own memory representation, which in turn arouses the associated word "cake." In this instance we might expect the cue "foz" to lead to better retrieval than the cue "cake," since "cake" as a response item should be more available.

A further study on possible retrieval differences between unitary and separate organizations was done by Barbara Bernabe (1981) as part of her doctoral dissertation at the Institute for Cognitive Studies at Rutgers. The research was inspired by Höffding's (1891) analysis of associative recall, which had been subsequently elaborated by Köhler (1940), Duncker (1945), Rock (1962), and Martin (1967). Höffding argued that recall involved a retrieval operation prior to associative recall itself. To illustrate this point, let us take the case where one learns to associate a face with a name. Presumably, this involves the storage in memory of the face–name trace. Later, when one again sees the face, one would have to locate the representation of the face in memory in order to recall the name since, of course, the name is associated not with the face itself but with the memory of the face. Köhler added the idea that the process of locating the trace given the original, of which it is a copy, is the fundamental operation in recognition. One can therefore regard recognition as an instance of within-unit retrieval, where the cue is not simply a part of the unit but is the entire unit. For example, retrieving the memory of the face upon seeing the face—how else would one know that the face had been seen before? Within-unit recall means recalling the entire face when only a part is given as a cue, for example, the nose. Associative recall, however, usually means between-unit retrieval. For example, one retrieves the name, given the face as a cue.

Given the descriptive correspondence between recognition and within-unit recall on the one hand, and associative recall and between-unit recall on the other hand, Bernabe asked whether there was also a functional correspondence between them. For example, one of the striking differences between recognition and recall is that recognition is much less susceptible to interference than is recall. The first indication of this phenomenon was the 1914 work of Rosa Heine (see Woodworth, 1938), who showed that retroactive inhibition disappeared when recognition was used to test memory (see also Postman & Stark, 1969). If the resistance to interference shown in a recognition task is due to the fact that it involves within-unit retrieval, then resistance to interference should also characterize recall when it is within-unit recall.

In order to test this idea, Bernabe ran an experiment in which subjects learned either unitary or separate material in either long or short lists. Her prediction was that separate stimuli would be recalled more poorly in long than in short lists, while unitary stimuli would be recalled as well in long as in short lists. In other words, interference would be found only for the separate stimuli. The materials used in her experiment are illustrated in Fig. 3. Both unitary and separate items had three properties: form, color, and mode (i.e., type of line). For the unitary stimuli the shape was described by the colored mode, while for the separate stimulus each property was represented in a separate unit. The long lists consisted of 10 such three-property stimuli, while the short lists had only 5. To control for possible differences in ease of learning, only the first five items of the long list were included in the analysis. These same first five items were also the first tested for recall, so that output order for the long list would be equivalent to the short list output order. An additional control procedure was that the short list actually consisted of 10 items. The first five were the form/color/mode stimuli and the second five were three-digit numbers. The numbers were added to the short list so that, after the critical first five items had been seen and before recall, the short-list subjects would have a period of time and effort comparable to that

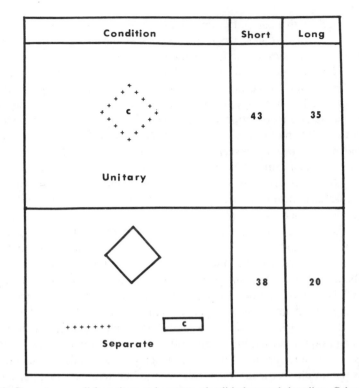

Condition	Short	Long
Unitary	43	35
Separate	38	20

Fig. 3. Percentage recall for unitary and separate stimuli in long and short lists. Colored figures are labeled c, others are drawn in black.

of the long-list subjects. At recall, subjects were given one of the properties from a card and were asked to recall the remaining properties. The recall cues for both groups were the isolated properties, as shown in Fig. 3, for the separate condition. Each property was used as a recall cue for one-third of the subjects, but the subjects did not know how they would be tested until the recall period began.

The results of the experiment are given in Fig. 3. The critical finding was that the recall difference between the unitary short- and long-list items was small and not significant, while the difference between short- and long-list separate items was substantially greater and significant. The results show that resistance to interference is not limited to recognition, but will also occur with recall when it is within-unit recall. It seems that interference is a characteristic of between-unit recall.

Unitization can also eliminate interference in transfer-type designs. Smith, Adams, and Shorr (1978) showed this in an experiment using verbal materials. Gilani and Ceraso (1982) presented a similar finding in a study which employed colored shapes in the two lists of a transfer study. The shapes were different in the two lists, but the colors were the same. This arrangement produced lists conforming to the A-B, A-C paradigm which consistently results in negative transfer. Two different groups learned these lists. One group learned the lists under conditions which encouraged the subjects to regard the shapes that had the same colors in the two lists as segments of a larger shape which they attempted to reconstitute. The second group of subjects regarded the shapes of the two lists as independent entities which shared the same colors, and they attempted to learn them as such. The result of the experiment was that negative transfer was only produced in the second condition. The conclusion drawn by the authors was that interference between temporally separated entities occurs only when they are treated as separate events. When these events are integrated they are learned and recalled without interference.

C. RETRIEVAL AND THE EMERGENT PROPERTIES OF UNITS

Units are often characterized by emergent properties, i.e., properties that arise from the relations between the components of the unit, and do not reside in those components themselves. Simple examples are symmetry in visual forms or tonicity in musical structures. These emergent properties were at the heart of the work of Gestalt psychology and have been of focal concern to contemporary investigators, most notably Garner (1981). Items to be recalled or recognized may combine with other items to form higher order units which have emergent properties. Crowder (1976) has summarized the evidence showing the consequence of this fact for recall. The idea is that whether an item is retrieved or not will be a function of how effective the retrieval cue is at getting at the higher order unit. It is this factor which may account for some of Tulving's encoding specificity effects, for example, those cases where recall is better than recognition. For example, it may be that "air" is a better cue for "airport" than is "port." In that case, if "airport" is the item learned, a higher recall score may be obtained when "air" is given as the cue for the recall of "port" than when "port" itself is given for recognition. Presumably, "port" will be difficult to recognize, since what has been stored is "airport," and recognition will not occur unless that higher order unit is retrieved. From this perspective, the phenomenon of encoding specificity is a modern version of the work of Gottschaldt (1938) on the recognition of embedded figures.

IV. Summary of Unitary Effects in Memory

At this point let us summarize the findings presented so far. First, it is clear that unitary organization facilitates coherence in memory as compared to sepa-

rate organization. Second, unitary organization, in contrast to separate organization or even grouping based on spatial proximity, seems to exert its effect on
memory under conditions of incidental learning. Third, unitary structures do not
show the same interference effects, either in transfer or in list length studies, as
do separate stimuli. Finally, unitary stimuli may have emergent properties and
cues which "resonate" with the emergent properties and are likely to be especially effective for retrieval.

It seems clear that the perceptual arrangement of material has powerful effects
on memory for that material. Does that mean that the structure of memory is a
direct result of perceptual processing? The studies which follow will attempt to
directly address that question.

V.   Memory for Unitary Stimuli Using Letters

The question of the relation between memory and perceptual processing arose
in an insistent way for us from a series of studies in which we compared memory
for unitary and separate stimuli, and where letters instead of geometric shapes
were used. Letters are interesting because of their inherent duality. They are
physical shapes and would be apprehended as such by one who did not know the
language. To one who is familiar with the language, however, the letter may be
apprehended as a sound or perhaps as a more abstract linguistic concept, but in
either case it would not be regarded as simply a shape. Does the difference
between geometric shapes and letter shapes result in a difference in the way in
which they are remembered? If memory is determined by the perceptual analysis
of the stimulus, one might not think so, since one would assume that on the
perceptual level a letter is analyzed as is any other shape.

The first study in this series was done by Robert Velk (1982) as part of his
dissertation research. In that study, Velk had two main conditions. In the let-
ter/color condition letters and colors were combined as unitary or as separate
stimuli. In the form/color condition the forms and colors were also combined as
units or as separate stimuli. Figure 4 gives an example of the four types of stimuli
involved. A different group of subjects was tested under each condition. Each
subject saw eight pairs, each pair for 5 sec. After presentation and a short period
when subjects worked on a distracting task, they were asked to recall as many
form/color or letter/color combinations as possible.

Figure 4 gives the data for this experiment. The results seem quite clear: When
colors and shapes were the stimuli the usual superiority of unitary to separate
pairs was obtained; when colors and letters were shown, however, there was no
significant difference between unitary and separate conditions. Furthermore, the
difference between form/color and letter/color stimuli is largely accounted for by

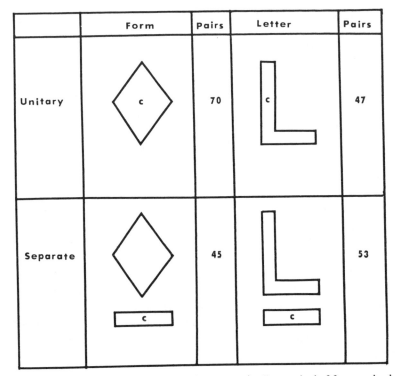

	Form	Pairs	Letter	Pairs
Unitary	c	70	c	47
Separate	c	45	c	53

Fig. 4. Percentage pair recall for unitary and separate stimuli comprised of forms and colors or letters and colors. Colored figures are labeled c, others are drawn in black.

the poor performance of the letter/color unit as compared to the form/color unit. The letter/color unit seems to act like a separate array.

Velk, in a replication study, again combined letters with colors in unitary or separate configurations. The stimuli were drawn as in Fig. 7. Fifteen subjects in each condition attempted to learn the pairs under the procedures described above. Correct pairing was 36% for the unitary condition, 53% for the separate condition, and the difference between the two was significant. Again, when letters are used in place of shapes, unitary pairs are not better recalled than separate pairs; in fact, in this study they are more poorly recalled.

I believe that the failure to achieve unitization effects with letter/color stimuli has to do with the fact that letters have meaning, but another possibility should be considered. It could be that the effect in some way stems from an asymmetry between letters and colors; for example, one might argue that subjects give priority to letters and ignore colors. It is not clear how this asymmetry would produce the particular results we obtained; that is, why would the substitution of letters for shapes adversely affect only the unitary condition and not the separate condition? Nevertheless, since this concern has often been expressed, Velk designed an experiment where only letters were used so that we would still have letter stimuli, but without the asymmetry of letter/color.

Examples of the letter/letter stimuli can be seen in Fig. 8. Eight pairs of these letter/letter stimuli were presented to 18 subjects in each condition. The learning and recall procedures were the same as those for the previous experiments. Note that the unitary stimulus is of the type which has been employed in perceptual studies of the local/global issue (Navon, 1977). This same type of stimulus, with shapes instead of letters, was studied extensively by Asch et al. (1960). In those form/mode experiments the superiority in memory of the unitary stimuli was well established.

The result of the experiment was that recall for unitary and separate pairs was identical at 52% for each condition. It does not appear that the failure to achieve a unitary effect is due to letter–color asymmetry, since that failure also occurs when only letters are used.

These experiments show that two arrays may look very much alike, for example, the letter/color and the form/color stimuli or the letter/letter and the form/mode stimuli, and yet show very different effects in memory. The results raise two important and related questions which are implicit in research on perceptual organization and memory, but which become salient in the light of the results just presented.

VI. The Perception of Units

The first question concerns the definition of a perceptual unit. Up to this point we have defined units pretty much by intuition in much the same way as one defines what is or what is not a grammatical sentence. A colored shape, a form/mode configuration—these we have called units. It seems clear that the grounds on which we designated those stimuli as units would also apply to the letter/color or the letter/letter conditions, yet these stimuli do not behave as units in memory. The first question is then "Is our intuitive judgment an adequate method for defining perceptual units, or is there some sense in which these presumably unitary letter arrays are not really units?"

The second question is "Is the structure of the memory trace established by processes involved in the initial perceptual apprehension of the stimulus, or rather, is it established by postperceptual processes?" Studies such as the one by Asch et al. (1960) show a relation between perceptual unitariness and coherence in memory. Not only are these effects substantial and very reliable, but it also seems quite sensible that memory and perception should be related in this way. Just as the levels of processing hypothesis (Craik & Lockhart, 1972) asserts that differences in memory for verbal materials can be related to differences in the way in which these materials are initially apprehended, so one can imagine that differences in the way visual materials are remembered are related to differences in their initial perception. If, however, one could be sure that the letter/color array, for example, is indeed a perceptual unit, then one would be forced to conclude that memory is not determined by the initial perceptual process and that the determinants of memory are postperceptual.

It is clear that the answer to these questions requires an objective, theoretically satisfying definition of a perceptual unit. The next studies to be reported were directed to the development of objective measures of perceptual unitization which could be related to the measures used in memory experiments. Most of the stimuli used in these perceptual studies were stimuli which had been used in previous memory investigations, so that we were studying the perception of stimuli for which we already had memory information.

I started with the assumption that the perceiver responds differently to perceptual units than to separate arrays and that the task is one of measuring these different behaviors; so the attempt was to develop measures of unitariness, just as Garner (1974) has done for good figures. The initial hypothesis, which came from the work I had done with Gilani (1982) and which was described earlier, was that a unit is the result of an integrative process, where the components of the unit are analyzed together so as to yield their joint meaning. As an analogy, one can think of the processes involved in the comprehension of a sentence where the words of the sentence have to be taken together so that the meaning of the sentence as a whole can be derived. Implicit in this idea is that the apprehender of the sentence (or the perceptual unit) first decides which words or attributes are to be analyzed together, that is, which properties are to be included in the unit, and only then begins the joint analysis. It might be possible to derive a meaningful idea by taking the words from one sentence and combining them with the words from another sentence, but that derived meaning would not be veridical, that is, it would not be faithful to the meaning intended in either sentence. It would be, to use Treisman's term, "an illusory conjunction." Treisman and Gelade (1980) have proposed that the perception of a unitary figure, such as a colored shape, requires special processes which accompany, or are perhaps identical to, focal attention. Pursuing the analogy with sentence comprehension, I assumed that the essence of those processes is that they are integrative in that properties are dealt with concurrently and the end product, for example, a perceived colored shape, can only be derived by dealing with shape and color jointly, just as the meaning of a sentence can only be derived from the words taken together. A separate form/color array (e.g., Fig. 4) consists of two units, with the form an attribute of the unit above and color an attribute of the unit below. If each unit is processed independently of the other, then I assume that they are processed successively, that is, first form and then color, or vice versa. Temporally separated processing would be one way to ensure the integrity of each unit of the separate condition. In short, the properties of perceptual units are assumed to be processed concurrently, while the properties of separate arrays are assumed to be processed successively.

A. Form/Color Units

The next series of studies to be reported were designed by George Laskaris as part of his dissertation research. In the first experiment, he used unitary and separate form/color stimuli, as in Fig. 5. The unitary form was described by a colored contour line. The separate form was drawn in black contour line and had an included color patch in its center. Asch (1969) has shown that form with included color acts as a separate stimulus in memory. Each subject saw a series of six cards in a three-channel tachistoscope. The shapes were drawn so as to fit within the foveal region, as is true of all the perceptual studies reported in this article. A fixation point was provided, located in the center of the target. When the subject was ready, the target card was presented and followed immediately at offset by a masking card. The mask contained black and colored lines and black and colored irregular shapes. The same mask was used for both unitary and separate stimuli and completely covered the area where the target stimuli had been. The subject's task was to report what he or she saw on each card as the card was presented. There was no constraint on the time allowed for each report. There were three conditions of report for both unitary and separate stimuli, and throughout the experiment each subject reported in only one of these ways: (1) Report both—the subject's task was to report both the form and color which appeared on the target card; (2) report form alone—the subject's task was to report only the form from each card; and (3) report color alone—the subject's task was to report only the color from each card. The set of cards was shown three times: The first time through the series each card was exposed for 25 msec, the second and third presentations were at 35 and 45 msec, respectively.

If the properties of the unitary stimulus are concurrently processed, we expect subjects to report as many forms and colors in the first condition (report both) as in the form alone or color alone conditions, since in either condition subjects would be processing form and color at the same time. If the properties of the separate stimulus are successively processed, then only form or color can be dealt with at any moment, and so we would expect superior performance in the alone as compared to the both conditions.

The relevant data are presented in Fig. 5. It is clear that form and color attributes of the unitary stimulus are reported as well in the both condition as they are in the alone condition, while, as predicted for the separate stimuli, color and form reports are poorer in the both condition than they are in the alone conditions. The data confirm our hypotheses regarding the processing of unitary and separate displays.

Report	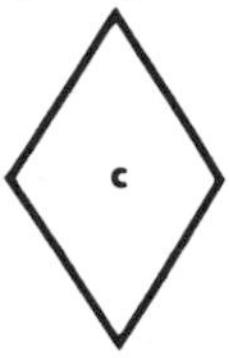 Unitary			Separate 		
Exposure in msecs	25	35	45	25	35	45
Form Alone	20	50	80	42	70	85
Form Both	23	61	77	25	48	73
Color Alone	25	58	83	27	53	83
Color Both	23	48	87	17	28	50

Fig. 5. Percentage correct report of the form and color of unitary and separate stimuli under conditions of reporting one property alone or reporting both properties. Colored figures are labeled c, others are drawn in black.

An important aspect of this result is that it shows that unitariness need not necessarily be measured along a continuous dimension as it usually is. For example, in the Asch *et al.* (1960) study, unitary stimuli are *better* paired than the separate stimuli. Horowitz and Prytulak (1969) define unitary pairs as those where, given one member of a pair, the other is recalled at least 60% of the time. Both of these measures could be interpreted to mean that unitariness is a continuous dimension, and a stimulus is more or less unitary. I would rather pursue the idea that the distinction between unitary and separate stimuli is a process distinction referring to whether properties are processed concurrently or not. If processing is concurrent, then the ratio of both to alone takes the unique value of 1.00, as in Laskaris's data.

B. FIGURE AND GROUND AS SEPARATE ENTITIES

There is an argument one could raise with respect to our analysis. The question is whether the results we obtained were due to the unitariness of the stimuli or whether they could be attributed to a difference in spatial proximity between the properties of unitary and separate stimuli. In the separate condition form and color are given at different positions of the visual field, while in the unitary condition form and color are spatially coincident. Perhaps it was the difference in degree of spatial proximity which determined the results we obtained and not the degree of unitariness. In the experiment to be reported, we attempted to tease apart these factors. We used two arrays which were structurally quite similar; that is, for both the unitary and separate conditions there was a solid figure on a background of a different color (Fig. 6). In the unitary condition the target color and form were part of the figure and the background was white, while in the separate condition the target color was the background and the form was white. The critical fact is that in both cases the form is delineated by the border between white and colored regions, so that as far as spatial proximity is concerned, form and color are equally proximal in unitary and in separate conditions. The well-known facts of figure–ground organization, however, are that the figure and its attributes constitute one perceptual unit, and the background and its attributes constitute another unit. With these stimuli we believe that unitary and separate conditions are equated for the factor of spatial proximity, but still differ in unitariness. A difference between the perceptual processing of unitary and separate stimuli under these conditions would implicate unit formation as the respon-

		Exposure in msecs					
		25		35		45	
Condition	Report	F	C	F	C	F	C
Unitary	First	42	46	72	68	88	82
	Second	48	36	74	58	90	82
Separate	First	36	24	60	52	76	72
	Second	18	28	36	36	58	58

Fig. 6. Percentage correct report of the form and color of unitary and separate stimuli under conditions of reporting one or the other property first. Colored regions are labeled c, white regions are labeled w.

sible factor. I should mention that Asch (1969) has shown that there is greater coherence in memory between a figure and its color than there is between a figure and its background color.

In the figure–ground experiment we used a different procedure than the previously described both–alone method. There were only two conditions of report: subjects were instructed either to (1) attend to and report color first and form second, or (2) attend to and report form first and color second. If processing is concurrent, then there should be no difference between first reported properties and second reported properties. Successive processing should result in superior performance for the property reported first.

The data for the four conditions of the experiment are given in Fig. 6. One can see that for the unitary condition there is little difference between first report and second report, and this is true for both form and color. For the separate condition, however, there is a large and significant difference between first and second report. The data are quite similar to those obtained in the previous form/color experiment, and suggest that it is the dimension of unitariness and not spatial proximity which produces differences in the processing of the two types of stimuli.

C. LETTER/COLOR UNITS

Here I want to return to a consideration of the letter/color stimuli discussed earlier. The reader will recall that when those stimuli were used, we did not find the usual superiority of pairing in memory for the unitary material over separate material. In light of the findings concerning the perceptual analysis of unitary and separate figures, it would be of great interest to ask about the perceptual analysis of unitary letter/color arrays. Based on the physical features of these arrays there is little to distinguish them from form/color arrays, so one might expect that they would be perceived in the same way; that is, concurrent processing should also characterize the unitary letter/color array. However, since we know that the letter/color units and the form/color units differ in the way they are remembered, the finding that these two kinds of stimuli did not differ in the way they were perceived would suggest that those memory differences were the result of processes occurring postperceptually. If, on the other hand, we were to find that unitary letter/color arrays are not processed concurrently, then it would suggest that memory processes are related to, or identical with, the operations responsible for the initial apprehension of the stimulus; that is, the finding would mean that letter/color units are neither remembered nor perceived as units. A striking aspect of the finding, however, is that it would demonstrate that the knowledge that a shape represents a letter plays a role in the initial perceptual analysis of that letter shape. To use the phrase of Kahneman and Henik (1981), it would mean that "the perceptual system is literate."

The experiments to investigate this issue were conducted by Robert Velk. Velk ran both a memory experiment (the results of which were reported earlier) and a perceptual experiment with unitary and separate letter/color stimuli. There were eight stimulus cards in each condition of the memory experiment, and five of these same cards were used in the perception experiment. The method used was the one described earlier, where subjects are asked to report both letter and color, letter alone, or color alone. Exposure durations of 25, 35, and 45 msec were used, and each exposure was followed by a 50-msec mask. Twenty subjects were in each of the six conditions of the experiment.

I want to remind the reader that the main question is whether the letter/color unit shows the same concurrent processing of properties which characterized the perception of the physically similar form/color unit.

Figure 7 gives the results of the experiment. The most important finding here is that performance in the alone condition is superior to performance in the both condition for the unitary as well as the separate stimuli. In the unitary condition the superiority is evident on the first two trials for letter, but is consistently

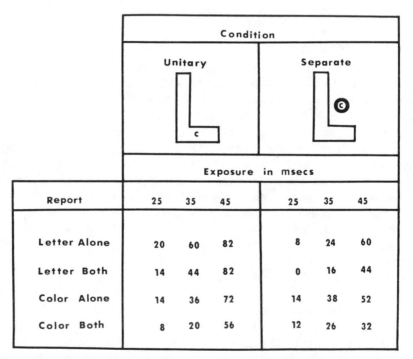

Condition					
Unitary			**Separate**		
Exposure in msecs					
Report	25	35	45	25	35	45
Letter Alone	20	60	82	8	24	60
Letter Both	14	44	82	0	16	44
Color Alone	14	36	72	14	38	52
Color Both	8	20	56	12	26	32

Fig. 7. Percentage correct report of the letter and color of unitary and separate stimuli under conditions of reporting one property alone or of reporting both properties. Colored figures are labeled c, others are drawn in black.

present for color. We believe that there is a preference for letter processing so that in the unitary both condition, even though subjects are instructed to report letter and color, letter processing receives priority; that is, letter preference would attenuate the alone/both difference for letter, and accentuate the difference for color. At any rate, the data are quite different from the data we obtained for the physically similar form/color stimuli and indicate that unitary letter/color stimuli are processed successively.

At this point, I want to put forth several ideas in an attempt to account for the data we have obtained on the relation between perception and memory. It seems to me that the critical fact is that unitary letter/color arrays are perceived differently and are remembered differently than are unitary form/color arrays. Physically the arrays are quite similar, but they differ in meaning, and it is reasonable to assume that the memory and perceptual differences arise from the difference in meaning. By a difference in meaning I refer to the idea that a form/color unit is coded as a physical object which has the attributes of form and color, while the letter shape is coded as a linguistic entity, that is, either as the abstract concept of a particular letter or as the phonemic representation of that letter. It is clear, however, that there is no schema which incorporates these linguistic entities with color. A subject could integrate a linguistic entity with a color, but it would have to be done metaphorically, through the use of a mnemonic. For example, in a pilot study we had the letter "J" paired with the color "blue." A few subjects were able to integrate the two through the use of the mnemonic, "bluejay." Ordinarily, however, letter and color are processed separately, with color abstracted from the stimulus as an entity independent of the linguistically encoded letter. Form and color can, of course, be integrated as attributes of the same unit, namely, as the attributes of a particular physical object. I want to emphasize the idea that our conscious experience of a visual event occurs only *after* that event has been interpreted; that is, rather than postulating that one first sees the letter and then looks up its meaning as a postperceptual event, the letter/color experiment seems to mean that the determination of the meaning of the visual letter is part of the process of perceiving it. Of course, one must postulate that the physical structure of the letter is determined before its meaning can be known, but it would seem that the analysis of the physical structure of the stimulus, including the analysis of unitariness, occurs preconsciously.

In any event, the letter/color experiment again shows agreement between our perceptual measure and memory; in this case we find correspondence in that the nominal "unitary" stimulus is neither perceived nor remembered as a unit.

D. FORM/MODE UNITS

The next experiment was motivated by findings which suggested a possible discrepancy between perception and memory. The form/mode unitary stimulus was the configuration most widely used in the Asch *et al.* (1960) study, and it reliably behaved as a unit in memory. More recently, psychologists (Navon, 1977; Kinchla and Wolfe, 1979; Martin, 1979) have been performing perceptual analyses of that configuration, calling it a global/local stimulus. The main issue in those studies has been whether the global property takes precedence in perceptual processing over the local property. The evidence suggests that under some conditions the global property is processed first, and under other conditions the local property is processed first (Pomerantz, 1981), but in either case the processing seems to be successive. If successive processing does characterize this array, then isn't that fact incompatible with the fact that the form/mode configuration is recalled as a unit? In other words, in form/mode we might have a case where, by the operational definitions we have been using, perception is of separate properties while memory is of unified properties. In thinking about this question, it occurred to us that experiments on the global/local issue have typically used letters for both form and mode, while in our form/mode experiments only geometric shapes were used. Given the result of our previous experiment where we found that letter/color arrays were processed differently than were form/color arrays, it is possible that, while letter/letter arrays are processed successively, form/mode arrays may be processed concurrently. If that were true, then of course the mode of processing of these arrays would agree with the way in which they are remembered, since letter/letter unitary stimuli are not remembered as units and form/mode unitary stimuli are remembered as units.

George Laskaris designed the critical experiment to see if the form/mode stimulus was processed as a unit or not. Unitary and separate versions of the form/mode stimuli were constructed. The unitary stimulus was drawn just as the unitary stimulus of Fig. 1. The separate stimulus had the mode drawn through its center, as in the separate stimulus of Fig. 8. Five cards were constructed for each condition and the procedure used was the order of report procedure described earlier, where, if the property reported second is perceived as well as the property reported first, then we infer that concurrent processing has occurred.

The results of the experiment are given in Table I. The results show clearly that properties which are to be attended to and reported first are better perceived than properties reported second, and this is true for both unitary and separate stimuli. We interpret the results to mean that the attributes of the form/mode stimulus are processed successively, and it is not the case that the results obtained by Navon and other were due to the use of letters in their displays.

An interesting side feature of the results is that global precedence, that is, the superiority of form over mode, is rather small in the unitary condition, but is quite pronounced in the separate condition, where the concept of global–local does not make any sense. In the present case, global precedence could simply mean that it is easier to perceive the larger stimulus. There is, however, a

TABLE I

REPORT (%) OF FORM AND MODE WHEN ATTENDED TO FIRST OR SECOND:
UNITARY AND SEPARATE CONDITIONS

Condition	Exposure (msec)	Form		Mode	
		First	Second	First	Second
Unitary	25	46	24	38	26
	35	66	44	54	42
	45	74	56	68	56
Separate	25	78	66	38	24
	35	92	76	48	38
	45	96	84	72	46

confound in the present experiment with respect to this question, since we did not counterbalance the properties used as form and mode.

It is also interesting to compare the results obtained with the unitary form/mode display of the present experiment to those we obtained with the unitary form/color display. Both displays have two properties which are spatially coextensive: in one a larger form described by the spatial distribution of a smaller form and in the other a form described by the spatial distribution of a colored line. Despite the similarity, they seem to be processed quite differently: form/color concurrently and form/mode successively. There is obviously something about the quality of the array where one form is nested within another which precludes concurrent processing.

VII. Hypothesis: Two Levels of Unit Formation

I believe that the form/mode results require a change in the way we have conceptualized the process of perceptual unitization and the way in which it affects recall. The altered scheme I will put forth is centered on the idea that the concept of a unit has application at two levels of analysis. I propose a first level where the physical array is scanned, and, based upon the rules of unit formation, the potential objects which comprise the visual field are selected before they are perceived so that their attributes are available for concurrent analysis. The rules of unit formation would certainly include some of Wertheimer's grouping principles, e.g., good continuation and closure. Many investigators of perception have proposed a preperceptual grouping level. Köhler (1947), for example, has suggested that following cataract surgery a patient would recognize the "thingness" of objects without being able to identify them. This is an idea similar to the "open file" concept of Kahneman and Henik (1981). Neisser (1967) also has argued that a preattentive grouping operation is necessary for veridical perception. Imagine, for example, that there are two circles in the visual field. If perceptual analysis merely involved the analysis of the features of the circles, then one would end up with an enumeration or listing of those features without knowing the number of circles involved. To know that, Neisser argued, one needs a process which separates the features into two sets, each set corresponding to one of the circles. Furthermore, it would not seem wise to depend on a preliminary listing of features followed by a process of sorting the features into units, since the same features may be put together in many ways. In fact, Treisman and Gelade (1980) and Prinzmetal (1981) have presented evidence which shows that under conditions of limited attention one may actually experience illusory conjunctions, i.e., one may see features, such as red and triangle, as part of the same object when these properties were in reality features of different objects. The processes involved in these illusions are not apparent, but they make clear the necessity of grouping operations for veridical perception. The fact that perceptual factors place constraints on attention has been demonstrated by other investigators such as Banks and Prinzmetal (1976), Garner (1974), Kahneman and Henik (1981), Pomerantz (1981), Treisman (1982), among many others, although one difference from most of those studies is that they deal with grouping while the present study has to do with unit formation. At any rate, I propose an early level of unit formation, at which point the properties that are likely candidates to be part of the same object are put together so that the assemblage can be analyzed concurrently for purposes of identification.

Of the arrays I have discussed so far, I believe that the unitary form/color and the unitary letter/color arrays are treated as units at the first level of analysis. This assumption is based on the fact that as physical configurations these two arrays are quite similar, and the first level is concerned with the physical structure of the stimuli. The arrays differ both in the way they are perceived and the way in which they are remembered, and I would attribute those differences to differences in the way they are treated at the second level of analysis. The separate conditions used throughout as control conditions are, of course, treated as separate stimuli at the first level of analysis, and I believe the unitary form/ mode display is also treated as a separate stimulus at this level; that is, I believe that form and mode are not concurrently available for subsequent analysis and therefore must be identified successively. That would account for the fact that perceptually the array behaves as a separate stimulus. The fact that it behaves as a unit in memory I would attribute to the way it is analyzed at the second level.

If properties are aggregated at the first level in preparation for identification of the object, it is at the second level that the process of identification occurs. Again, many psychologists have proposed a level of analysis concerned with the meaning of the stimulus. For example, Köhler (1947), following his chapter on sensory organization (level 1), has a chapter on organized entities, which deals with the stimulus as perceived (level 2). Similarly, Neisser (1967) attributes perceptual experience to analysis by synthesis, a process which occurs after the grouping operations. It is at the second level that the properties are concurrently analyzed to yield their joint meaning. The limiting factor, however, is that not every collection of properties can be integrated to make a sensible percept. Form and color can be integrated and they result in a shape with a colored contour, as in Fig. 5, or a colored shape, as in Fig. 6. The letter/color array is one in which integration is not possible at the second level of analysis because of the way in which the properties have been coded; that is, there is no higher order structure which combines a letter as a linguistic entity with a color; therefore, the perceiver must construct two independent percepts—one which represents the letter as a linguistic entity and one which represents the color. The form/mode case, I believe, is one in which the properties are aggregated separately at the first level but are integrated at the second level. The idea that properties which are at one point treated successively can be subsequently integrated is one which we used in an earlier study already discussed in this article (Gilani & Ceraso, 1982).

To briefly summarize the analysis, I am postulating that unitary processing occurs at two different levels. Unitization at the first level is based upon the physical structure of the stimulus, while unitization at the second is dependent on whether the properties can be integrated to form a higher order structure.

Coherence of the properties of an array in memory, however, is solely a function of whether that array is treated as a unit at the second level of analysis. Since, by definition, the second level of analysis results in the perceived stimulus, that is, the one the subject is conscious of, this assumption means that memory is tied to our conscious experience.

A.   AN INTERFERENCE MEASURE OF UNITIZATION

While the hypothesis of two levels of unitization enables us to account for the data obtained, it is to some extent ad hoc, and further evidence is needed to support it. The most useful evidence would be in the form of measures which would indicate how a given stimulus is processed at each level of analysis. At the present time we do not have such measures. However, we have developed a measure of interference which may help in investigating these proposed levels. The interference measure attempts to get at the amount of interference generated by the necessity of analyzing properties in succession. If a subject is asked to report both property X and property Y and if processing is successive, then, with limited time there should be some loss in reporting these properties compared to when they are reported alone. For the case of the alone/both procedure, the measure would be

$$\frac{[(X + Y \text{ alone}) - (X + Y \text{ both})]}{(X + Y \text{ alone})}$$

For the first/second procedure, one would simply substitute first for alone and second for both. The reader will recognize this measure as basically the same as that used in studies of retroactive and proactive inhibition.

Before proceeding with the presentation of the interference data for the perception studies I have described up to this point, I want to describe another experiment so that I can include those results in the analysis of interference.

B.   LETTER/LETTER UNITS

The experiment is one in which Robert Velt studied the perception of the letter/letter display. An illustration of the unitary and separate stimuli used in the experiment is given in Fig. 8. The reader will recall that earlier I reported a

Condition	Report	Exposure in msecs			
		25	35	45	55
Unitary	Large First	16	43	66	77
	Small First	28	48	79	90
	Large Second	12	36	55	72
	Small Second	6	19	41	64
Separate	Large First	70	93	97	100
	Small First	11	25	46	73
	Large Second	50	73	88	95
	Small Second	3	18	46	71

Fig. 8. Percentage correct report of the large and small letters of unitary and separate stimuli under conditions of reporting one or the other letter first.

memory study conducted by Velk where he used the letter/letter stimuli. Five of the eight stimuli which had been used in the memory research were used in the perception experiment. There are two reasons why we should expect the letter/letter array to be processed successively: first, it consists of letters; second, it is structurally similar to the form/mode array. These factors have led to successive processing in our previous studies. The procedure was the first/second report procedure where some subjects were asked to report the large letter first and small second, while others reported in the order from small to large. The results of the experiment are shown in Fig. 8. It is clear that for unitary stimuli first reports are better than second reports, although that effect is greater for small letters than it is for large letters. At any rate, the results show, as expected, that the letters of the unitary stimulus are processed successively. The interference measures for this study have been included in Table II.

C. An Analysis of the Interference Measure

Table II gives the interference measure calculated for the unitary and separate conditions of the five perceptual experiments we have reported. The idea behind the use of the interference measure is that the successive processing associated with separate stimuli at either level should produce interference, while the concurrent processing associated with unitary stimuli at either level should eliminate it. A stimulus that is unitary at both levels should therefore show zero interference, and that result is obtained for the unitary form/color and figure/ground stimuli—the stimuli which I have argued are unitary at both levels.

The hypothesis is that the unitary letter/color stimulus is unitary at the first level but separate at the second level. I assume that the separate conditions are

TABLE II

INTERFERENCE (%) FOR THE UNITARY AND SEPARATE
CONDITIONS OF FIVE PERCEPTUAL EXPERIMENTS[a]

Conditions	Unitary			Separate		
	25	35	45	25	35	45
Form/color	-2	-1	0	39	38	25
Figure/ground	5	6	-1	23	36	22
Letter/color	35	33	10	45	32	32
Form/mode	40	28	21	22	19	23
Letter/letter	57	39	34	36	22	7

[a]Exposure in milliseconds.

separate at both levels. That combination should produce a degree of interference for the unitary array which is greater than zero, but which is less than the interference generated in the letter/color separate condition. These expectations are confirmed in Table II.

I believe that the unitary form/mode stimulus is separate at the first level and then integrated at the second level. Therefore, I expected to see interference results like those of the unitary letter/color stimulus, which is also unitary at one level and separate at the other. In fact, Table II shows that the unitary form/mode stimulus suffers *more* interference than its separate counterpart. However, if the form and mode of the unitary stimulus are not organized at the first level so as to be available for concurrent processing at the second level, then that outcome may be reasonable. The perceiver would first have to turn his or her attention to one of the properties, let us say the form, then the process of generating the form percept would occur. Following form perception, attention would be switched to the mode, and the mode percept would be generated and integrated with the form. The point to realize is that it would take at least two sets of operations at the second level to achieve the final percept. In that regard the unitary stimulus resembles the separate stimulus, which also requires two sets of operations at the second level to generate the separate form and mode. These proposed mechanisms would account for the fact that the unitary stimulus suffers no less interference than the separate stimulus. A further complication, however, arises in that the unitary stimulus actually exhibits more interference than the separate stimulus. It is possible that that result means that switching attention from form to mode, or vice versa (zooming, as some have called it), is actually more difficult than switching attention between the different spatial locations of the separate array.

Finally, we turn to the letter/letter conditions. In this case, both the nominal unitary stimulus and the separate stimulus are assumed to be separate at both levels of analysis. Therefore, it is to be expected that the unitary stimulus should show no less interference than its separate counterpart. Again, the results of Table II go beyond what we might expect in that the unitary stimulus shows more interference than does the separate stimulus. As in the case of the unitary form/mode condition, the result could mean that zooming is a more difficult operation than is switching attention between two spatial locations.

Table II provides evidence that arrays which are physically similar also resemble each other with respect to the interference measure. The unitary form/color and letter/color arrays both show less interference than their separate counterparts even though they act differently in memory. The unitary form/mode and letter/letter stimuli show more interference than their separate counterparts, and they also act differently in memory. These similarities with respect to interference are consistent with the notion of a first level of grouping based upon physical structure.

Evidence for a second level of perceptual unitization is seen mainly in the difference between the unitary form/color stimulus and the unitary letter/color stimulus. These arrays resemble each other physically, but there is interference for letter/color and none for form/color. The interference for the unitary letter/color is attributed to separate processing for that stimulus at the second level. That interference is also consistent with the fact that letter/color does not act as a unit in memory. I have already given reasons why evidence for second-level unitization is not seen for the unitary form/mode array even though it acts as a unit in memory.

VIII.   Summary

The question that has interested me most in these studies was whether one could justify making a strong distinction between unitary and associative structures. A review of the evidence shows that there are important differences between them. Unitary structures are learned more quickly, unitization exerts its effect on memory even under conditions of incidental learning, units are less susceptible to interference, and finally, units have emergent properties through which they can be retrieved from memory.

The finding that units, in contrast to relational structures, persevere in memory even when experienced under conditions of incidental learning seems to indicate that the unitary trace is a direct product of perceptual experience. A result which appeared to challenge that conclusion was that colored letters, which resemble colored shapes physically, do not act as units in memory, while colored shapes do.

One could maintain the hypothesis of a direct relation between perception and memory, however, if it could be shown that a colored letter is not perceived as a unit. Accordingly, our work then aimed at the development of a more objective measure of perceived unitariness than we had used previously. This measure was based on the notion that a psychological unit was the result of a process of integration of lower level properties. Since integration entails dealing with properties concurrently, we proposed that the properties of a unit would be processed concurrently and the properties of separate units would be processed successively.

The perceptual measure based on the notion of concurrent processing showed that a colored form was perceived as a unit while a colored letter was not. This result made consistent the relation between perception and memory in that perceptually unitary arrays were recalled as units while perceptually separate arrays were not recalled as units. A further implication of these findings is that the concept of a unit is more directly tied to psychological processing that it is to the physical description of the stimulus. Of course, there must be rules and principles the perceptual system uses in deciding which arrays are to be integrated as units and which are to be segregated as separate entitities.

A further complication developed in our work, however, when we discovered that the unitary form/mode array, which consistently acts as a unit in memory, was not unitary by the perceptual measure we had been using. Given this finding, the status of the research was that arrays which are processed concurrently act as units in memory, but there is at least one array (form/mode) whose properties are not processed concurrently but which nevertheless acts as a unit in memory.

To deal with the form/mode case and also to account for the fact that the nominally unitary letter/color stimulus does not act as a unit in either perception or memory, two levels of perceptual unitization were proposed. The first level deals with the physical structure of the stimulus. At that level sets of stimuli which are potential components of the same object are segregated so that those stimuli can be integrated at the second level. At the second level the properties are integrated and the percept is constructed provided there is a scheme available which makes that possible. Objects such as colored shapes or form/mode percepts are constructions within the repertoire of the perceiver. In the case of other unitary stimuli, for example, letter/color, no meaningful construction can be achieved, and the observer perceives and remembers the letter and color as separate entitities.

Finally, to return to the distinction between units and associations, I assume that the kind of percept achieved at the second level is reflected in memory so that unitary percepts result in unitary memory traces and separately organized percepts result in separate memory traces. It follows from this analysis that the association between the properties of a unit is developed at the time the unit is perceived, while the association between separately organized entities occurs postperceptually and is the result of mnemonic elaboration.

REFERENCES

Asch, S. E. (1969). A reformulation of the problem of associations. *American Psychologist,* **24** (2).

Asch, S. E., Ceraso, J., & Heimer, W. (1960). Perceptual conditions of association. *Psychological Monographs,* **74** (3).

Banks, W., & Prinzmetal, W. (1976). Configuration effects in visual information processing. *Perception and Psychophysics,* **19,** 361–367.

Begg, I. (1978). Imagery and organization in memory: Instructional effects. *Memory and Cognition,* **6,** 174–183.

Bernabe, B. A. (1981). *List Length Effects as a Function of Stimulus Organization.* Unpublished doctoral dissertation, Rutgers University.

Bower, G. H. (1970). Imagery as a relational organizer in associative learning. *Journal of Verbal Learning and Verbal Behavior,* **9,** 529–533.

Bower, G. H., & Glass, A. (1976). Structural units and the power of picture fragments. *Journal of Experimental Psychology: Human Learning and Memory,* **2,** 456–466.

Bower, G. H., & Winsenz, D. (1969). Group structure, coding, and memory for digit series. *Journal of Experimental Psychology Monographs,* **80,** (2), 1–17.

Craik, F. I. M., & Lockhart, R. S. (1972). Levels of processing: A framework for memory research. *Journal of Verbal Learning and Verbal Behavior,* **11,** 671–684.

Crowder, R. G. (1976). *Principles of learning and memory.* Hillsdale, NJ: Erlbaum.

Duncker, K. (1945). On problem solving. *Psychological Monographs,* **58,** (270).

Garner, W. R. (1974). *The processing of information and structure.* Hillsdale, NJ: Erlbaum.

Garner, W. R. (1981). The analysis of unanalyzed percepts. In M. Kubovy & J. R. Pomerantz (Eds.), *Perceptual organization.* Hillsdale, NJ: Erlbaum.

Gilani, Z., & Ceraso, J. (1982). Transfer and temporal organization. *Journal of Verbal Learning and Verbal Behavior,* **21,** 437–450.

Gottschaldt, K. (1938). Gestalt factors and repetition. In W. D. Ellis (Ed.), *A Source book of Gestalt psychology.* London: Routledge & Keegan Paul.

Heindel, P. (1985). *Unitization, Grouping, and Intention in Memory.* Paper presented at the meeting of the Eastern Psychological Association, Boston, Massachusetts.

Höffding, H. (1891). *Outline of psychology.* New York: Macmillan.

Hogben, L. (1951). *Mathematics for the millions.* New York: Norton.

Horowitz, L. M., & Prytulak, L. S. (1969). Redintegrative memory. *Psychological Review,* **76,** 519–553.

Johnson, N. F. (1972). Organization and the concept of a memory code. In A. Melton & E. Martin (Eds.), *Coding processes in human memory.* New York: Holt.

Kahneman, D., & Henik, A. (1981). Perceptual organization and attention. In M. Kubovy & J. Pomerantz (Eds.), *Perceptual organization.* Hillsdale, NJ: Erlbaum.

Kinchla, R. A., & Wolfe, J. M. (1979). The order of visual processing: "Top-down," "bottom-up," or "middle-out." *Perception and Psychophysics,* **25,** 225–231.

Köhler, W. (1940). *Dynamics in psychology.* New York: Liveright.

Köhler, W. (1947). *Gestalt psychology.* New York: Liveright.

Laskaris, G. [The perception of unitary and separate stimuli]. Unpublished data.

Martin, E. (1967). Relations between stimulus recognition and paired associate learning. *Journal of Experimental Psychology,* **74,** 500–505.

Martin, M. (1979). Local and global processing: The role of sparsity. *Memory and Cognition,* **7,** 476–484.

Miller, G. A. (1956). The magical number seven plus or minus two: Some limits on our capacity for processing information. *Psychological Review,* **63,** 81–97.

Müeller, G. E., & Schumann, F. (1894). Experimentelle beiträge zur untersuchung des gedachtnisses. *Zeitschrift für Psychologie,* **6,** 81–190.

Müeller, G. E., & Pilzecker, A. (1900). Experimentelle beiträge zur lehre vom gedächtniss. *Zeitschrift für Psychologie,* **1,** 1–288.

Navon, D. (1977). Forest before trees: The precedence of global features in visual perception. *Cognitive Psychology,* **9,** 353–383.

Neisser, U. (1967). *Cognitive psychology.* New York: Appleton.

Pomerantz, J. R. (1981). Perceptual organization in information processing. In M. Kubovy & J. R. Pomerantz (Eds.), *Perceptual organization.* Hillsdale, NJ: Erlbaum.

Postman, L., & Stark, K. (1969). The role of response availability in transfer and interference. *Journal of Experimental Psychology,* **79,** 168–177.

Prinzmetal, W. (1981). Principles of feature integration in visual perception. *Perception and Psychophysics,* **30,** 330–340.

Rock, I. (1962). A neglected aspect of the problem of recall: The Höffding function. In J. Scher (Ed.), *Theories of the mind.* New York: Free Press.

Smith, E. E., Adams, N., & Schorr, D. (1978). Fact retrieval and the paradox of interference. *Cognitive Psychology,* **10,** 438–464.

Thorndike, E. L. (1931). *Human learning.* New York: Century.

Treisman, A. (1982). Perceptual grouping and attention in visual search for features and for objects. *Journal of Experimental Psychology: Human Perception and Performance,* **8,** 194–214.

Treisman, A., & Gelade, G. (1980). A feature-integrative theory of attention. *Cognitive Psychology,* **12,** 97–136.

Tulving, E., & Thomson, D. M. (1973). Encoding specificity and retrieval processes in episodic memory. *Psychological Review,* **80,** 352–373.

Underwood, B. J., & Schulz, R. W. (1960). *Meaningfulness and verbal learning.* Chicago: Lippincott.

Velk, R. J. (1982). *Perceptual and Conceptual Determinants of Accuracy in the Reporting and Recall of Symbolic and Nonsymbolic Stimuli.* Unpublished doctoral dissertation, Rutgers University.

Wertheimer, M. (1923). Untersuchungen zur Lehre von der Gestalt. *Psychologische Forschung,* **4,** 301–350.

Woodworth, R. S. (1938). *Experimental psychology.* New York: Holt.

HOW INFANTS FORM CATEGORIES

Barbara A. Younger

UNIVERSITY OF ALABAMA AT BIRMINGHAM
BIRMINGHAM, ALABAMA

Leslie B. Cohen

UNIVERSITY OF TEXAS AT AUSTIN
AUSTIN, TEXAS

I. Introduction

Imagine for a moment an organism faced with a novel environment without the benefit of concepts and categories. Imagine the tasks of perceiving, remembering, thinking, and talking without the ability to organize incoming information into existing category structures. Each percept, object, or event would be perceived as unique. Each would have to be remembered as different from all others, a different label applied to each object and event. The sheer diversity would prove overwhelming.

Categorization is an essential perceptual–cognitive activity enabling the reduction of the enormous diversity in the world to a manageable level. Through our categories, we relate new experiences to old; the unfamiliar becomes familiar. Each object and event in the world is perceived, remembered, and talked about, not as unique, but rather as a member of a category or concept that we already know something about. Category structures give meaning to incoming stimulation. Faced with a new situation, we are not confronted with a bewildering array of novel entities, but rather with lamps, clocks, tables, and chairs.

In addition, concepts and categories enable the observer to predict nonperceptible properties of objects on the basis of those properties that are perceived. For example, we can predict the functions of novel objects through inferences de-

211

rived through experience with other instances of the same category. Having identified an object as a chair on the basis of its perceptual properties, we can infer with some degree of certainty that we can sit on the object and it will support our weight. Similarly, having identified an object as a peach on the basis of perceptual properties, we can infer that the object is edible and, upon biting into its center, we will find its inedible pit.

As we have seen, categories and concepts play a crucial role in our everyday lives. They influence the very manner in which we perceive our environment, the way we remember, think, and talk about objects and events in the world. But what about the infant? Does the infant exist in a chaotic world without concepts and categories, i.e., a world in which each object and event is perceived as unique? When does the infant or young child come to partition his or her world into categories of like objects? And how does the infant or young child do it?

It is the thesis of this article that young infants, infants under 1 year of age, can indeed form a variety of different categories. Furthermore, we intend to show, through an examination of our research as well as research by others, some ways in which this categorization takes place. By assuming that each category item can be defined in terms of the set of features or attributes comprising that item, we have been able to explore such general theoretical questions as the ability to form a prototype, the sensitivity to the correlations among attributes, and the mechanism for segregating items into discrete categories. While our theoretical ideas have come primarily from the adult categorization literature, we do not mean to imply that infants at any age perform like miniature adults. On the contrary, we also will attempt to show that this ability to categorize develops dramatically during the first year.

Our plan for the article is to begin with an explanation of what we mean by categorization and then to move on to demonstrations that such categorization does indeed exist in infants. From there we shall examine how infants acquire and represent category information and how they are able to separate items into different categories. Finally, we shall explore how this ability to acquire categories develops during the first year and what precursors of these abilities may exist in infants who are not yet able to form actual categories.

II. Definition of Categorization

While it must be obvious to all that in order to deal effectively with the world around us we must organize objects and events into categories and concepts, it is much less obvious how we should define "category" or "concept." To some individuals, the terms appear to have been used equivalently (Bourne, 1966). To others a category is a subset of a more general concept (Anglin, 1977). We do not intend to enter into a semantic argument over the intrinsic meanings of these terms. Enough ambiguity exists in the literature already and that ambiguity is compounded when one includes the literature on infants. Nevertheless, the terms concept and category have been used a number of different ways in the infant literature and it would be helpful, for descriptive purposes at least, to distinguish among some of those different uses.

In the infant literature, the term concept most frequently appears in reference to infants' mastery of object permanence tasks. Usually a single object is presented and then hidden or moved. The infant's ability to retrieve the object despite its disappearance or transformation is taken as evidence for the existence of an object concept. In these situations, the infant is said to have a concept in the sense that his or her knowledge about the object transends the immediately available perceptual information. It includes some understanding about the existence of the object, its properties and uses, even when the object cannot be seen. For our purposes, it is sufficient to note that the notion of concept refers to the infant's extended knowledge about a unitary object.

In the present article we shall be examining those instances in which the infant's organization of information about objects (or pictures) goes beyond what is available from a single example, instances in which the infant must somehow organize multiple exemplars into discrete classes or categories. We shall define a category as a recognized equivalence among a group of stimuli, objects, or events that are discriminably different, where "group" refers to two or more exemplars.

This distinction between single and multiple exemplars may be critical for trying to assess how the infant organizes what he or she is seeing. As we shall demonstrate in the research presented below, infants often respond one way when presented with a single stimulus or object and a different way when presented with several stimuli or objects from the same general class. In fact, one of the most intriguing questions in the area of infant perception and cognition is whether our understanding of multiple examples coincides with the infant's understanding. Consider, for example, the case in which the infant first views the nipple end of a bottle and then turns it around to view the other end. In both instances we would assume we were viewing two sides of the same object, but what about the infant? For the infant is this a problem of object identity and permanence or a problem of equivalence and categorization? Thus, for the infant the dividing line between the concept of a single object and a category of different objects may not be well defined, or at least it may not be defined as an adult defines it. One goal of our research on the processes underlying infant categorization is to make progress toward answering that difficult developmental question.

Just as an infant may respond to a single object as if it were an entire category, so too may he or she respond to an entire category as if all its members were identical. In such cases the infant does not discriminate among the category exemplars. Assume for the moment that you were shown several different balls, each differing from every other in size, color, and texture. You probably would have no trouble distinguishing among them and also no trouble treating them equivalently by grouping them into a common category. But suppose the infant attended only to the spherical shape. Color, texture, or other distinguishing features were not noticed. For that infant the various balls would also be treated as the same, not because they were members of the same category, but because they were perceived as identical, as if they were the same object. In this case we would not want to claim the infant had formed the category "ball," but only that the balls were not discriminable from one another. It is for this reason that our definition of a category also includes the restriction that the stimuli or objects comprising the category should be discriminably different.

III. Demonstrations of Infant Categorization

Reduced to its basics, a typical categorization experiment involves two phases, training subjects with a set of exemplars from a given category followed by a test with a mixture of new exemplars from the same category and nonexemplars. The degree to which subjects correctly sort these test items into category members versus nonmembers is taken as evidence for categorization.

Research on infant categorization follows a similar procedure. Of course, one cannot ask an infant to sort pictures into two or more piles or to verbally indicate which items belong to a given category. However, one can "instruct" infants indirectly to respond on the basis of category membership. The procedure most often employed makes use of the infant's habituation or preference for novelty. In a standard habituation task the goal is to determine whether infants can discriminate between two or more stimuli. For example, in a visual habituation experiment, infants will be repeatedly shown a single visual pattern until it becomes familiar. They will then be shown either a familiar pattern or a novel one. Decreasing visual attention during the habituation phase followed by recovery of attention only to the novel pattern in the test is taken as evidence for recognition of the familiar pattern and for discrimination of the novel pattern from the familiar one.

With minor modifications this habituation procedure has been used to investigate infant categorization. Instead of habituating infants to a single, unchanging stimulus, they have been habituated to multiple stimuli that are all members of the same category. The test then involves presentation of a novel category member versus a nonmember. Recovery only to the nonmember provides some evidence for categorization. If it also can be shown that infants are able to discriminate the novel category member from those presented during habituation, then it can be assumed that the lack of recovery to the novel member in the multiple habituation task resulted from its being an example of the category and not from any failure to discriminate it from the habituation items.

A representative example of a category demonstration study was reported by Cohen and Caputo (1978). Using the habituation procedure, they tested 28-week-old infants on the category of stuffed animals. Color photographs of a wide variety of different stuffed animals and other common objects were used as stimuli. Infants were randomly assigned to one of three habituation conditions and all received a total of 10 habituation trials. Infants in the "same" condition were shown a photograph of the same stuffed animal on each habituation trial. Different infants saw different photographs, but any one infant saw the same stuffed animal on all 10 trials. In contrast, those infants in the "changing" condition were shown a different stuffed animal on each trial, and those in the "objects" condition received a totally unrelated object on each trial. The results of this habituation phase of the experiment are shown in Fig. 1. As one can see, infants in both the same and changing conditions clearly habituated while those in the objects condition displayed little, if any habituation.

In the test phase of the experiment, all infants were shown a novel stuffed animal (SA) and a rattle (R). The assumption was that if the infants had habituated to the category of "stuffed animals," their looking time in the test should remain low to the novel stuffed animal, since it was a member of the category, but it should increase (or recover) to a noncategory member, that is, the rattle. The test results are given in Fig. 2. For comparison purposes, responding to the last habituation trial (H) is shown along with responding to SA and R.

The most interesting comparison is between the changing and same groups. Habituation in the changing condition generalized to the novel stuffed animal,

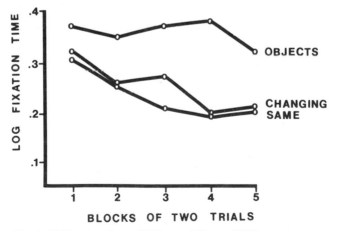

Fig. 1. Habituation phase of Cohen and Caputo (1978) experiment.

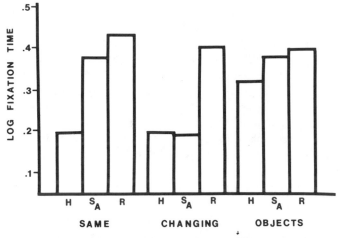

Fig. 2. Test phase of Cohen and Caputo (1978) experiment.

but not to the rattle. If the infants had seen several examples of stuffed animals during habituation, they responded to the novel stuffed animal in the test as if it were old rather than new. They behaved as one would expect if they had formed the category of stuffed animals. These infants had not simply been fatigued by the multiple habituation procedure, since their response recovered to the rattle, and infants in the objects group who saw as many different photographs as those in the changing group didn't even habituate.

In contrast, infants in the same condition recovered to both the novel stuffed animal and to the rattle. Their behavior indicated both that repeated exposure to a single exemplar is not sufficient to produce category-like responding and that infants at this age can discriminate between the set of habituation stuffed animals and the test stuffed animal. Taken as a whole, the results from this study have shown that by 28 weeks of age, infants are capable of responding equivalently to habituation and test items comprising a category even though they could discriminate between those habituation and test items. Thus, at least according to the definition of categorization given earlier, we would conclude that by 28 weeks of age infants had acquired the ability to categorize.

While the stuffed animal experiment just described may be considered representative, it certainly is not the only demonstration of infant categorization. Numerous other studies have also appeared in the literature within the past 10 to 12 years. The categories examined in these studies have ranged from simple figures (McGurk, 1972) to faces (Cohen & Strauss, 1979; Cornell, 1974; Fagan, 1976) and from food to furniture (Ross, 1977). In general, the experiments have shown that by 6 to 7 months of age, but probably not earlier, infants are able to organize a set of discrete objects into a perceptual category (e.g., Cohen &

Strauss, 1979; Cornell, 1974; McGurk, 1972); that by 12 or 18 months of age they can respond in terms of superordinate as well as basic level categories (McDonough, 1981; Ross, 1977); and that handicapped infants such as those with Down's syndrome or cerebral palsy have more difficulty forming categories than do normal infants of the same age (McDonough & Cohen, 1982; McDonough, 1984).

What these experiments fail to do is provide any information about the processes underlying category acquisition. Most of the categories were of common objects or faces, and it is unknown whether the infants formed the category during the experimental session or whether the experiments were only tapping preexisting category knowledge. Even if the category was acquired during the course of the experiment, it is not known what features, combinations of features, or relationships among features were abstracted to represent the category. In short, while these demonstration studies may have provided a necessary first step toward our understanding of infant categorization, the logical next step is to conduct process-oriented studies that require the infant to learn a new category and that manipulate the characteristics of individual category members.

The remainder of this article will be devoted to these process studies. Over the past several years we have been investigating issues related to infant prototype formation, the segregation of items into different categories, and the use of independent attributes versus the correlation among attributes in category acquisition. In the next section, we shall begin with a discussion of the formation of prototypes.

IV. Processing of Category Information by 10-Month-Old Infants

The first studies to look beyond simple demonstrations of the infant's categorization abilities and to investigate basic perceptual processes involved in infant categorization borrowed heavily from the adult categorization literature (e.g., Goldman & Homa, 1977; Neumann, 1974, 1977; Posner & Keele, 1968, 1970; Rosch, Mervis, Gray, Johnson, & Boyes-Braem, 1976). Rosch and her associates (Rosch et al., 1976) suggested that most natural categories do not have defining or criterial attributes, that is, attributes that are singly necessary or jointly sufficient to define category membership. Instead, they argued that category members are related by overlapping sets of attributes (i.e., attributes shared by most but not all members of a category). Those instances having the most features in common with other category members are the best, or prototypical, members of the category. The infant ''process'' studies are based in large part on a number of adult studies looking at how category-level information is abstracted from such ''ill-defined'' categories.

In a pioneering study, Strauss (1979) sought to determine whether 10-month-old infants abstracted features from category instances and integrated them into some type of schema or representation of the category. Based on the sizable literature on adult categorization processes, Strauss selected two principles by which different dimensional values contained in the various exemplars of a category can be psychologically integrated and stored as a central representation of the category.

The two principles involved the averaging of experienced featural values and the tallying of frequencies of occurrence of featural values across category instances. According to a feature averaging model, typical members of a category contain the average values of attributes varying within the category whenever those attributes vary on a metric for which an average can be calculated (e.g., size). According to a feature frequency model, typical members possess the most common or most frequently experienced values.

Studies in the adult literature have reported examples of both principles in adults' integration of features into a central category representation. As one might expect, adults abstract a modal representation of values varying along discontinuous dimensions (e.g., Hirshfield, Bart, & Hirshfield, 1975); however, values varying along continuous dimensions are sometimes "counted" to yield a modal prototype and at other times averaged to yield a mean prototype (Goldman & Homa, 1977; Neumann, 1977). In general, it has been found that adults count and form modal representations when featural values are easily discriminated, whereas they tend to average the values when the discrimination is more difficult.

Strauss (1979) used a visual preference paradigm in which two stimuli were presented side by side in front of the infant. During familiarization, the same face was presented on both sides. During the test, two different stimuli (e.g., a familiar and a novel stimulus) were shown. The observer simply recorded the amount of time the infant spent looking at each stimulus.

Ten-month-old infants were familiarized with one of two sets of 14 schematic male faces. As in the adult studies, artificial categories were used in order to control precisely the frequency and range of values along a limited number of dimensions. The face categories varied along four continuous facial dimensions—the length of the face, separation of the eyes, width of the nose, and the length of the nose. Five discrete values were selected along each of the four dimensions. The two sets of faces differed in the discriminability of the experienced dimensional values (i.e., values 1, 3, and 5 were used in the highly discriminable or wide condition, shown in Table I; values 2, 3, and 4 in the less discriminable or narrow condition). Strauss confirmed in a preliminary study that adults counted values in the wide condition (i.e., formed a modal prototype) and averaged values in the narrow condition (i.e., formed a mean prototype).

TABLE I

FAMILIARIZATION AND TEST STIMULI
USED IN THE STRAUSS (1979) EXPERIMENT

Facial dimension (trials)	Familiarization stimuli			
	Eye separation	Nose width	Nose length	Head length
1	1	1	5	5
2	5	3	1	5
3	1	1	5	3
4	1	3	1	5
5	5	5	3	1
6	5	1	1	5
7	1	5	1	5
8	3	5	1	1
9	5	5	1	1
10	3	1	5	5
11	1	5	5	1
12	1	5	3	1
13	5	1	5	1
14	5	1	5	3

Test pairs

1 1 1 1   1 1 1 1
or   vs. 3 3 3 3   Novel vs. 3 3 3 3   Novel vs.   or
5 5 5 5   5 5 5 5

The dimensional values were carefully selected such that, in each set of faces, the most frequently experienced (i.e., modal) values differed from the average values. In both the wide and narrow conditions, the extreme values (i.e., values 1 and 5 or 2 and 4) on each of the four dimensions were experienced six times each across the 14 category exemplars and the middle, or average, value (i.e., value 3) was experienced twice per dimension. Following familiarization with one set of 14 faces, infants received three recognition memory test pairs designed to determine whether a prototypical representation had been formed, and if so, whether it contained the average of the experienced values or the most frequently occurring values.

In the first test pair, a new face containing modal values (e.g., Stimulus 1111 or 5555) was paired with a new face containing all average values (i.e., Stimulus 3333). It was expected that if infants abstracted an average representation, the average prototype would be recognized as more familiar than the modal prototype, and consequently, a greater proportion of infants' looking would be directed toward the more novel, modal stimulus. In contrast, if infants abstracted a modal representation, a greater proportion of their looking would be directed toward the average prototype. In the second and third test pairs, the modal and average faces were each paired with an ''out-of-category'' face (i.e., a completely novel face containing qualitatively different features).

The pattern of results suggested that 10-month-old infants were capable of abstracting a prototypical representation of category members and that this prototype consisted of the average of the experienced dimensional values. In both conditions, infants spent a greater proportion of their total looking time (56.9%) viewing the modal prototype when it was paired with the average prototype ($p < .002$). In addition, infants directed a greater proportion of their looking (58.9%) toward the totally novel face when it was paired with the average prototype ($p < .001$). However, they exhibited no differential looking in the final contrast between the modal prototype and the totally novel face ($p = .13$).

Another finding that has emerged consistently in the adult literature concerns memory for prototypic versus nonprototypic category members. In both immediate and delayed recognition tests, previously unexperienced prototypes are recognized better than other novel nonprototypic exemplars (Goldman & Homa, 1977; Posner & Keele, 1968, 1970). In addition, after a delay, recognition of the prototype typically exceeds recognition of previously experienced exemplars (Homa, Cross, Cornell, Goldman, & Schwartz, 1973; Posner & Keele, 1970; Strange, Kenney, Kessel, & Jenkins, 1970).

In a second study, Strauss (1981) examined 10-month-old infants' memory for prototypic and nonprototypic category members. Infants were familiarized with eight exemplars of a face category similar to that employed in the 1979 study. The eight familiarization faces varied along the same four dimensions, although in this study, the faces were constructed using values 1, 2, 4, and 5. As can be seen in Table II, each value occurred twice on each dimension. The average value, 3, was never seen during familiarization. Following familiarization, infants received three test pairs: the average prototype (3333) paired with a novel, nonprototypic category member; the average prototype with an old familiarization stimulus (either the first or last familiarization item); and a novel, nonprototypic category member with an old familiarization face.

The results demonstrated that for 10-month-old infants memory for the average prototype exceeded memory for both previously experienced and novel exemplars. Infants showed a novelty preference for old exemplars (in either the initial or final serial position) when contrasted with the average prototype ($p < .02$), indicating that the prototype was recognized as more familiar. Remarkably, the average prototype appeared more familiar than the face they had seen on the previous trial. In addition, the average prototype was recognized as more familiar than the novel, nonprototypic member of the category ($p < .01$). Reli-

TABLE II

FAMILIARIZATION AND TEST STIMULI
USED IN THE STRAUSS (1981) EXPERIMENT[a]

Facial dimension		Familiarization stimuli			
		A	B	C	D
Face	1	1	1	5	5
	2	1	5	1	5
	3	2	4	2	4
	4	2	2	4	4
	5	4	4	2	2
	6	4	2	4	2
	7	5	5	1	1
	8	5	1	5	1
		Test pairs			
P vs. N		P vs. SP1 or 8		N vs. SP1 or 8	

[a]Under familiarization the letters A, B, C, and D refer to the dimensions of eye separation, nose width, nose length, and head length, respectively. In the test, P refers to the average prototype (3333), N refers to a totally novel face, and SP1 and 8 refer to serial position 1 and 8.

able differences were not obtained in fixation of previously experienced versus novel, nonprototypic category members.

These infant findings are consistent in many respects with findings typically taken as evidence of prototype formation in the adult literature. The evidence suggests that through experience with exemplars of a category, 10-month-old infants, like adults, can abstract a schema or prototype which is representative of the category as a whole. These studies also indicated that, like adults, infants recognize a prototype they have never seen before better than other novel category members and better than previously experienced exemplars.

One of the only discrepancies between the infant and adult findings is that Strauss (1981) found no evidence of infants' memory for individual instances, at least not under the conditions of brief (i.e., 5 sec) stimulus presentations that he used. Not only did infants recognize the average prototype as more familiar than previously experienced exemplars, but they showed no evidence of recognition of old over new exemplars. This would suggest that infants were abstracting an average representation during familiarization (i.e., during category acquisition). However, it should be noted that these findings did not hold up in a delayed test. In a test administered 15 sec after the end of familiarization, no reliable preferences were obtained (Strauss, 1981).

The emphasis of prototype research, both in the adult and infant literature, is on the principles involved in the abstraction of a central representation of category instances and on the classification of new items into existing categories. An equally important issue is how stimuli or objects become divided or segregated into different categories initially. In order to apply such principles as feature averaging or feature frequency in the formation of a prototype, it is necessary to have some means of determining which stimuli or objects are to be included as members of a given category and which are to be excluded.

In the typical prototype study, the experimental situation is structured in such a way that category segregation is not a problem for the subject. For example, in one kind of categorization task commonly used with adults, there is an initial period in which subjects must learn to categorize exemplars into two or more experimenter-defined categories. Subjects are given feedback and learning proceeds to some criterion. The subjects are then tested for generalization of these acquired categories to previously experienced exemplars, new exemplars, and the prototypic patterns. In another procedure commonly used with adults, only one category is used. Subjects are first presented a number of exemplars from a single category to remember. This phase is typically followed by a recognition memory test with the three types of test patterns.

The infant procedures strongly resemble this latter approach. In the typical demonstration study, infants are presented with a series of items, all members of the same adult category, then tested with a novel category member and a nonmember. In the prototype studies, infants first received a set of category instances derived from a single prototype and were then tested with the prototype and other novel or familiar instances of the category.

The standard experimental context differs in important ways from the natural environment encountered by the young category learner. In the typical laboratory situation, categories are explicitly taught (e.g., through feedback in a categorization task), or subjects are presented only with exemplars which they learn belong to a single experimenter-defined category. In the natural environment, category members typically are not organized spatially or temporally in this way for the young child. Instead, the child encounters objects from a variety of different categories at the same time and in the same general location. In addition, the child encounters different members of the same category at different times and in different locations.

So unless category membership is explicitly taught to the child, there must be some mechanism by which like objects are segregated into categories prior to the abstraction of a schema or prototype representing instances of a given category. Without such a mechanism for determining what is to be averaged in with what, the application of a feature averaging principle might lead the infant to form one all-inclusive category or several partially overlapping categories (e.g., some based on size, some based on rate of movement, etc.).

A possible mechanism that we have been investigating for the segregation of items into categories involves perceived structural relations among objects. Rosch (e.g., 1978) argued for the existence of a high correlational structure in the world. According to Rosch, "combinations of what we perceive as the attributes of real objects do not occur uniformly. Some pairs, triples, etc., are quite probable, appearing in combination sometimes with one sometimes with another attribute; other (combinations) are rare; others logically cannot or empirically do not occur" (Rosch, 1978, p. 29). According to Rosch, this correlational structure provides a basis for dividing objects in the world into categories. Though attribute values may vary continuously across objects, some combinations of those attributes are more likely to occur than others, forming breaks between clusters of correlated attributes. Rosch hypothesized that category boundaries occur at these breaks between correlated attribute clusters and, conversely, that the clearest cases of a category are those instances that best reflect the correlational structure of the category as a whole.

If correlations among attributes are to serve as the basis for infants' segregation of stimuli or objects into categories, it is necessary that infants be sensitive to correlational information. We recently conducted a study (Younger & Cohen, 1983a) to address this question. Specifically, we asked whether 10-month-old infants are sensitive to correlations among attributes, and if so, whether the presence of a correlational structure affects infants' learning. We used an habituation procedure. Infants viewed one of two sets of stimuli differing only in that one had a correlational structure and the other did not. It was expected that if infants were sensitive to the correlation and the correlated set was easier to learn, that difference in learning would be reflected in infants' habituation. For example, infants receiving the correlated set might habituate more rapidly than infants receiving the uncorrelated set, whereas infants seeing the uncorrelated set might not habituate at all. In addition, if both groups did habituate, differences in the kind of information they had processed could be assessed in the test. For example, the test results would indicate whether the infants were responding on the basis of independent features or on the basis of the correlation.

The stimuli were artificially constructed animals varying on five attributes—the shape of the body, tail, feet, ears, and the number of legs. The three possible values of each attribute are presented in Table III. Examples of the stimulus drawings are illustrated in Fig. 3.

Infants were habituated to one of the stimulus sets represented in Table IV. Each habituation stimulus was presented twice, randomized within two blocks of 6 for a total of 12 20-sec trials. As can be seen in Table IV, the two correlated and the uncorrelated habituation sets were constructed from values 1 and 2. The correlated and uncorrelated sets were identical with respect to specific featural information (i.e., values 1 and 2 for each attribute occurred equally often in each set).

TABLE III

STIMULUS DIMENSION VALUES FOR YOUNGER AND COHEN (1983a)
CORRELATED VERSUS UNCORRELATED ATTRIBUTE EXPERIMENT
WITH 10-MONTH-OLD INFANTS[a]

Dimension values	Body (a)	Tail (b)	Feet (c)	Ears (d)	Legs (e)
1	Giraffe	Feathered	Webbed	Antlers	2
2	Cow	Fluffy	Club	Round ears	4
3	Elephant	Horse	Hoofed	Human ears	6

[a]Key to abstract notation for stimuli used in Younger and Cohen (1983a) experiment.

The stimulus sets differed in the relationship among the attribute values. In the correlated sets, attributes a, b, and c were perfectly correlated. For example, in Correlated Set A, a value of 1 on a always occurred with a 1 on b and c (111). Similarly, a value of 2 on a co-occurred with a 2 on b and c (222). (The same pattern of correlation existed in Set B except that the correlations were 122 and 211. Both sets were used to allow us to control for any initial preference or bias the infants may have had for one of the test stimuli.) The two remaining attributes (d and e) were not correlated (i.e., values 1 and 2 occurred in all possible combinations). The actual attributes involved in the correlation varied across infants. For example, attributes a, b, and c could refer to the body, feet, and tail,

12221

21112   33333

Fig. 3. Stimuli used in Younger and Cohen (1983a) experiment.

TABLE IV

DESIGN OF YOUNGER AND COHEN (1983a) CORRELATED VERSUS UNCORRELATED ATTRIBUTE STUDY[a]

| | Habituation | | | | | | | | | | | | | |
| Correlated sets | | | | | | | | | | Uncorrelated set | | | | |
a	b	c	d	e	a	b	c	d	e	a	b	c	d	e
1	1	1	1	1	1	2	2	1	1	1	1	1	1	1
1	1	1	1	2	1	2	2	1	2	1	2	1	2	1
1	1	1	2	2	1	2	2	2	2	1	1	2	2	2
2	2	2	2	1	2	1	1	2	1	2	2	1	1	2
2	2	2	2	2	2	1	1	2	2	2	1	2	2	2
2	2	2	1	1	2	1	1	1	1	2	2	2	1	1
						Test								
2	2	2	1	2 (C)	2	2	2	1	2 (U)	2	2	2	1	2 (U1)
2	1	1	1	2 (U)	2	1	1	1	2 (C)	2	1	1	1	2 (U2)
3	3	3	3	3 (N)	3	3	3	3	3 (N)	3	3	3	3	3 (N)

[a]For key to abstract notation, see Table III. (C), (U), and (N) refer to the correlated, uncorrelated, and novel test stimuli, respectively. Since the uncorrelated set contained no correlation, two uncorrelated test stimuli, (U1) and (U2), were presented.

the tail, ears, and feet, or the ears, body, and legs. In the uncorrelated stimulus set, none of the attributes was correlated. Values 1 and 2 occurred in all possible combinations across all pairs of attributes.

Following habituation, infants received a single 20-sec presentation with each of the three test stimuli. In this study, the test stimuli were presented to the infant one at a time rather than in pairs. Infants in both conditions (i.e., correlated and uncorrelated) received the same three test stimuli. The first two (i.e., 22212 and 21112) were novel stimuli composed of equally familiar features. In the correlated stimulus, the correlation among the first three attributes were preserved (i.e., 222 for Set A, 211 for Set B). In the uncorrelated stimulus, however, the experienced pattern of correlation was violated (i.e., 211 for Set A, 222 for Set B). The third test stimulus, 33333, was a completely novel stimulus composed of all novel features.

If the infants in the correlated condition were sensitive to the correlation present during habituation, they should generalize their habituation to the test stimulus preserving the correlation (CORR), but not to the stimulus violating the experienced pattern of correlation (UNCORR). In contrast, in the uncorrelated condition, both of these test patterns contained equally familiar features, features that occurred in all combinations during habituation. Thus, the CORR and UN-

CORR stimuli should be equally familiar to the infants in the uncorrelated condition.

The results indicated quite clearly that infants were sensitive to the correlational structure. As can be seen in Fig. 4, infants in the correlated condition clearly showed a decrease in fixation over trials during habituation ($p < .005$). In contrast, infants in the uncorrelated condition showed little or no evidence of habituation ($p > .80$). These results alone suggested that infants were capable of processing a correlational structure, and that the presence of the correlational structure facilitated infants' learning.

The results of the test phase confirmed that infants were indeed processing correlations. As can be seen in Fig. 4, infants in the correlated condition generalized their habituation to the stimulus preserving the correlation. However, they

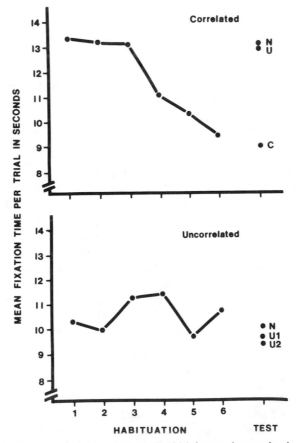

Fig. 4. Habituation and test results of 10-month-old infants under correlated and uncorrelated conditions.

clearly did not generalize to the stimulus violating the correlation. Infants in the correlated condition showed a marked increase in looking to both the UNCORR and NOVEL test stimuli ($p < .01$ in both cases). This pattern of results differed markedly from the pattern obtained in the uncorrelated condition. Consistent with their failure to habituate, infants in the uncorrelated condition exhibited no reliable differences in fixation of the test stimuli.

Younger (1984) conducted two experiments investigating 10-month-old infants' use of correlated attributes in the division or segregation of items into categories. The aim was, in a simple, well-controlled laboratory context, to structure a set of stimuli as described by Rosch, that is, to construct a stimulus set in which attribute values varied continuously across instances and to create a potential discontinuity by correlating restricted ranges of values across dimensions. Given experience with instances from such a stimulus set, would infants form category boundaries at this break between clusters of correlated values?

The experiments were based on the Strauss (1979, 1981) prototype studies. The goal was to use infants' preferential looking behavior to distinguish between the formation of a single category (e.g., by averaging experienced dimensional values) and the formation of two categories, with the boundary between categories falling at the break between clusters of correlated values.

The specific hypothesis under investigation was that the segregation of a set of stimuli into categories is based on the covariation of values experienced across dimensions of variation. To illustrate, consider a set of animals varying on two dimensions, for example, leg length and neck length. According to Younger's hypothesis, if dimensional values are uncorrelated (i.e., if the full range of values on leg length occur with the full range of values on neck length), a broad category would be formed encompassing the full extent of variation between the two dimensions (e.g., a category consisting of animals with any combination of leg and neck length). In this case, based on the Strauss (1979) findings, infants would be expected to form an average representation of category instances. Thus, an animal with average length legs and an average length neck would be expected to be most familiar to the infants.

In contrast, if restricted ranges of values on leg length are correlated with restricted ranges of values on neck length, narrower categories should be formed reflecting the covariation of values experienced among category exemplars. For example, if short legs always go with long necks and long legs always go with short necks, two categories should be formed (i.e., animals with short legs and long necks and animals with long legs and short necks). In this case, an animal with average length legs and an average length neck should fall at the boundary between the two categories. As such, animals falling within one category or the other (i.e., animals maintaining the experienced pattern of correlation among dimensional values) should be recognized as more familiar to infants than the "average" animal.

Younger's first experiment tested the segregation hypothesis with 10-month-old infants by manipulating the covariation of values across dimensions. Infants were familiarized with one of the two sets of artificially constructed animal drawings represented in Table V. The animals varied along four continuous dimensions—leg length, tail width, neck length, and ear separation. There were five discrete values along each dimension. As in Strauss (1981), values 1, 2, 4, and 5 occurred twice on each dimension in both familiarization sets. In the broad familiarization condition (taken from Strauss, 1981), the full range of values on any given dimension occurred with the full range of values on other dimensions (i.e., 1s went with 1s or 5s, 2s went with 2s or 4s, etc.). In the narrow condition, identical dimensional values were rearranged such that restricted ranges of values were correlated (i.e., 1s and 2s went with 1s and 2s, 4s and 5s went with 4s and 5s). The scaling of values on the different dimensions was arranged such that the animals in the two categories in the narrow condition were roughly of the same average size (e.g., long legs went with short legs, short legs with long necks).

TABLE V

FAMILIARIZATION AND TEST STIMULI
FOR EXPERIMENT 1 OF YOUNGER (1984)
REPRESENTED IN ABSTRACT NOTATION[a]

Familiarization stimuli							
Broad condition				Narrow condition			
L	N	T	E	L	N	T	E
1	1	5	5	1	1	2	2
1	5	1	5	1	2	1	2
2	2	4	4	2	2	1	1
2	4	2	4	2	1	2	1
4	4	2	2	4	4	5	5
4	2	4	2	4	5	4	5
5	5	1	1	5	5	4	4
5	1	5	1	5	4	5	4

Test pairs

1	1	1	1	1	or	5	5	5	5	vs.	3	3	3	3
2.		N			vs.	3	3	3	3					
3.		N			vs.	1	1	1	1	or	5	5	5	5

[a]Under familiarization, the letters L, N, T, and E refer to the dimensions of leg length, tail width, neck length, and ear separation, respectively. The numbers 1–5 refer to the values on the four quantitative dimensions as follows: legs, 1 = short, 5 = long; tail, 1 = thick, 5 = thin; neck, 1 = long, 5 = short; ears, 1 = narrow separation, 5 = wide separation. In the test, the letter N refers to a totally novel stimulus having qualitatively different features from those presented during familiarization.

Following familiarization, infants received the following three recognition memory test pairs: Stimulus 3333 paired with Stimulus 1111 or 5555; Stimulus 3333 paired with a novel or out-of-category animal (i.e., one containing qualitatively different features); and Stimulus 1111 or 5555 paired with the novel animal. The test animals are illustrated in Fig. 5. It was expected that if the familiarization items were segregated into categories on the basis of the covariation experienced among values, infants in the broad condition would form a single category containing all familiarization stimuli. Based on Strauss (1979), this category should be represented by the average of experienced dimensional values. Consequently, infants in the broad condition were expected to direct a greater proportion of their looking to the more novel, modal stimulus (i.e., 1111 or 5555) when paired with the average stimulus (3333).

In contrast, infants in the narrow condition were expected to segregate the familiarization items into two narrow categories on the basis of the experienced

NOVEL   1111

3333   5555

Fig. 5. Test stimuli used in Younger (1984) category segregation experiments.

correlations among dimensional values. Stimulus 1111 or 5555, which preserve the experienced pattern of correlation, was expected to be more familiar than Stimulus 3333, which falls at the boundary between clusters of correlated values.

On the other hand, if the items were not segregated into categories as predicted and all items presented during familiarization were grouped together into a single category, there should be no difference between conditions. Since the two familiarization sets contained identical dimensional values, infants in both conditions would be expected to form the same category representation. Again, based on Strauss's previous findings, all infants would be expected to form an average representation, directing a greater proportion of their total fixation toward the modal stimulus (1111 or 5555).

The pattern of results was consistent with the notion that the items were segregated into separate categories on the basis of the covariation experienced among dimensional values. In the comparison between Stimulus 3333 and Stimulus 1111 or 5555, infants in the broad condition directed a greater proportion of their total looking (59.5%) toward Stimulus 1111 or 5555, indicating that they recognized the average stimulus as more familiar ($p < .03$). In contrast, infants in the narrow condition spent more time (59.0%) viewing Stimulus 3333, indicating that the stimuli preserving the correlation (1111 and 5555) were more familiar to the infants than the stimulus containing values falling at the break between correlated values ($p < .02$). As expected, infants in both conditions recognized both the average and modal stimuli (3333 and 1111/5555) as more familiar than the qualitatively different animal ($p < .02$ in all cases).

While these results clearly indicated some sort of relational coding of dimensional information, it was not yet clear that infants in the narrow condition were forming two distinct categories. One potential problem was the discriminability among the "within category" or correlated dimensional values. In other words, it was not clear that values 1 and 2 and values 4 and 5 were discriminable to the infants. If they were not, then infants were in effect being familiarized to only two animals (e.g., 1111 and 5555) and tested with a familiar (i.e., 1111 or 5555) and a novel (i.e., 3333) stimulus. Since categorization involves a recognition of equivalence among a set of discriminable stimuli, such a test would have no clear implications for category formation.

A second experiment was conducted in an effort to provide a stronger test of the segregation hypothesis. In the second experiment, the correlated values were more discriminable, It was clear from the results of the first experiment that values 1 and 3 and values 3 and 5 could be discriminated. Infants in both familiarization conditions responded differentially in the comparison between Stimulus 3333 and Stimulus 1111 or 5555. As can be seen in Table VI, the familiarization set in the second experiment was like that of the narrow condition in the first experiment in that it contained two clusters of correlated dimensional values. In this case, however, values 1 and 3 and values 3 and 5 were correlated instead of values 1 and 2 and values 4 and 5.

TABLE VI

FAMILIARIZATION AND TEST STIMULI
FOR EXPERIMENT 2 OF YOUNGER (1984)
REPRESENTED IN ABSTRACT NOTATION[a]

Familiarization stimuli			
L	N	T	E
1	3	1	3
1	1	3	1
1	1	3	3
3	1	1	1
3	3	1	1
3	3	5	5
3	5	5	5
5	5	3	3
5	5	3	5
5	3	5	3

Test pairs

2 2 2 2 or 4 4 4 4 vs. 3 3 3 3

[a]Under familiarization, the letters L, N, T, and E
refer to the dimensions leg length, tail width, neck
length, and ear separation, respectively. The numbers
1–5 refer to the values on the four quantitative dimensions as follows: legs, 1 = short, 5 = long; tail,
1 = thick, 5 = thin; neck, 1 = long, 5 = short; ears,
1 = narrow separation, 5 = wide separation. Note that
the value 3 is also the average of the previously experienced values.

There is another important point to note about the second experiment. Recall
that the aim of the study was to demonstrate the segregation of items into two
separate categories as opposed to the formation of a single category represented
by the central tendency (i.e., the mean or mode) of experienced dimensional
values. In the first experiment, considering the full set of eight familiarization
items as a whole, the stimulus set was constructed in such a way that the mean
and modal values differed. Values 1, 2, 4, and 5 occurred equally often, thus all
could be considered modal values. In contrast, the average of the experienced
values (i.e., value 3) was never seen during familiarization. Although the response of infants in the two conditions clearly differed in the first experiment, we
could not conclude with any certainty whether the infants' performance in the
narrow condition reflected the formation of a modal prototype (i.e., one containing previously seen values) representing all eight exemplars or whether their
performance reflected the formation of two separate categories.

In the second experiment, the mean and modal values for the full set of familiarization items were equated. As can be seen in Table VI, value 3 was both the average of experienced values and the most frequently occurring value. Following familiarization with the 10 stimuli represented in the table, infants received a test trial in which Stimulus 3333 was paired with Stimulus 2222 or 4444. The greater familiarity of a stimulus containing previously unexperienced values but falling within the clusters of correlated values (i.e., 2222 or 4444) over the modal and average prototype (3333) would clearly indicate the segregation of the set of items into two distinct categories. The results were as expected. Infants directed a greater proportion (58.5%) of their total fixation toward Stimulus 3333, indicating the greater familiarity of Stimulus 2222 or 4444 ($p < .02$).

Together, the two experiments provided clear evidence of 10-month-old infants' ability to divide or segregate items into categories on the basis of perceived structural relations (i.e., correlations among dimensional values). The manipulation of the covariation of dimensional values in the first experiment had a clear and profound effect on infants' recognition performance. Those infants experiencing a broad range of covariation among values recognized the average prototype as more familiar than a modal stimulus. In contrast, infants experiencing correlations among restricted ranges of values recognized the modal stimulus as more familiar than the average stimulus. Moreover, infants in the second experiment recognized stimuli which contained values never before seen, but falling within the ranges of correlated values, as more familiar than a stimulus containing values which were both the average of experienced values and the values most frequently occurring among familiarization instances. Clearly, infants experiencing correlations among dimensional values were not forming a single category represented by the central tendency of dimensional values, but were using the correlations to segregate stimuli into two distinct categories.

V. Developmental Changes in Infant Categorization

From the "process"-oriented research presented in the previous section, we have seen that by 10 months of age, infants are already rather sophisticated in their categorization ability. They are capable of forming prototypic representations, they are sensitive to correlations among attributes, and they can use this correlational structure to segregate items into different categories. However, all of the research discussed so far has been conducted with 10-month-old infants. For a developmental psychologist, the next obvious question would be whether infants at younger ages also possess the same sophistication.

Our first developmental study examined 4-, 7-, and 10-month-old infants' abilities to perceive and base novelty responses on correlations among attributes (Younger & Cohen, 1983b). The design of the experiment was very similar to the correlated condition of the Younger and Cohen (1983a) study shown in Table

IV, and the stimuli were of the same type as shown in Fig. 3. The animals varied on the same five attributes (i.e., body, tail, feet, ears, and legs), and the same three values were used for each attribute (see Table III). In this study, four animals were constructed from values 1 and 2 for use in the habituation phase. These are represented in Table VII. As can be seen in the table, the first three attributes (body, tail, and feet) were perfectly correlated. For example, in Set A, an animal with a giraffe body (1) had a feathered tail (1) and webbed feet (1); an animal with a cow body (2) had a fluffy tail (2) and club feet (2).

The three test stimuli were identical to those used in the previous 10-month study. The correlated test stimulus preserved the pattern of correlation infants experienced during habituation, the uncorrelated stimulus violated that pattern of correlation, and the novel stimulus contained all new features.

Infants at all ages received two blocks of the four habituation stimuli for a total of eight 20-sec trials. The test stimuli in this study were presented singly rather than in pairs. Each was presented for a 20-sec trial. We expected that if infants had perceived the correlation, they would recover to both the novel and uncorrelated test stimuli. In contrast, if they were only remembering information about one or more specific features but not the relationship among them, they should

TABLE VII

HABITUATION AND TEST STIMULI FOR YOUNGER
AND COHEN (1983b) EXPERIMENT
REPRESENTED IN ABSTRACT NOTATION[a]

	Habituation stimuli									
	Set A values					Set B values				
Stimulus	b	t	f	e	l	b	t	f	e	l
1	1	1	1	1	2	1	2	2	1	2
2	1	1	1	2	1	1	2	2	2	1
3	2	2	2	1	1	2	1	1	1	1
4	2	2	2	2	2	2	1	1	2	2
Test stimuli										
CORR	2	2	2	1	2	2	1	1	1	2
UNCORR	2	1	1	1	2	2	2	2	1	2
NOVEL	3	3	3	3	3	3	3	3	3	3

[a]The letters b, t, f, e, and l stand for body, tail, feet, ears, and legs, respectively. Values 1, 2, and 3, respectively, for each of the five attributes are as follows: giraffe, cow, and elephant body (b); feathered, fluffy, and horse tail (t); webbed, club, and hoofed feet (f); antlers, round ears, and human ears (e); two, four, and six legs (l). © The Society for Research in Child Development, Inc.

recover to the novel stimulus, but not to the correlated or uncorrelated stimuli, since these contained equally familiar features.

The results of the habituation and test phases are presented in Fig. 6. Since reliable differences were not obtained between the 4- and 7-month-olds in the test ($p > .80$), the combined data are shown in the figure. As can be seen, infants at all ages showed a reliable decrease in looking over trials during habituation ($p < .001$). However, the patterns of performance in the test differed as a function of age. The 10-month findings replicated those in the correlated condition of the previous experiment (Younger & Cohen, 1983a). The 10-month-old infants demonstrated the ability to perceive the correlation, generalizing their habituation to the correlated test stimulus, but recovering to both the uncorrelated and novel test stimuli ($p < .01$ for both). In contrast, the 4- and 7-month-olds generalized habituation to both stimuli containing familiar features (i.e., the correlated and uncorrelated stimuli) and recovered only to the stimulus containing totally novel features ($p < .01$).

From the study just reported as well as from those of the preceding section, we know that when three out of five attributes are correlated, 10-month-old infants perceived the correlation while 4- and 7-month-old infants did not. These 4- and

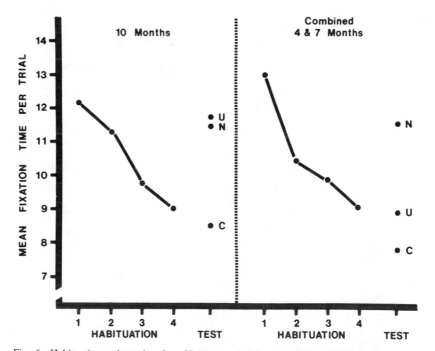

Fig. 6. Habituation and test data from Younger and Cohen (1983b) correlated attribute study. © The Society For Research in Child Development, Inc.

7-month-olds seemed to rely more on isolated attributes than on the correlation among attributes.

The next set of studies (Younger & Cohen, 1983c) was designed to shed more light on this apparent shift from processing separate attributes to processing the relationship or correlation among them. Considerable evidence is accumulating that this shift may represent a general developmental trend existing not only for infant category acquisition, but for simple patterns or objects as well (e.g., Bower, 1966; Cohen & Younger, 1984). If the developmental change in category acquisition could be substantiated, it might provide an important link between infant cognitive development on the one hand, and infant perceptual development on the other.

In our analysis of the previous experiment, we reasoned that the younger infants' failure to respond on the basis of the correlation could have been related to the category-like nature of the task. Inclusion of those two uncorrelated attributes meant that each animal was different. The infants not only had to perceive the correlation, but also had to retain it over a series of different exemplars. Perhaps infants younger than 10 months of age can process relations among the attributes of a single pattern or object, but have difficulty processing these relations in the context of a category.

In order to test this hypothesis, the design shown in Table VIII was used. The 4- and 7-month-old infants were given 10 20-sec habituation trials followed by 3 20-sec test trials.

The stimuli were the same drawings of imaginary animals used previously. The only differences were that, in the present experiment, three instead of five attributes varied from trial to trial, and when they varied, they maintained their correlation. Thus, if one looks at Stimulus Set A, when one attribute had a value of 1, they all had values of 1. When one had a value of 2, they all had values of 2. Another way of interpreting this study is that the category aspect of the task has been removed. The infants were simply being habituated to two discrete stimuli, 111 and 222. Set B was also correlated but, as can be seen, the correlated and uncorrelated test items were reversed for Sets A and B.

Results of the habituation phase are shown in Fig. 7. The only reliable effect was for trial blocks ($p < .001$), indicating that infants at both ages had shown a reliable decrement in fixation over trials. Even though it appeared that 4-month-olds looked longer than 7-month-olds, neither the effect of age nor the age × trial block interaction was significant.

Results of the test phase are presented in Fig. 8. At 4 months of age, infants recovered reliably only to the totally novel stimulus ($p < .01$), whereas at 7 months they recovered to the uncorrelated and the novel stimuli ($p < .01$ for both).

These results provide evidence that when the category aspect of the task has been removed, 7-month-olds are capable of processing the correlation among

TABLE VIII

HABITUATION AND TEST STIMULI FOR
EXPERIMENT 1 OF YOUNGER AND COHEN
(1983c) REPRESENTED IN ABSTRACT
NOTATION[a]

Stimulus	Habituation stimuli					
	Set A			Set B		
	a	b	c	a	b	c
1	1	1	1	1	2	2
2	2	2	2	2	1	1
Test stimuli						
Corr	2	2	2	2	1	1
Uncorr	2	1	1	2	2	2
Novel	3	3	3	3	3	3

[a]The stimuli varied on three attributes (represented as a, b, and c). Values 1, 2, and 3, respectively, for each of the three attributes were as follows: giraffe, cow, and elephant body; feathered, fluffy, and horse tail; webbed, club, and hoofed feet.

attributes. Since the values of the attributes (i.e., the 1s and 2s) were equally familiar for the correlated and uncorrelated test stimuli, it is reasonable to assume that the basis for the 7-month-olds' differential response to these two stimuli was the fact that the correlated stimulus retained the relationship among attributes experienced during habituation, while the uncorrelated stimulus did not.

The results also provided another dramatic illustration of an apparent developmental trend from processing independent attributes to processing the relationship among those attributes. While the 7-month-olds responded differentially to the correlated and uncorrelated test stimuli, the 4-month-olds did not. This pattern of results is consistent with the view that the 4-month-olds were processing one or more parts of the figure independently while the 7-month-olds were processing the figure as a whole.

The results for the 7-month-olds in this experiment were in direct contrast to those obtained for the same age group in the previous Younger and Cohen (1983b) study. It should be recalled that in that study the 7-month-old infants responded much as the 4-month-olds had done in this study. Of course, in the present experiment the task was simplified. Only three correlated attributes were used instead of three correlated plus two uncorrelated ones. One could argue, as we have done, that the critical difference between the tasks was the removal of

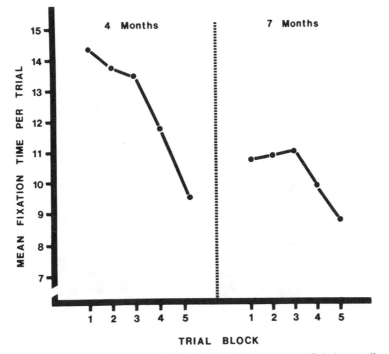

Fig. 7. Habituation data for 4- and 7-month-old infants on the simplified three-attribute (all correlated) experiment.

the two uncorrelated attributes, thereby eliminating the categorization aspect of the task.

However, a different explanation is also possible. It could be that removing any two attributes would make the task simpler. Seven-month-olds might just have been overloaded with variation in five attributes. Under those conditions they might have reverted to a more immature strategy of processing the attributes independently. If a reduction in number of attributes rather than removal of the categorical nature of the task was the critical factor, then they should process the correlation in a simplified category task, that is, in a task which involves variation in three rather than five attributes. On the other hand, if the category aspect were critical, the three-attribute category task should be just as difficult as the previous five-attribute task.

The design of the experiment to test these two interpretations is given in Table IX. The stimuli and procedure were the same as previously reported.

Infants were 4, 7, and 10 months of age. All infants were given 12 20-sec habituation trials with Stimulus Set A or B, followed by 3 20-sec test trials. As in

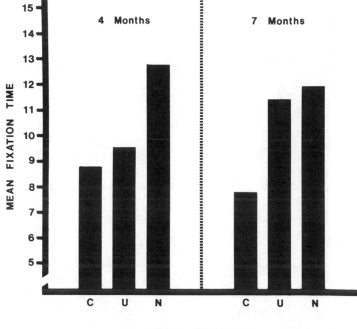

TEST STIMULUS

Fig. 8. Test data for 4- and 7-month-old infants on the simplified three-attribute (all correlated) experiment.

the previous study, only three attributes varied from trial to trial, but in this case, only the first two attributes were correlated.

Based upon our previous results, we expected 10-month-olds to have no difficulty with this task. They should habituate readily and recover to both the uncorrelated and novel test stimuli. We also expected the 4-month-olds to respond as they had consistently in the past; that is, we expected them to habituate, but to recover only to the novel test stimulus. The most interesting group was the 7-month-olds. They could perform like the 10-month-olds, processing the correlation in this simplified category context, or they could perform like they had in the five-attribute task (i.e., they could perform like the 4-month-olds and process the attributes independently.) A third alternative is also possible. From the results of the last experiment we have evidence that 7-month-old infants can process the relationship among three attributes. If they also do so in this experiment, then each habituation stimulus could constitute a totally distinct animal. For example, 111 would be perceived as a unique whole, different from 112, 221, and 222. The task would then become one of habituating to four different animals, and the test would be with three additional animals. Under such condi-

TABLE IX

Habituation and Test Stimuli for
Experiment 2 of Younger and Cohen
(1983c) Represented in Abstract
Notation[a]

| Stimulus | Habituation stimuli | | | | | |
| | Set A | | | Set B | | |
	a	b	c	a	b	c
1	1	1	1	1	2	1
2	1	1	2	1	2	2
3	2	2	1	2	1	1
4	2	2	2	2	1	2
Test stimuli						
Corr	2	2	2	2	1	1
Uncorr	2	1	1	2	2	2
Novel	3	3	3	3	3	3

[a]The stimuli varied on three attributes (represented
as a, b, and c). Values 1, 2, and 3, respectively, for
each of the three attributes were as follows: giraffe,
cow, and elephant body; feathered, fluffy, and horse
tail; webbed, club, and hoofed feet.

tions we would expect much slower, if any, habituation and no differences in
looking at any of the test items.

Results during the habituation phase of the experiment are presented in Fig. 9.
As this figure shows, both the 4- and 10-month-olds habituated rapidly (p
$< .001$). In contrast, the 7-month-olds (closed circles) displayed little, if any,
habituation. Because the apparent developmental shift from habituation to no
habituation to habituation again was so unusual, the study was rerun with an
additional group of 7-month-old infants (open circles). As can be seen, in this
replication the 7-month-olds again failed to habituate.

The test data are presented in Fig. 10. The 10-month-olds, as expected,
recovered to both uncorrelated and novel test stimuli ($p < .001$), the 4-month-
olds, also as expected, recovered only to the novel stimulus ($p < .001$), and,
consistent with their failure to habituate, neither group of 7-month-olds showed
differential responding to any of the test stimuli.

At this point, we feel reasonably confident about the reliability of our results.
Almost every pattern of responding at each age has been replicated at least once.
The theoretical account that seems to best fit this mass of correlated attribute data
is that a developmental progression exists from processing features of patterns to

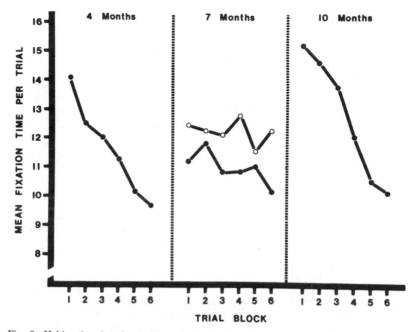

Fig. 9. Habituation data for 4-, 7-, and 10-month-old infants on the three-attribute (two correlated) experiment.

processing patterns as a whole to processing groups or categories of patterns. In none of our studies did 4-month-olds fail to respond in a way that would be inconsistent with the view that they process independent attributes. In none of them did 10-month-olds fail to respond to the relation among attributes embedded in a category-like structure. Although 7-month-olds could process relations among attributes in some conditions, they have consistently failed to respond in terms of those relations when they were presented in the context of a category.

However, before we can definitely conclude that 10-month-old infants are capable of processing correlations in a category context, there is one final issue that needs to be resolved. In all of the correlated attribute studies presented so far, we have been assuming that infants who respond to the correlated test stimulus as more familiar are doing so because they had previously experienced that correlation during habituation. There is one other possible explanation. By some theoretical accounts (e.g., Medin & Schaffer, 1978) the correlated test item would be more similar to the set of habituation items as a whole than would the uncorrelated item. This difference in similarity is due in part to the fact that the correlated item (e.g., 222) was actually presented during habituation, but the uncorrelated item (e.g., 211) was not (see Table IX). Although it would be a rather ad hoc explanation, one could argue that the age differences obtained in

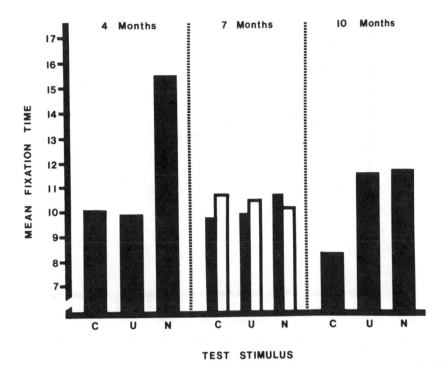

Fig. 10. Test data for 4-, 7-, and 10-month old infants on the three-attribute (two correlated) experiment.

these studies reflected nothing more than different novelty thresholds. Specifically, 10-month-olds may have a lower novelty threshold than younger infants. If that were true, then for 10-month-olds, the uncorrelated test item might have exceeded their novelty threshold while the correlated item might not have exceeded that threshold.

Recently, we have been able to test this "overall similarity" explanation experimentally and have found it to be inadequate. We simply replicated the experiment described in Table IX with 10-month-old infants except that the correlated test item (e.g., 222) was removed from the set of habituation items. Each infant received three presentations of the remaining three habituation stimuli (e.g., 111, 112, and 221) for a total of nine 20-sec habituation trials. The three 20-sec test trials remained the same (e.g., 222, 211, and 333). Under these conditions, the correlated test item continued to maintain the correlation seen during habituation, but now the uncorrelated item was more similar to the habituation set as a whole.

The results, as shown in Fig. 11, were unequivocal. The 10-month-old infants in this experiment continued to look longer at the uncorrelated than at the corre-

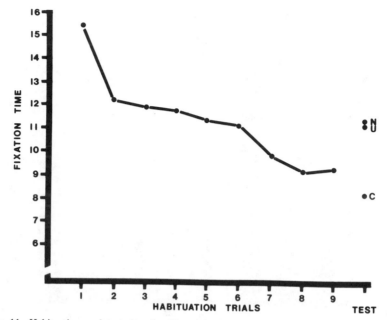

Fig. 11. Habituation and test data for 10-month-old infants on the overall similarity versus correlation experiment.

lated test stimulus ($p < .01$) despite the fact that the uncorrelated one was more similar overall to the set of habituation items. In fact, the infants seemed to display as much recovery to the uncorrelated test stimulus as they did to the novel test stimulus. Clearly, the presence of a correlation among attributes played a greater role in these 10-month-old infants' processing and categorization than did the overall similarity among habituation and test items.

VI. Summary and Conclusions

Altogether, the evidence we have presented suggests both that by 10 months of age, infants are rather sophisticated in their categorization abilities, and that infants' categorization abilities show considerable development over the course of the first year. The 10-month process studies demonstrated a number of similarities between infant and adult categorization processes. Infants, like adults, were able to abstract a prototypic representation containing the average of experienced dimensional values. In addition, 10-month-old infants were sensitive to correlations occurring among the attributes of category members, and they were able to use this correlational structure to segregate items into different categories.

Considerable evidence was also presented that infants' sensitivity to correlated attributes emerges in steps over the first year. The developmental studies supported the existence of two transitions across age in the perception of correlated attributes. First, there appears to be a developmental trend from the representation of feature-specific information to the representation of feature combinations. The 4-month-olds in our studies consistently responded on the basis of novel versus familiar features, but never to the relationship among those features. In contrast, the 10-month-old infants (and in one case, the 7-month-olds) responded on the basis of the correlation among features.

The findings also tended to support a second transition, namely, from processing relations among features of a single pattern or object to processing correlations in the context of a category. The 7-month-old infants clearly responded on the basis of relations among features when presented with only two patterns during habituation. However, they consistently failed to do so when the correlation occurred in a set of otherwise discriminable stimuli (i.e., when only a subset of the varying attributes were correlated). Yet, by 10 months of age, infants were sensitive to correlations occurring in a category context.

The final study we reported demonstrated clearly that the 10-month-olds were indeed relying on the correlations experienced during learning, and that they were not simply responding on the basis of the overall similarity among habituation and test items. This finding strengthens our interpretation of the developmental changes (i.e., the existence of a trend from part-to-whole processing) by ruling out the explanation of the reported findings that infants were responding only on the basis of overall similarity, since this view would imply that correlations play no special role even at 10 months of age.

What general conclusions can we draw concerning the way infants form categories? On the basis of the findings we have presented, we would like to suggest two possible approaches or "strategies" in infant categorization. The findings would suggest that the more mature strategy involves the representation and use of relations among features in categorization. The 10-month-old infants in our studies were clearly sensitive to a correlational category structure. They demonstrated a clear advantage for a correlational structure in category acquisition, as evidenced by rate of habituation (Younger & Cohen, 1983a), and they were able to use this correlational structure to segregate items into different categories (Younger, 1984). Such a strategy for category acquisition would seem particularly well suited for the young child's task of forming categories in the real world, since, according to Rosch (1978), correlated attributes represent an important structural characteristic of natural categories. In addition, there is now considerable evidence in the adult categorization literature that configural information (e.g., correlations among attributes) plays an important role in adults' category judgments (see Medin, 1983 for a review of this literature).

Perhaps a more immature form of categorization, one available to younger infants, involves a recognition of equivalence among instances based on independent properties of objects. In other words, younger infants may generalize across instances on the basis of a single, salient property common to all instances (or to multiple, independent properties). The 4-month-old infants in our studies responded in a category-like fashion to stimuli containing familiar features. Although it is difficult to say whether the 4-month-old infants' generalization to the correlated and uncorrelated items in these studies qualifies as categorization since it was not demonstrated that they could discriminate between these items and the habituation items, other studies have demonstrated categorization-like behavior in 3- to 4-month-old infants (e.g., Caron, Caron, & Carlson, 1979; Milewski, 1979). In these studies young infants apparently perceived invariant-form information across transformations in slant (Caron *et al.*, 1979; McGurk, 1972) and in size and position (Milewski, 1979).

Success versus failure in producing categorization at 3 months of age may be related to the type of stimuli presented and/or the nature of the category to be learned. For the most part, in the successful 3-month-old studies, infants have been shown very simple patterns and have had to generalize their response on the basis of a single perceptual feature such as overall size or shape. Several of these experiments more closely resembled tests of perceptual or object constancy than they did tests of categorization. Thus, these studies would be consistent with the view that young infants are attending to independent features. On the other hand, the demonstration and process studies mentioned above that have failed to find evidence of categorization in these younger infants have tended to use real objects, photographs, or multifeatured line drawings of imaginary faces or animals. In many of these studies, category formation would be facilitated by the ability to abstract and use the relationship among features, an ability that apparently does not develop until 7–10 months of age.

Of course, we recognize, a major unresolved question is what is the nature of a feature? This question is not unique to the infant literature and it has many different facets. For example, the research presented in this article has tended to manipulate structural characteristics of objects or pictures. In some cases those manipulations have involved quantitative changes (e.g., the degree of separation between the eyes or the length of the neck). In other cases, the changes have been qualitative (e.g., the type of tail or ears). But functional characteristics (e.g., the ability to move unaided or to support weight or to provide comfort) may be equally or even more important to the formation of certain categories (Nelson, 1973). How that importance may change over age and what role functional properties might have in infant category formation are significant but practically unstudied issues.

An even more basic question relates to the divisibility or indivisibility of perceptual features. In the research presented in this article we defined the features that were used in terms of facial characteristics or parts of an animal. But these definitions were arbitrary. One could rightly ask why we did not define the whole animal as a single feature or, conversely, an animal's tail as a collection of even finer features. No completely satisfactory answer can be given. The answer may depend in part on resolution of basic issues that have not yet been examined in infants, such as feature integrality versus separability (Garner, 1978), or the meaning of similarity (Tversky, 1977). However, the results of the experiments presented here lend some credence to the feature choices that were made. For one thing, it was clear that 4-, 7-, and 10-month-old infants processed the same visual input in very different ways, and that if one describes these developmental changes as going from processing independent features (as we have defined them) to processing correlations among features, much of the data can be explained. For another, it is unreasonable to assume that 10-month-old infants were just processing the animal as a whole. As we have already mentioned, data from the final experiment described here clearly showed that when overall similarity was pitted against correlated features, the results supported the correlated feature interpretation. Also, since in most studies the particular subset of features involved in a correlation randomly varied from subject to subject, one could not argue that the correlated features were somehow more intimately linked to one another than they were to the uncorrelated ones.

As with many programs of research, our investigation of the processes underlying infant categorization has led to as many new questions as it has answered. Some of the questions relate specifically to infant development. For example, does the 7-month-old infants' failure to habituate really represent a separate stage of information processing or only a transition from processing independent features to processing correlations among features? How general is this shift from independent features to correlations? Does it apply only to infants' processing of artificial perceptual categories or to their understanding of real-world objects and events as well. Other questions, such as those about the reality or use of features, transcend development to raise fundamental issues about our understanding of the nature of objects and how those objects may be related to one another. Our own research has drawn heavily from adult theory and research about categorization. We believe this strategy has paid off. While we may not yet be able to explain completely how infants form categories, our research has led to the discovery of several of the major processes involved. A more complete understanding of these and other processes will not only lead to a more accurate view of how infants form categories, it also will provide an important link between the world of the infant and the world of the adult.

Acknowledgments

Preparation of this article and much of the research reported in it were supported in part by Grant HD-15035 from the National Institute of Child Health and Human Development.

References

Anglin, J. M. (1977). *Word, object, and conceptual development.* New York: Norton.

Bourne, L. (1966). *Human conceptual behavior.* Boston: Allyn & Bacon.

Bower, T. G. R. (1966). Heterogeneous summation in human infants. *Animal Behavior,* **14,** 395–398.

Caron, A. J., Caron, R. F., & Carlson, V. R. (1979). Infant perception of the invariant shape of objects varying in slant. *Child Development,* **50,** 716–721.

Cohen, L. B., & Caputo, N. (1978). *Instructing infants to respond to perceptual categories.* Paper presented at the Midwestern Psychological Association Convention, Chicago, May.

Cohen, L. B., & Strauss, M. S. (1979). Concept acquisition in human infant. *Child Development,* **50,** 419–424.

Cohen, L. B., & Younger, B. A. (1984). Infant perception of angular relations. *Infant Behavior and Development,* **7,** 37–47.

Cornell, E. (1974). Infants' discrimination of photographs of faces following redundant presentations. *Journal of Experimental Child Psychology,* **18,** 98–106.

Fagan, J. F. (1976). Infant recognition of invariant features of faces. *Child Development,* **47,** 627–638.

Garner, W. R. (1978). Aspects of a stimulus. Features, dimensions, and configurations. In E. Rosch & B. Lloyd (Eds.), *Cognition and categorization.* Hillsdale, NJ: Erlbaum.

Goldman, D., & Homa, D. (1977). Integrative and metric properties of abstracted information as a function of category discriminability, instance variability, and experience. *Journal of Experimental Psychology: Human Learning and Memory,* **3,** 375–385.

Hirshfield, S. L., Bart, W. M., & Hirshfield, S. F. (1975). Visual abstraction in children and adults. *Journal of Genetic Psychology,* **126,** 69–81.

Homa, D., Cross, J., Cornell, D., Goldman, D., & Schwartz, S. (1973). Prototype abstraction and classification of new instances as a function of number of instances defining the prototype. *Journal of Experimental Psychology,* **101,** 116–122.

McGurk, H. (1972). Infant discrimination of orientation. *Journal of Experimental Child Psychology,* **14,** 151–164.

McDonough, S. C. (1981). *The use of habituation to investigate basic level and superordinate level categorization in cerebral palsied infants.* Unpublished doctoral dissertation, University of Illinois, Urbana.

McDonough, S. C. (1984). *Concept formation in motorically impaired infants.* Paper presented at the International Conference on Infant Studies, New York, April.

McDonough, S. C., & Cohen, L. B. (1982). *Use of habituation to investigate concept acquisition in cerebral palsied infants.* Paper presented at the International Conference on Infant Studies, Austin, March.

Medin, D. L. (1983). Structural principles in categorization. In T. Tighe & B. Shepp (Eds.), *Perception, cognition, and development* (pp. 203–230). Hillsdale, NJ: Erlbaum.

Medin, D. L., & Schaffer, M. M. (1978). Context theory of classification learning. *Psychological Review,* **85,** 207–238.

Milewski, A. (1979). Visual discrimination and detection of configurational invariance in 3-month infants. *Developmental Psychology,* **15,** 357–363.

Nelson, K. (1973). Some evidence for the cognitive primacy of categorization and its functional basis. *Merrill–Palmer Quarterly,* **19,** 21–23.

Neumann, P. G. (1974). An attribute frequency model for the abstraction of prototypes. *Memory and Cognition,* **2,** 241–248.

Neumann, P. G. (1977). Visual prototype information with discontinuous representation of dimensions of variability. *Memory and Cognition,* **5,** 187–197.

Posner, M. I., & Keele, S. W. (1968). On the genesis of abstract ideas. *Journal of Experimental Psychology, 77,* 353–363.

Posner, M. I., & Keele, S. W. (1970). Retention of abstract ideas. *Journal of Experimental Psychology, 83,* 304–308.

Rosch, E. (1978). Principles of categorization. In E. Rosch & B. Lloyd (Eds.), *Cognition and categorization.* Hillsdale, NJ: Erlbaum.

Rosch, E., Mervis, C. B., Gray, W. D., Johnson, D., & Boyes-Braem, P. (1976). Basic objects in natural categories. *Cognitive Psychology, 8,* 382–439.

Ross, G. (1977). *Concept categorization in 1 and 2 year olds.* Paper presented at the meeting of the Society for Research in Child Development, New Orleans, March.

Strange, W., Kenney, T., Kessel, F., & Jenkins, J. (1970). Abstraction over time of prototypes from distortions of random dot patterns. *Journal of Experimental Psychology, 83,* 508–510.

Strauss, M. S. (1979). Abstraction of prototypical information by adults and 10-month-old infants. *Journal of Experimental Psychology: Human Learning and Memory, 5,* 618–635.

Strauss, M. S. (1981). *Infant memory of prototypical information.* Paper presented at the meeting of the Society for Research in Child Development, Boston, April.

Tversky, A. (1977). Features of similarity. *Psychological Review, 84,* 327–352.

Younger, B. A. (1984). *The co-variation of dimensional values as a determinant of the segregation of items into categories by 10-month-old infants.* Unpublished doctoral dissertation, University of Texas, Austin.

Younger, B. A., & Cohen, L. B. (1983a). *The acquisition of correlated and uncorrelated categories in 10-month-old infants.* Paper presented at the meeting of the Society for Research in Child Development, Detroit, March.

Younger, B. A., & Cohen, L. B. (1983b). Infant perception of correlations among attributes. *Child Development, 54,* 858–867.

Younger, B. A., & Cohen, L. B. (1983c). *Developmental change in infants' perception of correlations among attributes.* Paper presented at the meeting of the Society for Research in Child Development, Detroit, March.

INDEX

CONTENTS OF PREVIOUS VOLUMES